THE DILEMMAS OF INTIMACY

The Dilemmas of Intimacy applies evidence-based, cognitive-behavioral interventions to therapeutic work with couples and individuals who have problems with intimacy. Karen Prager introduces a three-dilemma model that outlines the risks and rewards of intimate relating. A conceptual model for each dilemma is included and addresses the commonly presented problems, couple interaction patterns, and behavioral deficits, as well as many more factors that affect relationships. Strategies for building the therapeutic alliance; interventions with couple behavior, affect, and thinking patterns; and therapist–client dialogues help clinicians with the day-to-day issues that occur in their work.

Unique to this book is the author's Intimacy Signature, an assessment tool that incorporates general assessments of couple and individual functioning with additional measures added for assessing intimacy problems. Through use of the Intimacy Signature the behavioral, cognitive, and affective aspect of each couple's approach to handling intimacy and its dilemmas is laid out.

Visit the publisher's website at www.routledge.com/9780415816861 for access to additional clinical material, such as the Intimacy Signature basic intake, worksheet packets for each intimacy dilemma, initial formulation worksheets, therapist worksheets for in-session and at-home experiments, a couple's take-home packet, and individual partner and intimacy assessment interviews.

Karen J. Prager, PhD, ABPP, is a professor of psychology and program head for Gender Studies at the University of Texas at Dallas. She is also a diplomate in couple and family psychology, specializes in the treatment of troubled relationships, and offers supervision and continuing education for mental health professionals on couple therapy.

THE DILEMMAS OF INTIMACY

Conceptualization, Assessment, and Treatment

Karen J. Prager

Routledge
Taylor & Francis Group
NEW YORK AND LONDON

First published 2014
by Routledge
711 Third Avenue, New York, NY 10017

Simultaneously published in the UK
by Routledge
27 Church Road, Hove, East Sussex BN3 2FA

Routledge is an imprint of the Taylor & Francis Group,
an informa business

Library of Congress Cataloging in Publication Data

Prager, Karen Jean, 1952–
The dilemmas of intimacy : conceptualization, assessment, and treatment / by Karen J. Prager.
pages cm
(pbk. : alk. paper) 1. Intimacy (Psychology) I. Title.
BF575.I5P727 2013
158.2—dc23 2013003716

ISBN: 978-0-415-81685-4 (hbk)
ISBN: 978-0-415-81686-1 (pbk)
ISBN: 978-0-203-37537-2 (ebk)

Typeset in Garamond
by Apex CoVantage, LLC

CONTENTS

ACKNOWLEDGMENTS

I am deeply grateful to Greg Eaves, who listened to me read the entire book aloud over a period of weeks and offered many helpful comments. Monica Basco made detailed comments on an earlier draft of the book for which I am in her debt. I also appreciate very much working with Marta Moldavi and Denise File at Apex who were very helpful with the finishing touches on the final version of this book.

This book would not have been possible without the dozens of couples who shared their relationship troubles with me, and who have given me so much insight into the challenges of maintaining intimacy in a long-term couple relationship.

INTRODUCTION

Couples' problems with attaining and sustaining intimacy are some of the thorniest that a therapist will tackle. In my work as a couple therapist and in three decades of research on intimacy, I have noticed that couples' intimacy problems arise from one or more of three intimacy dilemmas. Each of these three dilemmas—joy versus protection from hurt, I versus we, and the past lives in the present—can be understood as an inevitable outgrowth of the rewards and risks of intimate relating. In turn, couple partners' responses to these intimacy dilemmas are individual and relational coping styles designed to increase rewards while minimizing the risks that intimate partners confront. Some couple partners withdraw and avoid intimacy whereas others sabotage it. Some individuals minimize their own aims to get along with their partners, whereas others attempt to mold their partners to fulfill their own needs. Still others break up one relationship after another to seek the partner who will fulfill all of their dreams.

My first intention in writing this book is to share this three-dilemma model with other therapists as a tool for organizing treatment for couples and individuals that struggle with intimacy problems. The assessment tools and interventions described in this book are designed to help clinicians conceptualize and treat couple and individual problems that emerge from partners' efforts to cope with these three intimacy dilemmas.

A second purpose of this book is to show that evidence-based, cognitive-behavioral interventions can be applied effectively to the treatment of couples and individuals who have problems with intimacy once intimacy is defined in behavioral and cognitive terms. If in years past, intimacy did not receive as much attention by cognitive-behavioral theorists as it deserves, it is perhaps because it has been difficult for psychologists to reach a consensus on exactly what being intimate entails. However, studies conducted in the last couple of decades or so have supported predictions about the benefits of intimate relating in couple relationships using behavioral definitions of intimacy (e.g., Cordova, Gee, & Warren, 2005; Laurenceau, Barrett, & Rovine, 2005; Prager & Buhrmester, 1998; Reis & Shaver, 1988). This book uses a behavioral definition of intimacy to create a treatment framework that is useful for clinicians.

Although my therapeutic home is in the cognitive-behavioral approach, treating intimacy problems has required that I broaden my perspective. As a cognitive-behavioral practitioner would predict, intimacy problems do arise from ineffective attempts to manage intimacy-distance cycles in a relationship, and from naïve or problematic assumptions about self and intimate relationships. However, they also stem from schemas that represent insecure attachment relationships earlier in life, and from a lack of self-awareness that compromises one's ability to communicate about feelings, wants, and desires. This book is an effort to integrate these components into a single approach that is not too complicated to be useful for clinicians and not too simple to account for the many variations in intimacy problems.

My purpose is not to supplant existing systems of cognitive-behavioral couple therapy. Rather, this book is part of a growing trend in couple therapy to target specific couple problems, an approach that Snyder (November, 2009) argues should hold an increasingly prominent position in the couple therapy literature. This application of evidence-based couple therapy to intimacy problems takes its place alongside other specifically-targeted therapies for couples, including Spring's (1996) and Snyder, Baucom, and Gordon's (2007) approaches for helping couples recover from extramarital affairs, Wakefield, Williams, Yost, and Patterson's (1996) system for treating alcohol abuse within the context of couple relationships, treatments for sexual dysfunction such as that devised by McCarthy and McCarthy (2003), and treatment for violent couples by Stith, McCollum, and Rosen (2011). Just as comprehensive approaches to treating individual problems have evolved into sets of specific treatments for identified individual disorders, so too are couple therapies now evolving into more specifically targeted treatments for particular sets of couple problems.

In Chapter 1, readers find a working concept of intimacy—what it is and why it is so important to couple relationships. This chapter introduces the three core intimacy dilemmas, each of which arises because of the coexisting joys and emotional risks involved in intimate relating. The *Intimacy Signature,* an assessment packet that lays out the behavioral, cognitive, and affective aspects of each couple's approach to handling intimacy and its dilemmas, is presented in Chapter 2. Chapters 3 to 6 lay out the interventions used in this book, including strategies and techniques for building the therapeutic alliance (Chapter 3), and for intervening with couple behavior (Chapter 4), affect (Chapter 5), and thinking patterns (Chapter 6) that interfere with intimacy. Chapters 7 to 10 each address one of the intimacy dilemmas, providing a conceptual model for understanding each dilemma, commonly presented problems associated with each, couple interaction patterns and behavioral deficits individual partner attitudes, beliefs, and expectations and problematic emotion regulation strategies in one or both partners. For each intimacy dilemma and associated problem, therapist–client dialogues demonstrate the use of the interventions discussed in Chapters 3 to 6.

Everyone needs some intimacy in their lives although not everyone wants the same type or level of intimacy. Regardless of whether we want our intimate connection with our partners to be based primarily on a verbal, sexual, or affectionate connection, there is little that is more gratifying in life than relationships that provide us with a deep, intimate connection with another. Intimacy promises that our needs can be known, accepted, and fulfilled; intimate partners reward us when they allow us to know them and when they participate with us in the give and take of support, love, affirmation, and joy. I hope that the approach in these pages guides therapists as they assist couples for whom these goals have been elusive to find their own path to a more rewarding and fulfilling intimate relationship.

INTRODUCTION

1

REWARDS, RISKS, AND INTIMACY DILEMMAS

When a couple shares a deep intimate connection they hold a source of meaning and purpose, happiness and companionship, relief from loneliness, and comfort and support (Prager, 1995; Prager & Roberts, 2004). When we have a confidante, someone with whom we can share our private thoughts and who offers us emotional support, tenderness, and devotion, we thrive, physically and psychologically. We handle stress more effectively, and we are more optimistic about life (Prager, 1995). The presence of a confidante in our lives boosts our life satisfaction and buffers us from the detrimental effects of life's daily stresses. Intimacy is one of the most treasured aspects of marriage and other couple relationships, and is at the heart of a couple's connection.

However, the promise of intimacy is also its risk: the more intimacy two people share, the more power they give to each other to cause hurt. An intimate who knows our fears and vulnerabilities can wound deeply with harsh words. Even a sensitive and thoughtful partner will sometimes act in callous, hurtful ways. Every individual seeks and finds his or her own balance between seeking the rewards of intimacy and defending against intimacy's inherent risks.

When individuals come together to form a couple, the partners together engage in a behavioral pattern of reciprocal influence that helps them to maximize intimacy's rewards and minimize its risks. A couple's pattern of intimate relating combines inviting, approach behaviors with defensive behaviors that protect against hurt. It is built from each individual's characteristic ways of handling stress and from the unique chemistry of the partners' influence on one another. Patterned interactions in turn shape an ongoing emotional climate for the couple that further influences their ability to maintain a deep intimate connection. In this chapter, I describe the rewards and risks that couples must weigh to form and sustain that deep intimate connection.

Intimacy can defy definition in that there is no single definition upon which scholars and clinicians agree (Prager, 1995). With the definition below, I hope to capture the characteristics of a single intimate interaction and the ongoing experience of intimacy in a long-term couple relationship simultaneously.

What Is Intimacy?

Intimacy has been difficult to define because the word refers to several different but related concepts. The most influential definition conceptualizes intimacy as a certain type of interaction (Reis & Shaver, 1988). According to Reis and Shaver, intimacy in interactions has two dimensions: (1) self-disclosure and (2) validation, caring, and understanding in the receiving of the other's self-disclosure. An intimate interaction is one in which we share ourselves, risking hurt should the partner make an insensitive response (Cordova et al., 2005). Second, two people are intimate when they share a kind of deep, warm, loving emotional connection. David Olsen and his colleagues developed a measure called the Personal Assessment of Intimacy in Relationships (PAIR; Schaefer & Olson, 1981) whose conceptual underpinnings highlight this aspect of intimacy. The PAIR measures the experience of connection in multiple aspects of the relationship, including recreational, intellectual, sexual, emotional, and spiritual intimacy. Intimacy can refer to the quality of the couple's interactions and feelings of connection within a specific relationship domain and can also refer to a type of relationship (Prager, 1995; Reis & Patrick, 1990), one that includes numerous and frequent intimate interactions and the warm, supportive relationship climate that permits such interactions to occur with safety. Finally, intimacy has been used to refer to the personal, private information that is only shared with select others.

What these three intimacy concepts have in common is the assumption that intimacy refers to the sharing of something personal and private about the self, something that is not ordinarily available or accessible without the person's invitation and consent. Part of what we cherish about intimate sharing is the understanding that our partners are sharing something exclusively with us, whether that intimate sharing is limited to exclusive sexual contact, or includes shared secrets and tearful confidences.

Dimensions of Intimate Interactions

Intimate interactions are defined by three aspects (shown in Figure 1.1): self–revealing behavior, positive involvement with the partner, and accurate, shared understandings (Lippert & Prager, 2001; Prager & Buhrmester, 1998; Prager & Roberts, 2004). Self-revealing behavior is the necessary defining feature of intimate relating and refers to verbal self-disclosure, sexual contact, physical closeness, and expressions of affection. Verbally intimate partners share themselves freely and unself-consciously, allowing the partner a window into their inner lives. Verbally intimate partners frequently express their positive feelings for the other.

Less verbal individuals can also enjoy frequent intimate interactions. Frequent sexual contact, frequent hugs, kisses, tender touches, caresses, and frequent hand-holding can all be intimate expressions. Positive involvement

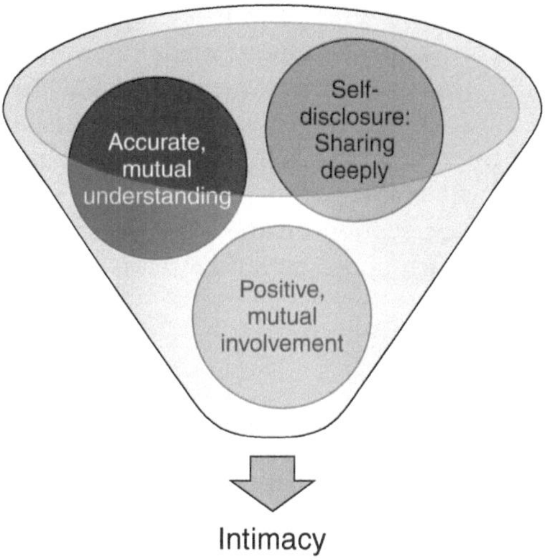

Figure 1.1 Three components of intimacy

refers to attentiveness and immediacy in communication and conveys positive regard for the other person. Immediacy increases the level of emotional contact between partners and includes the use of first person and present tense in verbal communication, as in the statement, "I appreciate everything that you do for me" versus "What you've done here is very much appreciated."

Positive involvement refers to an appreciative attitude toward the partner and the partner's disclosures. This does not mean that interactions are intimate only when partners are expressing positive emotions. Rather, intimate interactions can encompass the full range of emotions. Positive regard is an attitude that intimate partners have toward one another. Specific behaviors associated with positive involvement include listening to the partner's communication and demonstrating acceptance of the partner's expressions as his. It refers to affectionate touch that communicates pleasure from touching and being touched by the partner and an acceptance or appreciation for the partner's body. Intimate touches convey warmth, love, attraction, and affection. They convey positive regard.

Finally, intimate relationships are built upon shared understandings of each partner's inner self that are revealed in intimate interactions. In an intimate interaction, both partners gain access to or learn more about the other's inner experience—from private thoughts, feelings, and beliefs, to characteristic rhythms, habits, or routines, to private sexual fantasies and preferences. Intimate relating is at core two selves knowing each other deeply and thoroughly. This knowledge endures beyond a particular interaction and informs and deepens the intimate relationship.

In conclusion, an intimate interaction is one in which partners grant one another access to the most private aspects of themselves: to their bodies, to their psychological selves, and to that which they value highly. An intimate relationship is one in which partners have extensive mutual knowledge of one another's selves and offer each other a loving, respectful attitude toward that which is private and vulnerable within. The result of intimate interactions with the partner is the perception on the part of each that the one understands the other as they each understand themselves and accepts the partner's inner life as it is.

The Need for Intimacy

Although not everyone desires the same level of intimacy in their relationships, most people want some intimacy in their lives. We know that people feel positively about uncovering the mystery of an attractive stranger (e.g., Jourard, 1971; Montgomery, 1986; Vittengl & Holt, 2000), and they get excited about letting an attractive other know themselves. Harry Stack Sullivan (1953) concluded that human beings have a need for intimacy when he observed an early form of intimacy between schoolchildren and their friends. Sullivan judged this middle-childhood increase in intimacy as normative, a judgment that has been born out in later research (e.g., see review by Prager, 1995). The need for intimacy, then, grows and matures with the child as he or she develops.

There seems to be a drive in people to know others and to be known, even if this drive is only given expression with one other person as Rubin (1984) found was common for many American men with their wives. Intimacy fosters the hope that it is possible to know another fully. Maintaining at least one intimate relationship is part of being human.

As I have studied intimacy over the years, I have identified four interrelated needs that together compose the need for intimacy (see Figure 1.2). The first is the need to share ourselves with our partners. Through self-disclosure, through nudity and sexual contact, through holding, touching, and kissing, through living in close quarters, and through building lives together, we share our most private selves with our intimate partners. When the other is unavailable, we feel sad and become aware of our unmet needs.

Second, the need for intimacy is a need for another person to fully know and understand us as we know and understand ourselves. Research by Laurenceau, Barrett, and Pietromonaco (1998), Lippert and Prager (2001), Sprecher (1987), and Sprecher, Metts, Burleson, Hatfield, and Thompson (1995) shows that our partner's ability to listen sympathetically to our confidences contributes as much to our satisfaction with our relationship as does our partner's disclosing to us. When this need to be known by the other is not met, we feel lonely and misunderstood (Tornstam, 1992).

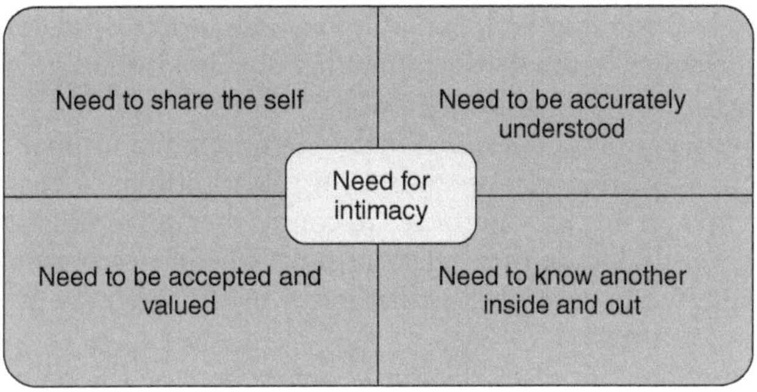

Figure 1.2 The need for intimacy and its components

Third, the need for intimacy is a need for that same person—the one that knows us and understands us as we understand ourselves—to fully accept us as we are. Couples who crave but do not give each other mutual acceptance behave defensively and express little appreciation for one another. Their arguments drag on as each gives the other endless evidence of how devoted and long-suffering he or she is and how unfair the other's accusations and criticisms are. These arguments reflect partners' yearnings to be accepted (and appreciated) for who they are and what they do (Jacobson & Christensen, 1996; Jourard, 1971; Reis, 2006; Reis & Shaver, 1988).

Fourth, the need for intimacy is a need to know another person, inside and out, and love that person. Intimate partners want to listen to each other's disclosures as much as they want their own to be heard (Sprecher, 1987). When our partners do not disclose to us, many of us can feel left out of our partner's life.

In sum, intimate relationships fulfill a fundamental psychological need in human beings. The absence of intimacy results in the state of psychological neediness that is loneliness. Most people will continue to yearn for or seek out intimate relationships despite disappointments, hurts, and losses from previous relationships.

Intimacy Dilemmas

The inherent rewards and risks of intimate relating can be usefully grouped into three overarching dilemmas that encompass the challenges of intimacy. For the purposes of this book, an *intimacy dilemma* is a conflict between two intimacy-related values or motives. These may be mutually exclusive in the sense that one cannot be wholly realized without jeopardizing the other or one may activate intimacy-related risks. Intimacy dilemmas can be internal to the individual or can play out as conflicts between partners. The three intimacy dilemmas are best understood when we recognize intimacy as a simultaneously rewarding and anxiety-provoking aspect of couple relationships. It is these three intimacy dilemmas that organize intimacy-related problems and their treatments in this book.

Relationship partners (and individuals) can respond to intimacy dilemmas adaptively, in ways that sustain satisfactory relationships. Often, however, people who present intimacy problems to couple therapists will be responding in such a way as to disrupt their relationship. They may even avoid initiating or sustaining intimate relationships altogether because they are overwhelmed by the risks of intimacy.

Each of the three intimacy dilemmas occurs because the rewards of intimacy are associated with emotional risks. The next few sections of this chapter explain each of the three intimacy dilemmas and its associated rewards and risks.

Intimacy Dilemma #1: Joy versus Protection from Hurt

Intimacy fulfills needs and offers compelling rewards yet, at the same time, makes us more vulnerable to hurt and loss. Intimate access and subsequent knowledge of another person's self provides us with joy and comfort and alleviates our very human existential loneliness (May, 1969; Sartre, 1956; Tillich, 1952). Intimacy's first built-in challenge is to balance the rewards of intimacy with the need to avoid being too vulnerable to hurt or shame, to feel psychologically safe.

Joy versus protection from hurt is intimacy's core dilemma. We confront Dilemma #1 because when we seek intimate contact, we must be willing to risk being hurt or abandoned. Dilemma #1 arises because intimate relating satisfies deep and abiding human psychological needs, but intimate partners are not perfectly reliable sources for fulfilling those needs. Rather, as noted by Cordova, Gee, and Warren (2005), our partners will eventually have an off-day and will respond insensitively or even cruelly to us when we are vulnerable. Those of us who sustain intimate relationships must be able to tolerate these disappointments and still approach our partners again for more intimate contact.

Intimacy's core dilemma comes from the following sources of joy and comfort and their associated psychological risks.

1. *Freedom to take off one's public mask.* People relax when they are with someone they know very well; knowing and being known gives us permission to drop our public roles and personas. When we drop our vigilance, we allow our private selves to be seen. We can breathe more easily.

Associated risk: Exposing our private selves to criticism, attack, or belittlement. Because our partner has access to ordinarily hidden parts of ourselves, criticism or belittlement from an intimate partner can take on a veneer of brutal truth and can be especially destructive to self-esteem and confidence.

Associated risk: Shaming the self. Even if our partners are supportive, we may ourselves feel shame when we reveal certain personal, private aspects of ourselves that we do not accept in ourselves.

Associated risk: Abandonment. When they get to know what we're really like, our partners may decide they don't want us and leave the relationship.

2. *Joys are more joyful when shared.* Intimacy brings excitement into a relationship (Aron, Norman, Aron, & Lewandowski, 2002). Excitement begins early in relationships when partners uncover the mystery of another person. Later, intimacy brings excitement when we involve our partner with the cutting edge of our personal growth (e.g., get a new perspective on an event from our pasts when we hear ourselves explaining it to our new love). Sharing joys intensifies positive emotions. When joyful moments come around, intimacy allows us to feel confident that the other knows just what it means to us.

Associated risk: Partners may not rejoice with us. Sometimes couple partners are competitive and begrudge some of the other's successes. Partners may also harbor anger and resentment, which dampens their generosity toward the other and may cause them to respond less than enthusiastically to the other's joys.

3. *Intimacy communicates love.* Intimacy reassures, accepts, and communicates love. Intimacy entails acknowledging the other's message and communicating to the other that they will not be abandoned, rejected, or frozen out because of their most private self. Love in combination with intimacy fulfills people's yearning to be lovable in the eyes of someone who "has known them forever" or "knows them inside out."

Associated risk: Lack of intimacy erodes love. To the extent that intimacy communicates love, dry spells without intimacy can communicate failing love. Even when there are other reasons for a lack of intimacy, we are at risk for feeling unloved.

Dilemma #2: I versus We

How much I versus how much we? Intimacy challenges us to maintain a balance between a desire to forge common life goals and aims with our intimate partner on the one hand and our desire to pursue individual dreams, interests, and friends on the other. Intimate relationships create pressure on us to give up some of our individual pursuits in the interest of couple harmony and our partner's well-being. Most intimate partners gladly trade some aspects of their single lives for a life shared with their intimate partner. However, this is where the dilemma lies: Some intimate partners will give up too much of themselves whereas others will attempt to change their partners so that their partner's aims harmonize more completely with their own. Some will even insist that their partners abandon their aims so that both can pursue a single goal or course of action.

Like Dilemma #1, Dilemma #2, *I versus we,* occurs because the rewards of intimacy carry with them associated risks. In this case, the risks stem from the way that individual partners manage the tension between the demands of their partner and the relationship and their needs for autonomy and individuality. Intimacy Dilemma #2 occurs because intimacy offers the following benefits to the self along with the associated risks:

1. *Intimate relationships provide a source of meaning and purpose for oneself.* Love is experienced as inherently meaningful. People will pursue individual goals in the name of love (e.g., to make someone proud, to support a family, to earn an education for a child). Harry Stack Sullivan (1953) argued that all human motivation is fundamentally interpersonal. A loved intimate partner's well-being can become one's *raison d'etre,* the overarching purpose to one's life endeavors.

Associated risk: Relying too much on a relationship for meaning and purpose. Expecting an intimate partner to completely fulfill one's need for meaning and purpose usually places too heavy a burden on that partner. The healthiest relationships are those in which partners have shared purposes but do not rely solely on each other to provide meaning for their lives.

2. *Intimacy affirms and validates the self.* Intimate interactions affirm our positive qualities by reminding us of our value to our partner. During intimate interactions, partners offer one another positive feedback; each helps the other perceive him- or herself as worthwhile, attractive, lovable, admirable, or competent. Intimate interactions offer encouragement and reassurance. Partners' extensive mutual knowledge allows each to know the other's aims for him- or herself, which maximizes the meaningfulness of affirmations offered.

We are validated when another person sees the world the way we see it. We feel validated when our own way of understanding ourselves and our world seems reasonable and acceptable to another human being. When a partner says, "Yes, that makes sense, I can understand why you see it that way," we are encouraged to trust our own reality testing (Jacobson & Christensen, 1996; Reis & Patrick, 1996; Reis & Shaver, 1988).

Associated risk: Relying too much on a partner to maintain self-esteem. Intimacy is so confirming of self worth that people are tempted to depend upon their partners for more than is reasonable to expect. Partners may unreasonably demand that the other compensate for what they cannot do for themselves (Horberg & Chen, 2010).

Associated risk: Intimate partners can invalidate. Partners who lack intimacy skills may inadvertently invalidate one another. Further, the more intimacy shared by the partners, the more information an invalidating partner has available to punish or undermine the other when angry.

3. *Intimate interactions enhance self-awareness and self-clarification.* Intimate self-disclosure offers us the opportunity for expanded self-awareness and self-clarification (Derlega & Grzelak, 1979). When talking about ourselves with a positively involved, attentive partner, we hear and can clarify our own

perceptions, beliefs, and values to ourselves. As theorists like Erikson (1950), Rogers (1958), and Sullivan (1953) have argued, self-exploration with a warm, accepting other increases our self-understanding while simultaneously letting our partners understand and know us better. In this way, intimate interactions encourage expanded self-awareness and self-clarification. Therefore, even as we engage in intimate interactions to be close to our partners, our intimate interactions paradoxically function to make us more aware of our individuality.

Associated risk: Self-awareness and clarification can uncover undesirable aspects of the self and make them available for inspection and evaluation. Because intimate interactions can increase self-awareness through a verbal self-clarification process, partners who shy aware from self-awareness may also end up avoiding intimacy.

Associated risk: Self-clarification punctures the illusion that two can become one. Just as intimate interactions can reveal to partners how very much alike they are in their thinking and their values, so too can intimate interactions reveal to partners how different they are. Partners who discover untenable differences or who have difficulty tolerating differences between them may either abandon the relationship or avoid intimacy to avoid dealing with differences.

4. *Intimate relationships allow us to share our dreams and our burdens.* Shared dreams are more obtainable when two work toward them. Our intimate relationship takes pressure off of us to do it all alone. We extend our dreams to include our partners and our partners help us to fulfill our dreams.

Similarly, our intimate relationship offers us an opportunity to piggyback on our partner's dreams. Love is a great motivator, and some of us like nothing better than taking on a loved one's ambition and making it our own.

Associated risk: Two partners' dreams are never identical. Dilemma #2 can reflect two simultaneous and potentially contradictory internal pressures: to invite our partners to share our own dreams and to celebrate and support our partner's dreams. Even when partners' dreams are remarkably similar, such as two partners who start a business and work together to make it a success, each may have a different vision of the final reality and how to get there. These different visions can clash and collide. How much more do partners struggle with this dilemma when each gets offered a plum job in a different state or when one's promotion means unemployment and lost opportunity for the other. Intimate partners end up being all too aware of their separate and conflicting individual interests.

Associated risk: One gives up a dream to maintain the relationship or couple harmony. The dilemma emerges because too much accommodating causes us to lose touch with ourselves.

Associated risk: One gives up the relationship in order to be oneself. Accommodating or not, some individuals start feeling claustrophobic and confined as soon as they get close to someone. These individuals often break off their relationships (for good reasons) to avoid feeling overwhelmed by the other person's wants and needs.

6. *Intimate relationships expand the self-concept.* We expand and extend our own identities through our partners, becoming indirectly associated with our partner's work, talents and competencies, accomplishments, and strengths (Aron, Mashek, & Aron, 2004). Further, through the intimate relationship, we incorporate new roles. Some of these roles can add to our prestige, such as "the Senator's wife." We can also add informal roles. As a result of two partners' unique combination of personalities, one will become the responsible one whereas the other is the dreamer; one will be the financially conservative one whereas the other lives for today; one is the neatnik, and the other is the slob. A partner can introduce us to new pursuits and teach us to be competent in new areas. For some of us, a partner may offer us the first opportunity we have had to be someone's beloved.

Associated risk: We can lose ourselves in our partner's identity. In the interest of harmony, some people will consent to giving up old friends, pursuits, and even values. Perhaps in the flush of new love, we go mountain climbing with our partner because we love being together. We assume we will pick up our old interests later, but somehow never do.

Associated risk: We may perceive our partner as an extension of ourselves. We can fail to respect our partner's identity (e.g., his or her friends, values, pursuits) and argue coercively that our partners should take on our own. We may be interested in how our partners complement us (e.g., a trophy wife or a breadwinner) but not sufficiently interested in our partner's unique perspective on life or his or her goals for him- or herself. We may even feel embarrassed because our partner is not presentable enough to do us credit (e.g., does not make enough money or has insufficient social polish).

Associated risk: An individual self-construal may clash with a relational self-construal. Researchers (Gore, Cross, & Morris, 2006) have identified two types of self-construals. The first type, independent self-construals, are ways of conceptualizing the self that emphasize one's independent, individual accomplishments, needs, motives, goals, and interests. Independent self-construals do not make reference to the individual's relationships. Relational self-construals conceptualize oneself in relationship to another (such as, "Johnny's mother," "Charlene's husband", "a person who needs people," or "a person who is thoughtful of others"). Some partners may shy away from intimacy (or from intimate relationships altogether) because they are too attached to being the "independent one" or the "player" or the "free bird." Further, individual identities (especially occupational ones) may be so important to one's self-esteem that one neglects his or her intimate relationship to fulfill the demands of the individual identity.

7. *Intimate partners fulfill one another's needs for intimacy.* Through the many ways that couple partners are intimate with one another, the partners can fulfill each other's needs for a best friend to talk to, for a willing and

enthusiastic sexual partner, and for a beloved person with whom to exchange hugs, kisses, and affectionate touches.

Associated risk: Partners have different needs. It is possible for each partner to find that his or her needs for intimacy and companionship or for autonomy and solitude are chronically unfulfilled because the other's needs are incompatible. When partners' needs are too different, one may settle for too little intimacy whereas the other feels suffocated. Collaborative problem solving around different needs can be a life-long challenge for the couple.

Dilemma #3—The Past Lives in the Present

Forming and sustaining intimate relationships require skills and resources that draw on the psychological acquisitions of childhood, both in the family of origin and with peers. Sustaining a deep intimate connection over time is especially challenging when one or both partners, because of their developmental histories, lacks significant personal resources to tolerate and manage intimacy's normative dilemmas. Sometimes, when a couple fails to attain the intimacy that they desire, it is because one or both partners have brought intense negative affect into the relationship that is fed by dysfunctional cognitive and behavioral habits. Because these reactions and the habits that go with them were consistently reinforced in earlier relationships, they have not yet been adapted to the current relationship.

The skills and resources that intimacy demands vary depending upon the stage of the relationship. Some individuals have problems deepening relationships once they begin whereas others have problems sustaining intimacy once it is initially attained. Some individuals have no trouble forming deep and abiding intimate friendships but balk at the challenges created by romantic relationships. Still others are lonely because they lack the skills and the resilience to go out and meet new people. The benefits and risks that create Dilemma #3 are as follows:

1. *When we meet people and form new relationships, we create the opportunity to meet the person who can be a lifetime intimate partner.* A willingness to meet and reach out to new people opens doors to meeting potential partners.

Associated risk: As soon as we go out to meet new people, we are confronted with the risk of rejection. To reach out and become emotionally available for an intimate relationship, the individual must be able to tolerate the inevitable rejection that can occur at different points in a developing relationship. Depending on when the rejection occurs, the individual may be hurt in a particularly vulnerable aspect of the self (e.g., feeling unattractive, feeling unfeminine, believing that one has little to offer, holding a conviction that one is unlovable in some aspect).

2. *Adult intimate relationships can give adults the love and intimacy they missed out on in their youth.* It is commonplace for people who felt unloved,

undervalued, neglected, or abused as children to dream of the romantic partner whose love would soothe the hurts of those early deprivations.

Associated risk: Adult intimate relationships can also cause us to reexperience the pain and disappointment from our past. When events in the adult intimate relationship elicit negative feelings similar to those experienced in past relationships, people will try to feel better using the same behaviors that seemed to work in the past. These outmoded relationship behaviors may consistently undermine the couple relationship.

Associated risk: Impoverished relationships in one's past may have failed to provide the interpersonal skills needed to initiate or maintain an intimate adult relationship. The individual may find that the problems of the couple relationship overwhelm his or her meager resources for resolving them.

3. *Intimate relationships can soothe hurt feelings and lift us out of a blue mood.* Intimate interactions can soothe us when we are agitated or distraught. Adults who are prone to feelings of depression, anxiety, or loneliness can find comfort in the presence of a supportive intimate relationship partner (Beach, 2001). Emotionally supportive intimate interactions allow partners to share their stresses and burdens with one another in exchange for psychological bolstering and soothing. Many relationship partners depend on one another for support, nurturing, and reassurance in the face of stress, exhaustion, and other normal challenges of daily life.

Associated risk: Because a partner is soothing, we fail to learn to soothe ourselves. Because intimacy is such an effective source of soothing and emotional support, it is tempting to demand more soothing than a partner can give and fail to soothe oneself. Expecting or demanding that a partner function "like a Valium" (as one wife put it) puts a strain on a relationship and may sabotage intimacy and contribute to a relationship's demise.

Associated risk: Erosion of intimacy exacerbates loneliness. It is a truism that a bad relationship is lonelier than being without a relationship. When partners lack the skills to soothe one another, when partners fail to develop mutual understanding or cannot share themselves, partners are lonely within the relationship.

4. *An intimate romantic relationship is also an attachment relationship and thereby provides a secure base and a safe haven from the demands placed upon our public selves.* Ample evidence now demonstrates the close connection between feelings of security and intimacy in close relationships (e.g., Mikulincer & Shaver, 2007; Reis & Patrick, 2006). Research suggests that secure partners are willing to risk more intimacy with one another, whereas partners who enjoy more frequent intimate contact feel more secure.

Associated risk: A history of insecure attachments may lead us to accept an insecure adult romantic relationship too readily and leave us wanting more security and intimacy. Individuals who are anxious about their partners' emotional availability and commitment to the relationship seek more intimacy to be reassured but do not always find what they are looking for (Campbell,

Simpson, Boldry, & Kashy, 2005). Further, they tend to be hypersensitive to signs of rejection and abandonment. In contrast, avoidant individuals, who cope with their insecurities by avoiding emotionally arousing interactions with the partner whether those are positive (intimate) or negative (conflict), are disproportionately likely to find themselves in relationships with anxious partners and unable or unwilling to provide them the reassurance they need. Further, avoidant individuals are prone to leaving their relationships when their partners make demands upon them. Whereas individuals with insecure attachment histories can learn to be more effective and contented romantic partners, they may require help from a therapist to do so (Johnson, 2005).

Conclusion

Intimacy at its best fulfills our need to share our deepest selves to a caring, interested, and understanding other and to know another person inside and out as well. Intimacy fulfills our needs to be known and accepted for who we are. In our dreams, our intimate relationships offer us an ongoing source of sexual intimacy, of self-affirmation, and of validation and support. What we encounter in a couple relationship is less than what we imagined. Even more, we find ourselves struggling within ourselves or with our partners over one or more intimacy dilemmas that seem to have no permanent solution. Further, we may find that our efforts to resolve these dilemmas only make them worse and damage the relationship besides. It is because of intimacy's dual nature, its promise of fulfillment, and its threats of hurt and frustration, that people have intimacy dilemmas. Moreover, some people have their own particular intimacy problems that stem from the hurts and deprivations of their individual relationship histories.

Intimacy problems have been some of the thorniest that couple therapists have encountered, and their complexity has defied efforts to understand or treat them from the perspective of any one theoretical orientation. This intimacy-focused therapy offers clinicians a cognitive-behavioral system for assessing and treating intimacy problems that draws from humanistic and family systems approaches in order to best address the ebb and flow of intimacy in ongoing relationships. It also draws from developmental theories such as attachment theory and Sullivan's interpersonal theory to understand the skills and resources that individuals bring to their relationships to cope with intimacy dilemmas.

2

THE ASSESSMENT OF INTIMACY-RELATED PROBLEMS

Just as each person's signature is unique, so does each couple have a unique configuration of individual and relational characteristics that combine to form their conjoint *Intimacy Signature*. The uniqueness of each Intimacy Signature comes from the particular adaptations that the couple and the individual partners make to the three intimacy dilemmas, both those that are nearly universal and those that are unique to their relationship.

The Intimacy Signature assesses proximal and distal contributors to a couple's (or individual's) characteristic ways of relating. It assesses behavioral, cognitive, and affective aspects of the couple relationship and individual psychological functioning that affect couple satisfaction, harmony, and stability along with individual partner mental health and well-being. Behavioral measures assess intimate expressive communication and listening skills, couple problem-solving, and intimacy-distance regulation. Cognitive assessment targets intimacy-relevant thinking patterns and intimacy schemas. Affective assessment examines emotion regulation.

The Intimacy Signature is divided into (1) a set of measures for therapists' use, relevant to each of the three intimacy dilemmas, (2) packets for clients to take home, one most appropriate for couples and one more appropriate for individuals, and (3) a small packet for therapist formulations and treatment planning. The measures work well in concert; however, each assessment tool stands on its own. Experienced clinicians will likely want to choose those tools that are most useful to them in their work with couples and interpersonally troubled individuals. Clinicians who are just starting out should try the whole package at first.

The Assessment Process

With the *Intimacy Signature*, the clinician assesses both the couple and each individual partner. Comfort and ease with intimacy requires both individual and relationship resources and it is important to do an assessment of each.

Ideally, the assessment process begins with an initial conjoint interview, during which the clinician gets an initial impression of the relationship and establishes a rapport with each partner. Following this, the clinician meets with each of the partners separately to get information about each partner's history and to get an impression of each partner's take on the relationship problems without the other present. Finally, the assessment process concludes with a second couple session during which the therapist shares his or her impressions with the couple, obtains their feedback, and establishes a therapeutic contract with them. Meeting with each partner individually before meeting with the couple is a viable alternative, as one partner is often more motivated and wants to meet with the therapist first. The individual partner assessment can also be used for individual clients who are without partners and want to find and sustain an intimate relationship.

The Structure of the Intimacy *Signature*

Intimacy is only one aspect of a couple relationship, however central and important. Its evaluation must fit seamlessly into a broader assessment of couple functioning in order to be useful to clinicians. The Intimacy Signature is a general assessment of couple (or individual) functioning with additional measures added for assessing intimacy problems. Comprehensive introductions to couple assessment can be found in Datillo (2010), Epstein and Baucom (2003), Gottman (1999), and Karpel (1994).

The first goal of the Intimacy Signature is to identify the presenting problem and the individual and relational factors that contribute to it. An analysis of the presenting problem helps the clinician determine whether a focus on intimacy is appropriate for a particular couple. Second, information from the Intimacy Signature provides a prognosis for a couple's relationship; it allows a clinician to make predictions about the couple's potential for happiness together in the future or, conversely, the likelihood that they will separate. Finally, the Intimacy Signature suggests treatment interventions. By analyzing couple problems into their behavioral, cognitive, and affective components, the Intimacy Signature can be used to develop a comprehensive plan of treatment. The presentation of the Intimacy Signature in this chapter begins with prognostic indications and concludes with targets for intervention.

The Initial Couple Interview

Before the clinician assesses the presenting problem, the initial couple interview can put the couple relationship into the broader environmental context of the couple's extended family, children, employment status, and work satisfaction and obtain information about previous mental health treatment sought by either partner [see Datillo (2010) or Gottman (1999) for thorough discussions]. The Intimacy Signature Basic Intake contains a checklist for summarizing the information obtained through the interview and the prognostic implications of the couple's responses. These prognostic implications are derived from research on marriage and divorce.

Assessing the presenting problem. Problems with intimacy may be manifestations of other, more pervasive, underlying themes (e.g., struggles for control), or they may themselves underlie various dysfunctional interaction patterns (e.g., withdrawal and avoidance). Assessment of intimacy problems must begin with the presenting problem(s). The presenting problem is what brought the couple into treatment and is either what the partners are most urgently distressed about, or it is what they are willing to talk about initially.

The presenting problem should be assessed in the context of the couple's whole relationship. The therapist should ask what prompted the couple to seek help at that time and determine which partner, if not both, is suffering the most from the problem. Table 2.1 lists questions therapists may ask regarding the history of the presenting problem and indicates the significance of the couple's responses. Problems that are precipitated by an event are more amenable to treatment than problems that were part of the relationship from the beginning. If the relationship was functioning adequately before

Table 2.1 Determining the history of the presenting problem

Question	*Potential Therapeutic Benefit*
When did you first notice (this problem)?	If the problem was precipitated by an event, therapy can focus on the outcomes of the event and its meaning for the partners.
Has this always been a problem or has it come up recently?	If the problem was caused by a change in one or both partners or their circumstances, focus on the meaning of the change for the partners.
If it came up recently, was there a turning point or trigger event?	A trigger event may illuminate problems that were tolerable and are now worse. The trigger event overtaxes existing coping mechanisms and forces couples to try something new or dissolve their relationship. The crisis offers the couple an opportunity to improve their coping skills.
If it has always been a problem, what makes it especially bad right now, compared with in the past?	If partners are fighting over the same issues that once attracted them to one another, therapeutic focus can shift to acceptance and "people are packages" (see "Irritating Things Come in Attractive Packages," Chapter 6).
What, if anything, have you tried in order to solve the problem?	Helps partners and therapist separate problems from their attempts to resolve them (i.e., assesses their problem-solving skills).

the crisis, the couple may bring strengths that the therapist can channel into resolving the crisis. In the case of problems that existed from the beginning, however, the therapist is more likely to be facing problems that are not resolvable through ordinary problem-solving methods. Rather, the partners may simply be coming to the end of their efforts to mold each other into the ideal spouse each hoped the other would be. The couple may question whether there has ever been a basis for them to love and decide if they want to be together now that they know each other better and are more realistic about the possibilities for change. These are not hard and fast rules, but they demonstrate why it is important for therapists to assess the history of the presenting problem, as different pathways demand different approaches. A checklist of prognostic indicators can be found in Appendix A, Intimacy Signature Basic Intake. The therapist may go over the sheet with the couple to ensure that she or he has identified the correct issues.

Identifying Intimacy Issues in the Presenting Problem

Karpel (1994) reported that the most common presenting problems in couple therapy are (a) lack of intimacy, (b) conflict over intimacy, (c) repetitive, unresolved conflict, and (d) lost love. Of these, the first two are explicitly characterized by intimacy dilemmas. The second two may have other causes but are often direct outcomes of problematic efforts to resolve intimacy dilemmas. This section describes some of the more common forms taken by intimacy-related presenting problems and offers examples to illustrate the processes by which presenting problems emerge from misguided efforts to resolve one or more of the three intimacy dilemmas.

Lack of intimacy. Couples who complain of lack of intimacy often resemble Cuber and Haroff's (1965) devitalized couples. They live like roommates. Sometimes there is little conflict; they have mastered the art of staying on an even keel by increasing distance to the point where they do not obstruct one another's aims. Neither takes much initiative to increase romance or engage in sexual activity. One may be more dissatisfied than the other, but neither reports that the relationship is very satisfying. One or both experiences need deprivation and may think of becoming involved with others. One wife described the lack of intimacy in her relationship by saying, "It doesn't feel like there is a special bond between us. He treats me the same way he treats his soccer buddies." Further questioning of this husband indicated that he struggled with Dilemma #1, joy versus protection from hurt. He felt odd and uncomfortable with too much intimacy and had created enough distance so that he did not have to experience discomfort.

Lack of intimacy is often most acutely apparent in the couple's sexual relationship or lack thereof. One or both partners may have little or no desire for sex; the desexualized client may want the other to "just accept it." Sometimes, the problem is lack of desire; one husband described himself as going "sexually dormant" because he worked hard and could go for months without thinking about sex.

Lack of sexual intimacy may reflect Dilemma #3, the past lives in the present. Inappropriate, unhealthy exposure to sexuality in childhood is traumatic, resulting in attitudes and emotions that make it difficult to sustain a sexually intimate relationship (Johnson, 2005). Negative messages about the body, about one's attractiveness, about sexuality itself, or about the legitimacy of sexual pleasure-seeking can leave their mark on an adult's comfort with sexual intimacy.

In some low-intimacy relationships, one partner has been labeled (perhaps by both) as the *bad guy* who is identified as having problems with intimacy. The bad guy partner often finds him- or herself in the role of resisting the other partner's efforts to make intimate time for the couple. It is important that the therapist not buy into a pattern of blaming one partner, as this way of understanding has not been helpful to the couple or they would not be seeking the therapist's help. Careful observation of the couple's interactions (discussed below) will often reveal that the resisting partner is not the only one contributing to the couple's lack of intimacy. The therapist may discover that the other partner rarely initiates intimate contact because he or she has given up. The couple then goes along, sometimes for years, rarely having intimate contact of any kind. They are friendly with each other but are not really friends. Karpel (1976) has argued that partners in such relationships collude to maintain a low level of intimacy, one in which the ideal, perfect conditions for them to come together never happen in real life. In this way, they protect themselves and one another from the risks embodied in Dilemma #1, joy versus protection from hurt. A checklist for assessing lack of intimacy is part of the Intimacy Signature Basic Intake (Appendix A).

Conflict over intimacy. Partners who lack intimacy in their relationship do not always have conflict about it. To determine if a couple's conflict is intimacy-related, clinicians can use the checklist for assessing lack of intimacy and circle any of the problems that cause conflict in the couple's relationship. If one or more of the above problems is a source of conflict, it is likely that a couple's problems with intimacy should be further explored and made a focus of treatment.

Sometimes, both partners claim to want more intimacy, but the partners fight about when, where, how, and under what circumstances. One partner may complain about the lack of sexual intimacy, whereas the other complains that he or she rarely feels sexual because there is so little emotional intimacy in the relationship. If these couples also experience a lack of intimacy, their inability to resolve their conflicts seems to be the source. Their arguments leave both feeling intensely frustrated, unappreciated, and deprived of intimate contact.

Couples are more likely to have conflict over intimacy when they find themselves unable to cope effectively with Dilemma #2, I versus we. Irresolvable I versus we conflicts stem from partners being unable to accept that they are two distinct individuals in one intimate relationship. An argument over intimacy can reflect partners' erroneous belief that they should want (exactly) the same things, which leads them to struggle to change each other's wants and preferences. For example, one husband complained, "She always wants to do everything with me. I don't understand why she can't make some other friends and do more on her own." His wife counter-complained that, "He makes plenty of time to go out and have a beer with his friends or take his clients out to dinner, but then he comes home tired and begs me to understand how busy he is and how he doesn't have time for me. I'm on the bottom of his priority list." This pair was *polarized* around the issue of time together versus time for separate pursuits: Each believed that the other should be more like him (or her)—more independent or spending more time with each other—and each believed the other was destroying the relationship. The wife interpreted her husband's desire for separateness as a personal rejection of herself instead of a difference that needed to be worked out. The husband similarly misunderstood how rejecting his behavior was in his wife's eyes. The impact of the partners' difference thereby snowballed and brought with it increasing frustration.

It is the unresolved I versus we intimacy dilemma that often explains the intensity of the partners' struggle. Intimate relationships threaten loss of self in vulnerable individuals because couple partners are identified with each other and thought of by others as a unit. Most people can enjoy being part of a couple unit and assume that this is not all that they are (i.e., each is also viewed as an individual in his or her own right in one or more domains of activity). However, those individuals who are especially prone to feeling that they are losing themselves may believe that they must schedule significant numbers of activities that do not involve their partners. The result is that the other partner feels left out and lonely.

Conflict over intimacy may stem from poorly functioning intimacy-distance regulation. One or both may lack good initiation skills: Perhaps the more eager partner approaches the other in ways that guarantees his or her getting rejected. They may also fail to decline the other's initiatives tactfully; the more reluctant partner may decline in a way guaranteed to injure the pride or tender feelings of the other. One partner may have low desire because he or she is struggling with Dilemma #1, joy versus protection from hurt. The failure to cope effectively with the intimacy dilemma may create a negatively charged atmosphere around initiating and reciprocating intimate contact.

Finally, partners' conflicts over intimacy may involve bitter blaming and recriminations over the effects each partner's moods exert over the other. One husband complained, "She always seems to be angry with me," even though his wife denied that this was the case. He complained further that when she was angry, she was not affectionate, warm, or concerned about him. In his case, the conflict over intimacy reflected unresolved issues with Dilemma #2, how much I versus we? This husband blamed her for being emotionally unavailable, believing that she could be available if it weren't for her desire to punish him for his misdeeds by withholding from him. When he gained the ability to perceive her as another sojourner in life with her own struggles and moods, he developed more realistic expectations of her availability for intimate contact with him.

Repetitive, unresolved conflict. Repetitive irresolvable conflict is the most common complaint of distressed couples. It can be contrasted with conflict over intimacy in that intimacy-related issues are not the primary focus of quarreling. In fact, the focus of arguments in couples with this complaint is often mercurial, with the only constant being the frustrating repetition of the quarreling itself. Even when intimacy problems are not the focus of quarreling, however, and especially when quarreling does not have any other consistent focus, it is worthwhile to assess whether frustration and intimacy deprivation fuel the fury of the quarreling. The frustration of unmet intimacy needs creates simmering resentments, and frustrated, lonely partners are often tempted to blame one another. Alternatively, if intimacy needs are being frustrated indirectly as a result of other unresolved problems (e.g., a lack of cooperation in caring for home, children, and so forth), one or both spouses will feel that they have no time or energy for fun. In any event, destructive conflict erodes the positive sentiment that is the fertile ground in which intimacy grows and thrives.

The pathway from intimacy deprivation to repetitive, destructive conflict has several intervening steps. It begins with a need for intimacy that motivates us to approach our partners or to remain open to their approaches. It progresses when intimacy needs are frustrated consistently and relationship partners feel deprived. Initially, partners may pursue and cajole each other, but if these friendly tactics don't work well enough, they come face to face with Dilemma #1, joy versus protection from hurt. To protect their tender advances from suffering further rejection, and because tender advances have not worked, they may behave more coercively to get the other's attention and time. Coercive behavior stresses the relationship, and partners feel increasingly motivated to hide their vulnerable, needy selves from each other and fight about safe issues. The coercive fighting allows them to engage one another, but it is a poor substitute for intimacy. The clinician should be on the lookout for frustrated intimacy needs, as these can underlie partners' motivation to engage in attack-and-defend communication. The following dialogue illustrates how this can work.

Jayden: She's just so angry all the time, about everything. She holds on to it for days, and everyone in the house feels it.

Ariana: So why do you do the things that make me so mad? We've been giving dinner parties for 22 years, and he still acts like I don't know how to entertain. I hate that.

Jayden: So I have to be so careful what I say because otherwise you'll be mad for days, at every little thing I say that's wrong. . . .

Therapist: He's got a point, you know—was that remark [about the table] really at the root of it all?

Ariana: You know, you've seen him, how he tosses off these little put downs all the time. I just get tired of hearing them, and then I shut down; I just can't keep going with him doing that.

Therapist: So there's a cumulative effect of these remarks?

Ariana: Yes, I feel like I can't do anything right.

Therapist: So what happened at dinner the other night, it's part of a pattern in which he doesn't treat you like an equal, his wife?

Ariana: He treats me like I'm his servant or something.

Jayden: I don't get it; I'm always telling you how much I appreciate everything that you do.

Ariana: Yes, you say those words, but let me do one thing that doesn't fit his exact standards, and he's putting me down.

Therapist: You know, I'm getting the impression that this anger that Jayden complains about, it's not just about him being critical and demanding. It's about something more, that you don't feel close to him.

Ariana: Exactly—we're not friends; we're just business associates who happen to live together.

Therapist (to Jayden): What do you think? I'm beginning to think that this problem is ongoing. It's chronic, and at some level she's always mad about it. Then these little things bring it all to the surface.

Ariana: That's it, that's really it.

Therapist: I suggest that we spend some time getting to the bottom of this ongoing problem. I say that [to Jayden] because I think that your problem with her anger might be greatly reduced if this issue were resolved. You know, in most marriages, people are inconsiderate and say thoughtless things when they're tired or under pressure. And most partners can take it in their stride

> because they have a foundation of intimacy and friendship. I'd love to see us work on building that foundation for your relationship together. As we build that up, I think these miserable little quarrels will either go away or stop being such a problem.

In this example, Ariana was chronically angry with Jayden because of her loneliness and her feeling of being rejected by him. Her apparent overreactions to his day-to-day, annoying behaviors actually reflected her anger and frustration with the lack of intimacy in their marriage. Until both partners understood that lack of intimacy was at the core of their unsatisfying, repetitive quarrels, they could not address their conflicts constructively.

There is another way that unresolved Dilemma #1 (joy versus protection from hurt) issues can sabotage intimacy and create chronic, nonproductive conflict. Sometimes couples communicate the way they do because they cannot tolerate the risks associated with higher levels of relational intimacy than what they have already. Negative, coercive communication pushes the partner away and precludes intimacy, making the coercively communicating spouse feel safely distant. There is an irony in this situation because, from the clinician's perspective, it is often clear that the nonproductive arguing has created an atmosphere that is poisonous to intimacy. Given this obvious fact, clinicians reasonably assume that couples want more of intimacy's joys and would have them if only they argued less frequently. However, individual partners each have their own capacities for tolerating the risks of intimacy, and if the demands of intimate interaction exceed their tolerance levels, they experience anxiety. Further, higher levels of intimacy may force them to face their fears (e.g., that they will have to make a significant change, that the partner might leave, and so forth). They are afraid to hear what their partners might tell them.

Sometimes irreconcilable conflict reflects long-standing interpersonal problems on the part of one or both partners. In this case, the couple's problems may stem primarily from Dilemma #3, the past lives in the present. For example, one partner may get extremely emotional regarding the distribution of domestic responsibilities, with the intensity of his or her emotions seeming to be disproportionate to the issue. The emotions may be triggered less by the unreasonableness of his or her partner's behavior and more by an unarticulated, unevaluated assumption about the partner or about relationships, such as "Others (like my partner) are indifferent to my needs" or "I have to be vigilant or everyone (including my partner) will take advantage of me." Similarly, partners who are willing to engage in no-holds-barred conflict, in which they attack basic aspects of each other's character, have likely experienced situations that led them to believe, consciously or not, that "My partner has all the power." The belief justifies the extremely punitive conflict tactics.

Repetitive, nonproductive conflict may not appear to stem from unresolved intimacy issues when first encountered. If it resists straightforward intervention techniques, such as communication and problem-solving training, it may be that the clinician will need to help the couple identify unresolved intimacy issues before the couple can make progress in treatment.

Lost love. Partners who complain of lost love feel as if they are no longer in love and perceive themselves to be emotionally detached from the other. Sometimes partners report a loss of romance, perhaps feeling a brotherly or sisterly affection toward their spouse but little romantic or sexual interest. The waning of romantic feelings may stem from ineffective efforts to cope with Dilemma #1, joy versus protection from hurt. Many individuals feel intensely emotionally vulnerable when they feel romantic and find these vulnerable feelings difficult to tolerate. They may be tempted to wall themselves off from their romantic feelings, with the result that they believe that they are no longer in love.

People who avoid their own romantic feelings could also be coping with Dilemma #3, the past lives in the present. Early deprivations of love, affection, or attention—abuse or neglect—can interfere with a young person's acquisition of the emotion-regulation skills that are required for managing the anxieties associated with building romantic relationships (Grossman, Grossman, & Waters, 2005). The resulting suppression of romantic feelings, in turn, sabotages the individual's efforts to form lasting romantic relationships (Murray, 2005). In this case, the person is protecting him- or herself from reexperiencing the all-too-familiar and painful emotions of his or her younger years, ironically preventing him- or herself from having different experiences as an adult.

Partners may also experience lost feelings of love as a result of their method of coping with conflict. People commonly find conflict with a romantic partner to be anxiety provoking or simply aversive. In order to avoid it, they might passively acquiesce to their partner's wishes, avoiding anger with the partner by distancing themselves. Conversely, they tell themselves that the partner is not so important to them or that they do not need to be so close. They may also be unaware of their distancing behavior.

Sometimes intimacy-related conflict underlies complaints of lost love. This can occur if intimacy is poorly regulated (that is, if partners have been unable to work out a mutually satisfactory intimacy-distance regulation rhythm). Intimacy-related conflict becomes lost love if a pursuing partner gives up trying to engage a withdrawn partner and discovers in the giving up that he or she has no feelings of love left. Years of effort without fruit can result in despair on the part of the pursuer. Whereas the withdrawn partner may sometimes rally to fill the gap, the couple may also drift farther apart. Eventually, the lack of intimacy in the relationship causes one or the other to fall out of love.

Table 2.2 gives some examples of linkages between these four presenting problems and the three intimacy dilemmas. Assessment links presenting

Table 2.2 Presenting problems linked to intimacy dilemmas

Presenting Problem	*Example of Intimacy Dilemma Involved*	*Cognitive-Emotional Process Linking the Two*
	Lack of Intimacy	
"When we can't resolve a disagreement, we'll spend hours and sometimes days barely speaking to each other."	Dilemma #1, *joy versus protection from hurt.* Intimacy fulfills needs and offers compelling rewards yet, at the same time, makes us more vulnerable.	Outside of awareness: "When I'm angry and distant, I feel strong and safe from hurt or humiliation. Once I'm secure in my strength, I can move back closer again."
"There's no connection between us. It's like we're roommates, we have fun, we do things, but when we come home, we go our separate ways."	Dilemma #3, *the past lives in the present.* One or both partners, because of their developmental histories, lack personal resources needed for rewarding and sustained intimate relating.	Outside of awareness: "When it's just the two of us, I'm at a loss for words or gestures. I do fine with socializing but get tongue-tied and uncomfortable when it's just the two of us. It's like I never learned how to be a husband."
	Conflict over Intimacy	
"She won't give me any space; she takes everything I do without her as an indication that I don't love her."	Dilemma #2, *how much I versus how much we?* It can be challenging to create harmony between intimacy and preserving the distinct identities of the partners.	Within awareness: P1: "I have to fight you so hard any time I want to do something on my own. You want to suffocate me." Within awareness: P2: "It seems like I never see you, and when you're around, you're trying to get away. You must not love me."
"I don't have much sexual desire, and he gets so mad at me when I'm not in the mood that I'm in the mood even less often than I would have been."	Dilemma #2, *how much I versus how much we?* It can be challenging to create harmony between intimacy and preserving the distinct identities of the partners.	Within awareness: "He's so critical of me; I feel like I'll never be the wife he wants me to be." Outside of awareness: "I'm slightly disgusted with my own body and sexuality and need enormous amounts of reassurance. From him, I get just the opposite."

	Irresolvable Conflict	
"He doesn't talk to me anymore. As soon as he gets home, he's on that computer. He says he'll change but he never does."	Dilemma #3, *the past lives in the present.* One or both partners, because of their developmental histories, lack personal resources needed for rewarding and sustaining intimate relating.	Outside of awareness: "I got used to being alone as a small child, because my mother abandoned our family after my parents divorced. Now, anytime I get too close to my wife, I reexperience my anger at my mother and my fear of once again being abandoned. So I have to keep my distance."
"She won't pick up after herself, and she won't make the kids pick up their toys." "He doesn't accept that a house with small children is going to be messy most of the time."	Dilemma #2, *how much I versus how much we?* It can be challenging to create harmony between intimacy and preserving the distinct identities of the partners.	Outside of awareness: "I'd love to put my eyes in her head so she can see how this looks to me. Then, she'd have the same reaction I do, and she would change and I could stay the same."
	Lost Love	
"I got over involved with the kids. We started being parents, and we stopped having fun together as husband and wife. I thought it was temporary, but now he wants to leave."	Dilemma #3, *the past lives in the present.* One or both partners, because of their developmental histories, lack personal resources needed for rewarding and sustained intimate relating.	Within awareness: "The kids were small and demanding. I thought he would be more understanding about that." Outside of awareness: "Being a wife, being romantic and sexual, was difficult for me. I felt uncomfortable. Having kids was a relief because I could refocus on them and not deal with those other feelings."

(*Continued*)

Table 2.2 (Continued)

Presenting Problem	*Example of Intimacy Dilemma Involved*	*Cognitive-Emotional Process Linking the Two*
"I really don't want a divorce, but I don't feel like I love her any more. I'm especially aware of not wanting to have sex with her and looking for excuses to avoid it. But I know that she's a good person at heart, and that it would be better for the children if we could stay together."	Dilemma #3, *the past lives in the present.* One or both partners, because of their developmental histories, lack personal resources needed for rewarding and sustained intimate relating.	Within awareness: "There was a woman who really hurt me when I was in college. She was hot and cold, but I was crazy about her. She eventually dumped me, and I realized later that she was only nice to me when she wanted something. I swore that I would never again love someone who wasn't nice to me. So after [my wife] wasn't nice to me a few times, I just turned off to her." Outside of awareness: "I must do everything I can do to avoid feeling that humiliation again, even if it means losing my marriage. I couldn't stand feeling those feelings again."

problems to intimacy dilemmas via intimacy-related thinking patterns and their associated blueprints for behavior.

The Relationship History

The assessment of the relationship history can function as both a data gathering mission and a therapeutic intervention. The relationship history is a way of documenting (and helping the couple remember) how their relationship developed and what brought them together. It also helps them identify intervening events that caused stress in their relationship, possibly precipitating the decline in the relationship's functioning.

Couples will usually talk readily together about their initial attraction and courtship, allowing the therapist to determine whether the problems are recent or date back to the beginning of the relationship. Recent problems may stem from the couple's reactions to recent changes in one or both partners or their lives (e.g., new job, new baby) and are therefore more amenable to behavior change efforts than more long-lasting problems that may reflect personality differences and require acceptance-oriented strategies (such as those described by Jacobson & Christensen, 1996).

Aspects of the partner's personality that were attractive in the beginning can later become irritants. It is a truism in couple therapy that the things that attract a couple to one another are the same things that frustrate them when they have been married for awhile. These frustrating aspects of the other can often be understood as powerful growth possibilities in the relationship. For example, a wife who was attracted to her husband's ability to see the humor in everything may now be frustrated because she cannot persuade him to engage in serious problem solving with her. The therapist may perceive the wife as someone whose life would be enriched if she were able to develop her own sense of humor. By refusing to face her own humorlessness, the wife creates a humor vacuum in the relationship that the husband all too readily rushes to fill. In this way, the characteristics that draw the couple together often become difficulties. Part of what is going on when partners turn off to qualities that once turned them on is that they are resisting the pressure toward growth that their partner's characteristics offer, the same pressures that promised growth at the beginning. Therefore, resistance to a partner characteristic that was once attractive can be identified as a target of intervention for the complainer.

Current Relationship Functioning

Part of the relationship history involves assessing the couple's current relationship functioning in key areas outside of the presenting complaint. It is useful to assess strengths and weaknesses in the following areas: social life and friends, decision making (e.g., regarding division of labor, child-rearing, finances), relations with extended family and in-laws, demands of work versus family, sexual relationship, shared leisure activities and interests, religious or spiritual life, and level of intimacy. The interview assessing current relationship functioning includes the Intimacy Assessment Interview (Intimacy Signature Basic Assessment, Appendix A; a client self-report version, Appendix B). The Intimacy Assessment Interview asks about frequency of expressions of affection, presence of couple time and intimate contact, emotional support partners seek and provide, romantic and sexual functioning, and the couple's ability to have fun together. In the Basic Assessment, the therapist can also find an intimacy behavior checklist to use to assess problems with specific kinds of intimacy in the couple's relationship.

The Individual Partner Interviews

The individual interviews provide an opportunity for the therapist to form an independent trust relationship with each partner as well as one with the couple. In the private interview, partners can talk to the therapist about issues that they are not prepared to share with the other partner. The therapist can also use the individual partner interview to find out more about each partner's life and relationship history. As one's parents' relationship (or lack thereof) can provide a model or set of expectations for one's adult couple relationship, it is useful to find out what it was like while the individual was growing up. That the individual's relationship with each parent and with other significant caregivers also shapes expectations of love relationships, as has been borne out by research on adult attachment (e.g., Grossman, Grossman, & Waters, 2005; Mikulincer & Shaver, 2007). A parent-offspring relationship that improves over time and offers satisfactions in adulthood that were not forthcoming during childhood suggests that there are resources in the individual partner and his or her family of origin that can be drawn upon in the couple therapy. Conversely, parent-child relationships that were demoralizing, abusive, or neglectful set up expectations for love relationships that affect adults in profound ways and can suggest points of intervention for the therapist.

Finally, individual partners frequently have insights about each other that they do not have about themselves. Although the therapist must always double check the partners' impressions of each other against his or her own observations, the partner's perceptions of each other can offer valuable shortcuts for the therapist as he or she formulates a treatment plan.

The individual assessment interview provides the therapist with an opportunity to build his or her alliance with the individual partner. This is best accomplished by the therapist accepting and validating the client's point of view and current method of managing stresses and unmet needs. Starting with acceptance of the client's current mode of being with others, the therapist can later work step-by-step to help the client acquire the resources and skills that will lead to more satisfying and sustainable intimate relationships. Acceptance and validation is most therapeutic when it acknowledges the individual's needs and emotions as normal, human, and understandable and affirms the logic of the coping style without affirming psychopathology. The alliance is furthered by the therapist affirming the client's strengths and coping efforts and avoiding behavior that controls, judges, or handles the patient.

Interviewing the individual patient requires that the therapist balance three aims: to appropriately follow up on the client's statements, to use the structured interview (see Basic Assessment, Appendix A) to get as much useful information as possible, and to give the client new topics to consider. The disadvantage of too much structuring is that the therapist misses hearing what the client's associations are as the client's conversation moves from one topic to the next. The client's associations provide useful information about his or her thought processes, assumptions about the relationship, and hopes and expectations, the assessment of which will be discussed later.

The confidentiality dilemma. Interviewing each partner separately creates a confidentiality dilemma. The therapist must decide whether to guard the confidentiality of the material shared by the partners in the individual sessions or to use it openly in the couple sessions. The therapist must make a judgment about whether he or she can work with the couple effectively, knowing the secrets that they shared in the individual sessions.

To maintain the trust relationship between the therapist and the partners, it is helpful if the therapist lays out the confidentiality policy during the initial couple therapy session. Maintaining confidentiality carries with it several risks. One risk is that the therapist will inadvertently refer to something in the couple session that one of the partners shared in the individual session, breaking confidentiality. A second risk is that the therapist will hear secrets that make it impossible to treat both partners together. For example, if one partner is actively engaged in a secret extramarital affair, the therapist cannot conduct therapy with both partners as if the affair does not exist without colluding with the betraying partner; nor can he or she take it upon him- or herself to share a secret that could break up the marriage. A third risk is that mistrustful partners may imagine that the therapist is keeping weighty secrets from them that can undermine the therapist's alliance with one or both partners. My experience suggests that the advantages of confidential individual partner interviews outweigh the risks. The therapist may decide, however, that the risks outweigh the advantages with some couples. Partners who distrust the therapy process out of hand, or who distrust one another, may find that the possibility of secrets between the spouse and the therapist causes more anxiety than they can tolerate and still remain in therapy.

Assessing individual needs and fears. Dilemma #2, how much I versus how much we, exists in part because intimate interactions require two partners, but partners' individual needs for intimacy, privacy, and separateness will never be perfectly compatible. Underlying the framing of this dilemma is the assumption that individuals have relatively stable need strengths that function as motives driving behavior. Further, partners may have different ways of fulfilling their needs for intimacy and related provisions. In the Intimacy Signature Take-Home Couple Packet (Appendix B), there is a form called "Thoughts on Our Relationship" that goes home with each partner after the first session for purposes of assessing significant differences in their needs and the consequences of those differences. It is less useful to discover absolute need strengths for each individual and more useful to assess how fulfilled each partner's intimacy needs are (Ryan & Deci, 2010). The form asks partners how much closeness and intimacy they like, compared with the other partner, whether their preferences have changed, and whether they feel lonely in their relationship. It asks couples when they feel closest to one another and when they are most likely to feel distant. It also contains a checklist of intimacy problems for each partner to complete.

Observations of In-Session Behavior

A cornerstone of traditional behavioral couple therapy is systematic direct observation of the couple's communication in the session (Epstein & Baucom, 2003; Jacobson & Margolin, 1979). Traditionally, behavioral observation is used to assess the couple's communication and problem-solving skills. Observations of communication behavior reveal deficits and illuminate targets for communication and problem-solving skills training. For some couples with intimacy problems, practice in using effective communication skills will help them to address and resolve problems with intimacy.

Direct observation is critical, as it is rare that couples are able to report accurately on all aspects of their communication. It is nearly always essential to observe (a) how the couple solves problems together, (b) whether either is able to listen to the other empathically, (c) how they express themselves on an important or emotionally charged issue (e.g., how they handle anger and frustration, called *emotion regulation*), and (d) how they express wants or preferences. In order to communicate effectively, couples must be able to express themselves clearly and specifically without demeaning or attacking the other. Skillful expression minimizes defensiveness in the other and encourages him or her to listen and convey understanding. Partners also need to be able to verbally confront and resolve their problems while sticking to their agenda and avoiding emotional escalation.

Assessing intimate communication. No couple is intimate all the time, but couples often discuss highly personal, private topics in their therapist's office. Under these circumstances, the therapist can observe couples' skillfulness with intimate communication. Therapists can encourage couples to talk to one another by asking each to think about or respond to something the other has just said. For example, the therapist might say, "You look surprised like you're hearing this for the first time. Am I reading you right? . . . ask him more about that" or "She's just given you some important feedback—try checking with her now to ensure that you've understood her correctly." The therapist can also ask the couple to interact around a first homework assignment during the fourth session. For example, "You were each asked last session to come up with a list of gifts [that you are willing to give to your partner, that you think would make your partner happy]." Talk with each other about your lists, and communicate with each other about which of the gifts on the other's list would be most meaningful to you and why" (see Jacobson & Christensen, 1996, for more information on this intervention). The Intimacy Signature Basic Assessment includes a checklist for observations of intimate communication that includes all three components of intimate interactions discussed in Chapter 1: self-revealing (expressive) behavior, positive involvement, and shared understanding.

When intimacy issues are at the forefront, it is useful for the therapist to pay attention to whether partners are able to express "soft emotions" (Johnson & Greenberg, 1994). Because intimate interaction, by definition, involves the revelation of private, usually vulnerable aspects of oneself, it is instructive to observe partners' responding to one another's vulnerabilities as they are expressed. Johnson and Greenberg (1994) call the emotions of sadness, fear, pain, and anxiety the "soft" emotions because their expression tends to reveal vulnerabilities, minimize defensiveness, and focus attention on intimate experience. Soft emotions can be contrasted with anger, which is often self-protective and can be used to hide more vulnerable emotions.

Partners' responses to the expression of these feelings, when they are talking directly to each other (as opposed to talking through the therapist), should reveal each person's ability to express empathy and sensitivity and to communicate their understanding of their partner's message. The therapist can observe the couples' interactions to (a) assess behavior directly, (b) observe signs of unexpressed affect in facial expressions, gestures, and voice tone, and (c) make inferences about the partners' thinking patterns based on what they say.

Structuring the session to elicit specific behaviors. The therapist can structure intimacy-focused problem-solving dialogue in order to elicit specific conversation sequences that he or she suspects are contributing to the couple's problems. For example, the therapist can ask the partners to talk with each other for a few minutes about a thorny intimacy-related problem in their relationship. Alternatively, a conversation about any presenting problem that appears to stem from unresolved intimacy issues can, when observed by the therapist, reveal the couple's typical mode for addressing intimacy concerns.

If a couple will not get near their intimacy issues, and the therapist strongly suspects one or both partners has difficulties in that area, the therapist can ask the partners to discuss one of the following topics in the session, each of which can reveal typical and problematic communication patterns in couples who are having difficulty with intimacy:

1 Planning something pleasurable to do together;
2 Listening and supporting the other as he or she expresses a concern or problem unrelated to the relationship;
3 Make a sex date.

The therapist can begin the discussion as follows: "If you wanted to have some couple time tonight, just to be together, to be close, maybe to have sex, who would start? . . . OK, what I'd like you to do is to initiate some couple time—plan it for the next night you have available—so that I can see how this goes with you two. . . . See if you can get her to make some couple time for the two of you this Thursday night." An alternative instruction that is also useful, depending upon the couple's complaint, is: "If Julie wants some couple time, Kenneth, but you really need some time to be quiet and not interact, how would that go? Would you be willing to show me how it usually goes between you when she tries to get your attention under those circumstances?"

It can be useful for the therapist to structure the interaction in order to observe the couple's communication under optimum conditions (Jacobson & Margolin, 1979). Optimum conditions allow the therapist to determine whether partners lack communication skills or whether they have them but are not able to make use of them within the context of their interactions. By observing how well the partners respond to instructions, the therapist can tell whether there is a gap between the partners' ability to communicate effectively and their performance of effective behavior. Therapists can structure an optimum communication environment through one of the following sets of instructions:

1 Instruct one partner to listen quietly while the other speaks;
2 Instruct the listening partner to repeat what he or she heard the other say;
3 Stop the speaking partner from attacking or blaming;
4 Instruct the speaking partner to use "I" language to be specific and to pause so the listener can respond.

The assessment questions addressed here are: (1) are they unable to communicate effectively or do they understand each other all too well; and (2) can they demonstrate skillful, effective communication under controlled conditions or are they already doing the best that they can? Often, partners with intimacy problems are getting their messages across quite clearly, and each knows very well already what the other wants. Instead, what appears to be a lack of communication is defensiveness, in which one or both partners protects themselves from the other's influence, attacks, or demands.

Assessing intimacy-distance regulation. Because many romantic partners live together and occupy the same physical space for numerous hours each day, the potential for intimate contact is theoretically continuous. It is, therefore, necessary that couples develop coordinated strategies for moving in and out of intimate relating. These strategies together form the couples' *intimacy-distance regulation process.*

Linda Roberts and Karen Prager (Prager & Roberts, 2004) have defined intimacy-distance regulation processes as those behavioral sequences that move partners back and forth from intimacy to separateness and back again to embrace intimate contact. There are three intimacy-distance regulation sequences that are worth assessing: (1) One partner initiates and the other reciprocates or otherwise responds positively; (2) one partner initiates and the other postpones, declines, or begs off; and (3) the partners conclude their interaction when one gets up or does something else, and the other objects or resists. Regulation sequences are taken for granted in well-functioning couple relationships. For these couples, intimacy-distance regulation behaviors will quickly become automatic, well coordinated, and mutually acceptable. For others, maintaining intimacy in conjunction with other relationship demands and individual needs may be an overwhelming task or one riddled with conflict. Poorly functioning intimacy-distance regulation causes and sustains intimacy problems whereas it also reflects unresolved intimacy dilemmas.

Like any behavioral sequences that are repeated time and again, intimacy-distance regulation sequences shape and confine the couple's relationship. Characteristic intimacy-distance regulation sequences are represented by each partner in the form of self-fulfilling, behavior-outcome expectations associated with intimate relating. Treatment implications of these processes are covered in more detail in Chapter 7. The Intimacy Signature—Dilemma #1 packet (Appendix C) contains a checklist that clinicians can use to assess a couples' intimacy-distance regulation process. It asks about specific behaviors associated with initiating, reciprocating, or declining intimate contact.

If the clinician suspects that there are intimacy-distance regulation problems, but has not observed them in the couple's interactions in the session, the clinician can instruct the couple to try one of the following in-session exercises:

1. Ask the couple to describe or demonstrate how they usually initiate intimate interactions (i.e., sexual encounters, bids for verbal intimacy, requests for hugs and kisses, and so forth). Couples who complain of low intimacy or lost love may say that neither has initiated anything in ages. Others may report initiation behaviors that seem to guarantee rejection. A common example is one in which an angry spouse who has been waiting for the other to initiate sexual contact, complains, "I can't remember the last time you showed any interest in having sex with me." This kind of initiation is unlikely to elicit a positive response from the partner.

2. Ask the couple what they do when one of them is ready to stop talking, stop having sex, or stop spending time together. Parting with a kiss or an affirming statement, such as, "I hate to break this up, but I have to get back to work," or "I enjoyed that" allows movement out of intimacy to be a positive experience.

3. Ask the couple to describe how they typically say "no" to sexual contact, intimate conversation, or time together and how the other typically responds.

Using problem-solving discussions to assess couple's intimate communication. Therapists nearly always have the opportunity to observe couples' problem-focused interactions. Problem-focused interactions have the potential to become intimate interactions if the couple resolves a problem or if the interaction is fair, nonblaming, and nondefensive (Jacobson & Christensen, 1996). Interventions directed at couples' problem-focused conversations also have the potential of helping couples have better intimate interactions. The Intimacy Signature—Dilemma #2 packet (Appendix C) contains a checklist of problem-solving interaction behaviors for the clinician, with strengths and targets for intervention side by side to ensure easy use of the checklist for treatment planning.

Assessing partners' schemas and associated thinking patterns. Intervention with partner thinking patterns is central to ameliorating intimacy problems, and it is important that clinicians have multiple options for assessing beliefs and attitudes. The Intimacy Signature includes three methods for assessing cognitions: (1) paper-and-pencil inventories, (2) in-session assessment via behavioral indicators of beliefs and attitudes, and (3) open-ended interview questions.

Paper and pencil measures have the advantage of being quick to administer and offer rapid insight into partners' thinking about their relationship. They can offer targets for intervention early in therapy and offer a means by which clinicians can offer immediate feedback to partners about the attitudes that may be harming their relationship.

The Inventory of Relationship Beliefs (Eidelson & Epstein, 1982) assesses beliefs about couple relationships that are likely to have global, nonspecific effects on partner's day-to-day interactions with one another. Don Baucom and his colleagues (Baucom, Epstein, Daiuto, Carels, Rankin, & Burnett, 1996; Baucom, Epstein, Rankin, & Burnett, 1996) developed the Inventory of Relationship Standards (IRS) to measure three different dimensions of relationship standards: boundaries, time investment, and power/control. A third possibility is Knee, Patrick, and Lonsbary's (2003) Implicit Theories of Relationships (ITR) measure that assesses people's beliefs about relationships as destined (or not) and as having growth potential (or not).

Because schemas and automatic thoughts are often under specific stimulus control, they are effectively accessed via couple interactions. Although people occasionally lay out their intimacy-related assumptions and expectations for the therapist, it is more common for the therapist to infer people's thinking patterns from their verbalizations. Observations of the couple's interaction behavior can help the therapist generate hypotheses about partner's intimacy-related automatic thoughts and schemas and the impact of those on each partner's emotional reaction and consequent behavior with the other.

The Intimacy Signature Basic Intake includes a checklist of behaviors that are especially likely to reveal underlying intimacy schemas. The left-hand column of the checklist gives some examples of behaviors that frequently signal the presence of an intimacy schema whereas the right-hand column lists the schemas.

Here is an example from a couple interview in which the therapist developed a hypothesis about one partner's intimacy schema after listening to the couple's in-session exchange:

Lillian: You know, I end up being the one who's in charge of the house, of the finances, of all the work that needs to be done. He gets to play. And when I want a little help, when I want to teach our boys that they have to help, he's the one who gets upset because his game has been interrupted. He's always been like that though, toys and games first, playing first, everything else second.

Harold: You know she says that about intimacy too. I can't get her to sit down and relax with me. I can't remember the last time we had sex. She's always running around, and she's usually in a bad mood.

Lillian: If he would only help me more, I wouldn't be as angry. I also don't understand why he can't see the things we do together around the house as time together? When we're cooking together or cleaning up together, or last summer, when we were painting the boys' bedrooms, we were together. We talked and laughed while we did it. It wasn't so bad, was it?

Harold: I'm OK with all of that, and I've said I'd help you more. But you know, none of that replaces for me time in front of the fire, just the two of us, with a cup of hot chocolate and the music on . . . it's not intimacy to me to paint. I want more intimacy.

Lillian: He has a point, I've always had trouble sitting still. I feel guilty because I can always think of things that need to be done. I'm always thinking about the boys and what they'll need to do to be ready for school the next day. I just don't understand how he can put all that aside and not think about it.

Therapist: When you think you're ready to sit down with him, what kinds of thoughts come up that get in the way?

Lillian: I feel responsible and partly that's because I can't count on him to be thinking about it. But I believe that our responsibility for our boys is our number one priority. That's just how I was raised.

Therapist: Do you worry about that when you're at work, too?

Lillian: Well, not as much, because then, I believe I'm fulfilling a different set of responsibilities, of contributing to our family's income, of doing what I'm supposed to do at work.

Therapist: So it's the hardest to forget when you're just goofing around, like maybe that's a waste of time or too selfish?

Lillian: You know it's been so long since I did that, I can't remember.

This therapist, by listening to the connections that the partners made in their conversation and by asking questions that followed the couple's dialogue closely, generated a hypothesis about Lillian's problematic intimacy schema, "Pleasure-seeking is shameful."

An advantage to observing behavior with an eye to uncovering influential cognitions is that a "causal chain" can be identified that, on the one hand, connects one partner's behavior to the other partner's schema and, on the other, connects the second partner's schema to his or her own emotional reaction and defensive behavior. Once the therapist identifies a causal chain, he or she can share the perceptions of the linkages with the clients and begin working with them on each of the links in the chain in an effort to change them. Figure 2.1 illustrates the causal chain from schema to emotion to behavior.

Certain open-ended questions can help the couple to explore any assumptions, perceptions, expectations, or attributions that accompanied their verbal or affective expressions. These questions, useful for either couple or individual sessions, can help to identify cognition-emotion-behavior chains and are listed in Table 2.3.

Dilemma #2, I versus we, stems in part from a paradox in which intimacy appears to be most attainable when partners are together, sharing their aims, their lives, and their selves, while at the same time wanting to continue to fully be themselves as individuals. Psychological differentiation is what Bowen (1978) called the set of psychological resources that are required to maintain this balance (see Chapter 8). *Psychological differentiation,* according to Schnarch (1997), involves "balancing . . . individuality and the drive for

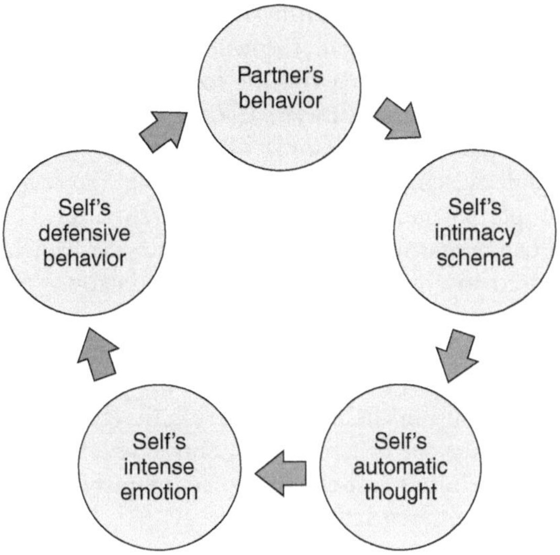

Figure 2.1 Process from partner's behavior to self's defensiveness

Table 2.3 Questions that help identify causal chains

Is there anything in particular that your wife (husband) does that sets you off? Gets you really upset? What do you feel when he or she does that? What do you think it means?
What does that mean to you that is upsetting?
Is this similar to anything you experienced growing up? In another relationship that didn't work out?
Do you think there's a connection between what you experienced growing up and your reaction to X?
Is there anything else that your wife (husband) does that particularly upsets you? And so forth.

togetherness. Individuality propels us to follow our own directives, to be on our own, and to create a unique identity. Togetherness pushes us to follow the directives of others, to be part of a group. When these two life forces . . . are expressed in balanced, healthy ways, the result is a meaningful relationship" (p. 55–56). Differentiated individuals are able to be close without feeling that they are being overpowered by the partner and can therefore disagree without "feeling alienated and embittered" (Schnarch, 1997, p. 56). There are two undifferentiated responses to Dilemma #2. The first is called *enmeshment*, in which partners each perceive the other as having overwhelming power over themselves and their actions. Enmeshed partners fight like their disagreements were a life or death matter. *Unrelated partners* increase distance and even cut off communication to avoid the feeling that they are losing themselves to their partner's desires (Bowen, 1978).

The Intimacy Signature—Dilemma #2 packet includes a checklist that is designed to aid the clinician in thinking about the level of differentiation of each couple partner. Psychological differentiation is associated with three groups of behaviors and emotion management skills, which are listed in column 1 and used to organize the behavioral indications of differentiation versus enmeshment versus unrelatedness. The three groups are: (1) assert and care for the self within the intimate relationship; (2) maintain accommodating, respectful, and accepting behavior toward the partner; and (3) maintain the intimate relationship in the face of I versus we challenges. The checklist offers sample behaviors for differentiated, enmeshed, and unrelated coping with I versus we dilemmas to help therapists identify specific intervention targets for increasing differentiation.

Conclusion

The Intimacy Signature captures the combination of couple interaction processes and individual patterns of thinking and reacting that together constitute the couple's unique approach to intimacy. The Intimacy Signature combines self-report, interview, and behavioral observational measures to gather information on the couple's primary complaints and the individual, relational, and historical factors that contribute to and sustain their problems. The Intimacy Signature offers a systematic conceptualization of intimacy and the factors that influence a couple's efforts to cope with its risks and inherent dilemmas.

3

GETTING STARTED AND BUILDING THE THERAPEUTIC ALLIANCE

Intimacy-oriented treatment takes intimacy dilemmas and translates them into sets of problematic cognitions, emotions, and behaviors, and by doing so, makes them accessible to intervention. Intimacy-oriented interventions are organized here and in the next three chapters according to the target of the intervention: the therapeutic alliance, behavioral, cognitive, or affective change. One of the goals of these chapters on intervention is to demonstrate that intimacy problems, however complex, can be understood and treated systematically as sets of specific thinking patterns, emotional reactions, and maladaptive behaviors and can together be understood as responses to one of the three intimacy dilemmas.

Evolution of This Treatment

The therapeutic approach described in this volume stands on the shoulders of existing cognitive-behavioral systems of psychotherapy. Research supports the notion that negative, distorted thinking patterns are associated with emotional distress and mood disorders (Beck, 1976; Beck, Rush, Shaw, & Emery, 1979; for a review, Haaga, Dyck, & Ernst, 1991). Intimacy problems in turn may be exacerbated and maintained by unnecessarily negative, pessimistic, or unrealistic attitudes and expectations about the self, the partner, and intimate relationships (Campbell et al., 2005). Unrealistic expectations elicit disappointment and anger when they are not fulfilled, whereas pessimistic expectations lead to sadness, defeatism, and depressive symptoms. Couple intimacy problems can be treated with evidence-based, cognitive-behavioral strategies and techniques for intervening with faulty thinking patterns that have proven effective in the context of individual therapy (e.g., Beck et al., 1979; Datillo, 2010) and are currently being tested systematically as tools in couple therapy (Datillo, 2010; Epstein, 2006; Snyder, Castellani, & Whisman, 2006).

Although the interventions described in this book are primarily cognitive-behavioral, it is helpful to borrow certain concepts and interventions from family systems, humanistic, and attachment theories for the treatment of intimacy problems. Family systems theory was the first to discuss the *interdependence* of partners' behavior that is now recognized by all approaches (e.g., Bowen, 1960; Kelley, 1984; Satir, 1967), meaning that each partner's behavior is not only a product of his or her own personality but also a reaction to the other's behavior. From this perspective, both partners' behaviors work together to ensure *homeostasis,* which is a balance between forces in the relationship. Intimacy-distance homeostasis is maintained when each partner behaves in such a way as to maintain his or her optimum (or most comfortable) level of relational intimacy. The homeostatic balance between too much distance and too much closeness is a product of both partners' intimacy needs, fears, and behaviors.

From humanistic approaches comes the notion of communicating complete self-awareness as a pathway to intimacy. The humanistic perspective emphasizes the importance of complete, moment-to-moment awareness of one's psychological state as a critical contributor to mental health. Some humanistic writers (Maslow, 1968; Rogers, 1959) have recognized the additional potential offered by fully symbolized or articulated self-awareness for creating deep intimate connections with others (Prager & Roberts, 2004). Some interventions discussed in this book emphasize self-awareness as a path to intimate communication.

Finally, from attachment theory comes the notion that interpersonal capabilities are acquired developmentally and depend upon appropriately nurturing and sensitive relationships with caregivers and affirming relationships with peers to develop normally (e.g., Mikulincer & Shaver, 2007). Recent research demonstrates connections between early experiences of attachment security and intimacy in adolescent and adult relationships. Also well-documented are the difficulties faced by insecure adult romantic partners when they must manage conflict and emotion or sustain open communication (see review by Mikulincer & Shaver, 2007).

In sum, the intimacy problems of couples and individuals can be effectively treated with a cognitive-behavioral approach that is supplemented with selected interventions from family systems, humanistic, and attachment approaches. In this chapter, I provide specific recommendations about establishing a therapeutic alliance, the role of the therapist, intervening early in therapy, and recognizing therapeutic progress. Therapists who are new to couple therapy may want to supplement the descriptions of treatment in this book with a detailed manual like that provided by Epstein and Baucom (2003).

Building the Therapeutic Alliance

Building the therapeutic alliance begins as soon as people sit down with the therapist. The Intimacy Signature is both an information-gathering venture and an opportunity to introduce new perspectives to clients who are stuck in shop-worn ways of thinking about their relationship. By the fourth assessment session, the couple (or individual) will have gotten a good idea about how the therapist is thinking about their problems even before the therapist shares his or her formulation with them, because the therapist will have planted the seeds during the three previous assessment sessions. Table 3.1 summarizes the alliance building strategies and techniques used with couples.

Create a safe environment. The therapeutic alliance should create an atmosphere of safety for both partners, to encourage open expression and nondefensive responding. With a strong alliance, both partners should be able to trust the therapist's ability to help them improve their relationship and to control the interaction in the session. Each should experience the therapist as fair to both partners.

In my experience, many of the couples who switch therapists do so because they perceive the previous therapist to be taking sides unfairly. Inappropriate

Table 3.1 Alliance building interventions

Type	*Phase of Therapy*	*Intervention*
Alliance	Early	Therapist creates safe therapeutic environment.
Alliance	Early	Therapist supports and validates: Create a safe environment for discussion and disclosure by supporting and validating each partner's perspective.
Alliance	Throughout	Therapist reinforces: Provides positive reinforcement for clients' efforts, courage, devotion, and love.
Alliance	Early	Therapist fulfills needs: Therapist stands in to fulfill needs temporarily when partners are unable to do so. Therapist offers understanding, acceptance, validation, warmth, and caring.
Alliance	Early	Therapist creates hope: Therapist creates hope by acknowledging each partner's perspective and showing clients they can solve their problems and reconnect.
Alliance	Early	Therapist normalizes: Offers reassurance, shows that partners' needs and concerns are normal and human, models "de-catastrophizing" of problems.
Alliance	Early	Therapist sets goals: Collaborates with the couple to set goals.
Alliance	Throughout	Therapist gives capsule summary: Summarizes work of current or previous sessions to reinforce learning.
Alliance	Early	Therapist calls a stop: Asks partners to stop when their behavior is counter-therapeutic.

taking of sides can be prevented when the therapist views the couple's problems as joint creations in which each partner's personality plays a role. A therapist who fully understands the interdependence of the partners' behavior is best able to avoid taking sides.

As helpful as it is to avoid taking sides overall, it is also helpful to take each partner's side alternately, depending upon the issue under discussion. Therapists who alternate taking sides, first with one partner and then the other, are able to provide needed validation to both. In specific behavioral terms, taking a partner's side translates into a therapist's communicating acceptance for a wide variety of strategies by which partners seek to meet intimacy needs.

Therapists support each partner in turn by acknowledging their feelings and their respective predicaments, and validating each by demonstrating that their feelings and perceptions are understandable. The therapist does not have to condone inappropriate behavior to provide this validation.

It is important in couple therapy that the therapist use Rogerian skills of empathic and accurate reflection of content and affect in clients' communication. Reflection should affirm each partner's best intentions. Empathic reflection can also include interpretations if the therapist invites the clients to correct his or her impressions of them. Both reflection and interpretation convey understanding to the partner who has just spoken and validate his or her concern as understandable. Jacobson and Christensen (1996) advocate therapists finding ways to validate both partners' perspectives, both for each partner's own sake and in the interest of helping each partner to see the validity in the other's concerns.

Interpretative reflection can demonstrate the therapist's awareness of the strength and courage it takes to try as each partner is trying. The therapist's attention to these efforts reinforces what may remain unappreciated by a partner during times of couple distress. Further, it is often the case that the most vituperative partners still love one another, and the intensity of their efforts in therapy reflects that love. The therapist can affirm the visibility of that love to each partner which in turn gives hope to the couple. The therapist can also affirm positive motivations even when behavior is negative. Here is an example showing how to use Rogerian listening techniques to affirm positive motives in the face of negative behavior:

Therapist: OK stop a minute. As this is our first session, I want to express my appreciation to you for getting so many issues on the table for us to work with as it is very helpful for me to know where the problems are in your relationship. Also, although I sense that this arguing that you're going through here is a pretty painful process for both of you, I want you to know that, at least for now, it is beneficial for our work together, because it shows me just what happens when both of you are trying so hard to get understanding and acknowledgment from each other. And although I can see

> how frustrated you get with one another, I sense that some of your frustration is with yourself that you can't make these conversations go the way you'd like them to.

In this example, the therapist affirms the partners' openness with the therapist and, through interpretative reflection of the partners' feelings, expresses sympathy and understanding about each person's effort and perspective. By reflecting both partners' feelings simultaneously, the therapist also suggests to the couple that they are facing their challenges together and have similar feelings about what is going on.

Temporarily fulfill partners' intimacy needs. Clients with intimacy problems often feel that their partners have not heard them accurately and do not know or understand how they really feel. In the early stages of therapy, and often longer, the therapist serves as a "stand-in" for the fulfillment of that need. The therapist provides one or both partners with an intimate experience when he or she reflects what each says and shows empathy and understanding. Because the partner is present as the therapist does so, the therapist can also help the partners to hear and understand one another without attacking and blaming or defending. The therapist models good communication, but more, the therapist gives intimacy-hungry clients enough acceptance, affirmation, validation, and understanding to assuage unmet intimacy needs temporarily, which thereby allows the partners a reprieve from neediness as they inevitably wait longer to experience it in their relationship.

Help discouraged couples have hope. Couples who have hope will more readily participate actively in therapy and experience the therapy as helpful. Part of fostering hope is effective goal setting; in order to persuade their clients to buy into therapy, therapists must be able to formulate goals that speak directly to their clients' concerns. Nothing is more effective in helping clients get hopeful about therapy at the beginning than for the therapist to provide them with a new way of understanding their problems, one that therapy can help them to fix. One effective approach to inspiring hope is for the therapist to emphasize each partner's responsibility for the problems while simultaneously indicating a definite course of action that the partner can take to improve the relationship, one that is within the partner's power to activate. A therapist is most effective with this approach when he or she can push individual partners to take responsibility for their part of the problems while also helping both to see that the overall problem is jointly created. That is, the relationship problems are described and conceptualized systemically, but the individual contributions to those problems are clearly distinguished and each individual's responsibility for his or her contribution is established.

Establishing compelling treatment goals provides hope, because the subtext for articulating goals is the belief that they can be met. Below is an example of how a therapist simultaneously maintains a systems interpretation of the overall problem, while also letting each partner know how he or she sees their individual contributions to it.

Therapist: It sounds to me like you all fight, in part, because both of you feel unappreciated and misunderstood in the relationship. Possibly, this is because you're still angry with each other over the ways that each of you has disappointed the other. Sheryl, I hear Dennis saying that he gets a lot of complaints from you without your recognizing his efforts to contribute his share to your relationship and raising your children. . . . Dennis, I hear Sheryl acknowledging that she criticizes you frequently, and wants to cut back on all that, but I also hear her saying that you don't respond to her requests until she's all over you. So now she starts right up with the angry complaints, which feels really unfair to you. I'm afraid, that this is her response to your not hearing her when she asks nicely. When she demands loudly, you do hear and you are very cooperative, Dennis, but at that point, Sheryl is convinced you would have never done what she asked unless she made a big fuss. . . . Both of you are caught in this miserable cycle of arguments in which most of your communication with each other is angry, and neither of you feels much like praising or complimenting the other. . . . I see each of you having your own changes to make to stop this pattern. Sheryl, you and I can work together, with Dennis' input, to find a way to let Dennis know what you want that doesn't have to start a fight. Dennis, I'd like to work with you work on hearing and responding to nice requests from Sheryl and communicating clearly with her regarding when you are available to carry them out or, absent that, why you would like to beg off.

This therapist has let Dennis and Sheryl know that their negative interaction cycle is repetitive and predictable and that they each contribute to it. The therapist has also let each of them know what they can do to prevent this pattern from repeating itself and has offered to serve as a resource to help them do so.

Reassure the Couple or Individual That Their Struggles Are Normal

Because the intimacy dilemmas introduced in Chapter 1 are a normal part of intimate relationships, educating partners about one or more of them can help reassure the partners that their struggles with intimacy are normal. Following

Albert Ellis's (1962) notion that it is not so much events as it is our interpretations of events that create severe emotional upset, I believe that it is not so much the intimacy problems as the catastrophic interpretations couples make about their problems that causes a good portion of their upset. When the therapist is matter-of-fact about the couple's problems, for example, the therapist is modeling "de-catastrophizing" as Ellis calls it, when an unpleasant reality about the marriage is acknowledged but is not treated as catastrophic. Taking a matter-of-fact attitude and modeling it contributes to the therapist's efforts to normalize what is currently so upsetting for them. It can be reassuring to combine normalizing of problems with validation of partner needs as worthy of being fulfilled.

The role of the therapist in normalizing is that of a teacher and information resource. The therapist is providing the clients with knowledge and experience about couple relationships and intimacy that the couple would not necessarily possess. The therapist tells the couple, when normalizing, that certain dilemmas are built into couple relationships.

There are several issues that can be normalized when couples have problems with intimacy.

1 *Human needs for intimacy are normal and healthy.*

In American culture, normal needs for intimacy may be seen as weaknesses. Men may perceive normal emotional needs as compromising their masculinity, whereas women may fear that their needs for intimacy from their husbands set them up to be too dependent on them. Partners can both be reassured that their intimacy needs are normal and healthy, and each may find it useful to explore the origins of their reluctance to accept their intimacy needs as such. A dialogue between therapist and client, Socratic style, can encourage this self-exploration. Often, the process of questioning their own motives results in a client's increased acceptance of his or her needs for intimacy.

2 *It is normal for partners to have different intimacy needs.*

Individual partners often differ in the way they seek to fulfill intimacy needs. Prager (1999) reported data from 133 cohabiting couples indicating that people get their intimacy needs met in a variety of ways. Some get intimacy needs met via self-disclosure, some via an attentive and accepting listener, some via affectionate touching, and some via sexual contact. Others were more idiosyncratic (e.g., they felt intimate with their partners when the partner avoided initiating sexual contact). It would be relatively easy for partners to find that they favor different ways of fulfilling their intimacy needs. The therapist can accept each partner's intimacy need-fulfillment process as appropriate for that partner (e.g., sexuality is an excellent path to intimacy;

e.g., verbal expressions of positive feelings about the other is an excellent path to intimacy).

Therapist: I think that what's going on here is that Julie is different from you, and that in order for her to stay happy, there are things you need to give to her that you do not need for yourself. It's tempting to think, "Oh my God she'll never get enough." It's really easy for people who have the difference that you two have to get into that. . . . In every marriage—I want to normalize this—there is one person who wants a little more intimacy, a little more closeness than the other person. Unless you marry your identical twin, that's just the way it is. And we never marry our identical twin. I would guess, Edward, that you did not by accident marry someone [who wants more intimacy], I know you well enough to know that that's part of the appeal of Julie.

Edward: Oh absolutely (laughing).

Therapist: Just as that's part of the appeal it's also part of your obligation. . . . As a husband, to give more than you may feel you yourself need.

The therapist reassures Edward that it is normal for him and Julie to have different intimacy needs, and that their differences constitute a real-world problem that they will have to cope with day-to-day. It is likely that Edward will spend more time with Julie than he might need to do for himself.

3 *People are more easily hurt and feel more vulnerable with their intimate partners than with anyone else.* Heightened emotional vulnerability has at least three sources.

Vulnerability due to intimacy. Perhaps because dominant American culture valorizes emotional toughness and independence, especially for men, relationship partners frequently do not accept their own emotional vulnerability in relationship to the other partner and may create problems in their relationships through their own defensive behavior. They may unrealistically expect themselves to be cool in response to potentially hurtful behaviors on the part of their partners and engage in defensive behavior to hide their vulnerable emotions both from their partners and from themselves. Therapists can help partners relax maladaptive defensive behaviors by normalizing emotional vulnerability in intimate relationships. They can reassure clients that a stronger individual can tolerate the vulnerability of intimacy whereas a weaker one finds it necessary to hide.

Vulnerability due to interdependence. The high levels of interdependence in the typical couple relationship also increase vulnerability to hurt. Vulnerability to anxiety or even panic is increased when the other's actions have consequences for oneself (e.g., "if he keeps spending money like this, I won't have any security for my future").

There are several types of interdependence shared by couple partners. Some kinds are obvious: Couple partners have children together, pool their financial resources, and depend upon one another for shared leisure, vacations, and possessions. However, they are also highly interdependent in the intimacy arena. In particular, they are interdependent due to their choice to depend solely on each other for romantic intimacy, especially sexual intimacy.

Because they rely primarily on each other, couple partners may perceive the other as controlling their gratification in the area of romantic and sexual intimacy. High levels of interdependence lead partners to interpret one another's actions in this arena as deliberately and maliciously withholding. Therapists can help partners perceive their mutual dependency as normal by reassuring them that most couple partners are concerned about their partner's behavior and the way it affects them, and most couple partners depend heavily on each other for intimacy and sexual gratification.

Vulnerability due to attachment. Adults' intimate couple relationships are attachment relationships (e.g., see Ainsworth, 1989). Adults with their romantic relationship partners, like young children with their parents, feel a sense of belonging and of being at home with their relationship partners; similarly, they feel sad during an extended separation, and relief or joy upon reuniting. Attachment theorists argue that a romantic relationship provides adults with a "secure base" that allows them to take chances and try new things at work and in their communities (Mikulincer & Shaver, 2007).

For all they provide, attachment relationships also create emotional vulnerabilities. Permanent separation or divorce from the partner activates an extended grief reaction that most adults anticipate and want to avoid. Most adults feel fear at the thought of losing their partners, and some, who are not securely attached, perceive abandonment by their partners as a perpetually imminent possibility. The latter group may adapt to that possibility by engaging only in low-risk behavior with their partners. Inevitably, an unwillingness to take risks results in reduced intimacy in the relationship, and often, along with intimacy, satisfaction is reduced. It can, therefore, be helpful to normalize people's reactions to their attachments, their fears of being without their partners, and their associated fears of taking risks.

When building the alliance and fostering hope, the therapist reassures the partners that the dilemmas they face in their relationship are normal, and that it is primarily their method of coping with those dilemmas that creates problems. The therapist "de-catastrophizes" the dilemmas themselves in an effort to reduce the partners' anxieties about their relationship. Reassurance and anxiety-reduction help the partners focus on resolving their problems and, when necessary, trying out new ways of behaving that will help them achieve the intimacy that they crave.

Set Goals Collaboratively

Once the therapist has begun building an alliance with the couple and assessing their strengths and vulnerabilities, they are ready to collaborate and establish mutually agreed upon goals. In couple relationships, the tendency of partners each to blame the other for the problems in the relationship means that the therapist must find a compelling rationale to help each partner see his or her own role in the problems and to willingly work toward changing problematic behavior. Because intimacy problems are nearly always manifestations of both couple and individual dynamics, the therapist's best strategy is to help partners identify one or two couple goals, and then help each identify an individual goal that is compelling enough to motivate them to maintain a sense of personal responsibility for their own progress in therapy.

In sum, when couples have intimacy problems, it is usually beneficial to help them identify both couple-level and partner- or individual-level goals. Couple-level goals help both partners have hope that the other partner can be more responsive to their needs, whereas individual goals help each partner take responsibility and work to improve his or her own responses to relationship problems.

Use Capsule Summaries to Reinforce Learning

As part of any cognitively oriented treatment, the therapist should provide the couple or individual with capsule summaries that summarize the agenda and the accomplishments of the current or previous sessions (Beck, 1976). Capsule summaries help couples stay focused on their stated goals for therapy and help them perceive their own progress in therapy. For example, here is the capsule summary that Edward and Julie's therapist provided for them.

Therapist: In our last session, Edward, we worked on the anger you often feel toward Julie that wasn't completely comprehensible to you; we worked on understanding better where it came from. We came up with this notion that you unknowingly were expecting Julie to maintain a nurturing, warm, and cheerful presence for you all the time and that you got mad at her when she was tired. You realized that this was not a realistic expectation and that her tired or grumpy moods were not actually directed at you at all, especially if you avoided attacking her when she was in one of those moods. You predicted that this realization would help you be less reactive to Julie's moods and better able to avoid fighting with her when she is in one of those moods. Does that fit with your recollection?

Structuring Therapy

With each couple, therapists must make judgments about whether to see the couple conjointly, to see one or both partners individually, or to mix conjoint and individual sessions. The therapist must also decide whether to recommend individual therapy for one of the partners with a different therapist or whether all the work can be accomplished with a single couple therapist who is allied with both partners.

Conjoint versus individual treatment. Because intimacy dilemmas stem from a combination of individual factors grounded in developmental history (i.e., Dilemma #3, the past lives in the present, see Chapter 10) and relational factors grounded in partner interaction quality, intimacy-oriented treatment must target both couple and individual processes, sometimes simultaneously. When compelling individual partner issues are as salient as couple issues in creating couple problems, combined conjoint and individual therapy sessions may be called for.

The cognitive focus of intimacy-oriented therapy sometimes calls for mixing individual and conjoint sessions over the course of treatment. Powerful, influential ideas about the self, the partner, and intimate relationships in general, or *intimacy schemas,* are individual and different for each partner, necessitating some individual sessions to help individual partners evaluate and possibly change their intimacy schemas, the associated behavior, and the impact of that behavior on their relationship. Intimacy-related behavior is difficult to address effectively until the schemas that drive the maladaptive behavior are identified and "worked through" by the individual partners. This is because intimacy schemas are often acquired early in life and are applied to numerous situations over time, becoming habitual and resistant to change. Individual sessions can offer the focus that the therapist and client need to address those schemas without interruption.

There are several ways to combine individual and conjoint sessions with a single couple. In one pattern, one partner who is symptomatic, particularly one who is suffering with an Axis I disorder that needs attention, works with a different mental health professional to receive medication and if necessary, individual therapy that will be focused on the disorder itself. The most common disorder to receive this pattern of treatment is depression, but I also recommend this course of action if one partner is abusing a substance, or has a severe anxiety or eating disorder, or if there has been abuse or violence in the relationship.

In a second pattern, the couple therapist can take advantage of one partner's greater motivation to change by working with that partner to change his or her way of thinking, feeling, and behaving with the partner. In this second pattern, the individual treatment is part of the couple treatment. However, it is usually important to avoid framing these sessions as a way to change one partner to make the other partner happier. If the client construes his or her individual work as being primarily for the partner's benefit, he or she may resist the treatment when he or she is angry with the partner and may be tempted to view the partner's well-being as not being worth the effort. A better strategy is to frame the individual work as a process that will help the more motivated partner feel empowered (or less upset) within the relationship. The individual work then focuses upon the psychological growth of that partner, helping him or her to feel more content and to expand his or her behavioral repertoire. Individual sessions also have the benefit of drawing attention away from blaming the partner for one's troubles and toward taking charge of one's own well-being. Here is an example of a rationale recently given to a wife who wanted to save her marriage but whose husband had one foot out of the door and little or no energy for therapy: The couple was in their fourth assessment session with the therapist.

Therapist: The thing that strikes me about your marriage is not only that you two are not having sex, although that is notable. It's that you two don't touch each other: You don't kiss, hug, hold hands, rub shoulders, anything, and this has been going on now for a long time. It's not that you two don't get along, right? You get along fine, as you said, like roommates. . . . I think a good way to start would be for Harriet to work with me individually for three or four sessions on getting more comfortable with initiating touch and get the touch back in your relationship. Harriet is the one who has the energy and motivation to work right now. Harriet has expressed a desire to be less inhibited about initiating affection and sex, and our work together can help you do that, Harriet, whether the two of you continue together or apart. . . . In truth it could be either one of you that needs this work, but I perceive Harriet as being the driving force behind the therapy right now, is that your perception? . . . I'd like both of you to return in three or four weeks to talk about how things are going and we can reevaluate at that time whether Harriet should continue with the individual or whether we should take a new course of action.

In this example, Harriet and the therapist have identified an individual goal for Harriet that, if accomplished, would further her own personal growth and also benefit the relationship. The husband, who was feeling depressed and hopeless about the relationship, gets to experience the changes that Harriet, who is not depressed but is energized, can bring to their relationship. In this way, the husband gains some hope for the treatment for himself. The therapist is careful in this case not to pinpoint Harriet as the "identified patient," but says instead, that while both of them could benefit from individual work, there are good reasons for letting Harriet begin the process.

In a third pattern, the therapist works with the couple until it becomes clear that the therapy cannot progress without significant individual work by one spouse. This becomes apparent when the spouse keeps repeating the same dysfunctional thoughts or behavior, session after session, despite feedback from the therapist. For example, one husband still blamed his wife for her bad moods, failing to recognize the connection between his reaction to her moods and his tendency to personalize them. In this case, individual sessions with the husband, in which he monitored his moods and automatic thoughts as in traditional cognitive therapy (Beck et al., 1979) taught him to be more aware of the connection between his interpretations of his wife's moods and his own feelings of anger, deprivation, and loneliness. Further, he learned to deliberately modify his interpretations to fit more readily with what he had learned in therapy. The husband's individual work helped him to feel more consistently content in the marriage and to feel less upset with the ups and downs of his wife's moods.

When clients focus on shoring up their own strengths and shift their focus away, even if momentarily, from controlling how the partner thinks and behaves, they are better able to provide a safe climate for each other. Partners in couple relationships often seem unable to resist attacking each other, just when the partner is self-confronting. Sometimes this self-defeating behavior seems to be motivated by an "I told you so" desire to show who was right. The effect, however, is to distract the other from his or her work on self and refocus it on the partner whose behavior was provocative and no doubt merits an angry response. The therapist can help the unsupportive partner to let go of being right. Perhaps that partner can at that moment be helped to see that the partner is being courageous and attempting to do his or her part in the joint effort to move past their stalemate. Here is one example of how a therapist may intervene when one partner's response to the other partner's work threatens to be anti-therapeutic:

Therapist: In other words, you're interpreting Harry's being less interested in pursuing intimacy with you than you are with him, you're interpreting that . . .

Joan: No . . . not intimacy.

Therapist: OK—let's talk about undivided attention, is that better?

Joan: Yeah.
Therapist: You're interpreting [the fact] that Harry needs less undivided attention than you as Harry's putting you lower, low down on his priority list.
Joan: Yeah, I guess so, yes.
Therapist: You're interpreting it as a priority issue and what I want to know is, what's the advantage of interpreting it that way? As you being less of a priority?
Joan: You know, I don't think I make an issue of this.
Therapist: I'm not saying you make an issue of it. This is inside of you.
Harry: I just wish Joan could see the positive; she's so sad, so negative.
Therapist: Harry, let me work with Joan on this because this is Joan's issue.

The therapist was working on helping Joan change the way she interpreted inattention from Harry, and Harry used this opportunity to jump on the bandwagon and attack Joan for being so negative. The therapist asked him not to jump in but to let Joan do her own work. Harry was potentially creating an unsafe climate for intimacy by attacking Joan when she was sharing herself openly. It is also interesting to notice how Joan resists the word *intimacy* (often associated with sexuality) but accepts the word *undivided attention*. It is important for the therapist to use the words that fit for the client.

Separate therapists or one therapist. Couple therapists often prefer to refer out when individual partners seem to need their own therapy. Most couple therapists are familiar with the reasons for this separation. First, issues of confidentiality can get complicated, with therapists finding it difficult to separate individual partner confidential material from material brought up in couple sessions that can be discussed freely with both partners. Second, a therapist who works both with the individual partners and with the couple may have difficulty maintaining a therapeutic alliance with both partners. One partner may resent the therapist having secrets with the other partner as a result of their individual therapy. Conversely, depending upon the therapist's confidentiality policy, the individual client may resent it that the therapist encourages him or her to bring up issues raised in the individual sessions in the conjoint sessions. The therapist may more easily be seduced into taking sides under these circumstances. Further, even if the therapist is not taking sides, one or both of the clients may perceive the therapist taking sides. This risk is always present in conjoint therapy and may be greater if the couple therapist is also the individual therapist. One partner may make it appear that the therapist has taken sides against the other partner in an effort to win an argument and can claim special knowledge of the therapist's attitudes because of the individual sessions.

I do not deny that there are risks to the therapeutic alliance when therapists work with a couple while simultaneously working with one or both of the partners individually. With intimacy-oriented therapy, the advantages of working simultaneously with one therapist often outweigh the disadvantages. Under the following conditions, I believe that the risks are less and the advantages even greater: (1) Both partners perceive the individual's personal therapy as being part of the couple therapy, with the potential to contribute to the well-being of the other partner and the couple; (2) the partner (or partners) perceive their individual therapy as being secondarily for the relationship and primarily for themselves, that is, as being focused upon their own growth and well-being; (3) partners have no history of using third parties (in-laws, children, friends, therapists) to give themselves an advantage in disputes; and (4) neither partner has paranoid ideation. When couples are working toward improving the intimacy in their relationship, they are in part working toward each partner feeling empowered to get his or her needs met, which in turn means that they must feel empowered as individuals. What works for the relationship, therefore, also works for the individual.

Combined couple and individual treatment can backfire if there are reasons for partners to mistrust one another. If one partner has recently had an affair and the couple is still working actively on trust-building, it will likely be difficult for the hurt partner to tolerate the other having any privacy, and indeed, the straying partner has often forfeited the right to privacy by betraying the other's trust. In the absence of an affair, it is problematic if one or both partners have a history of telling lies. Even when the therapist is not taking sides against anyone, a deceptive partner could be tempted to tell a fib about something the therapist said in an individual session that, if believed or taken the wrong way, would destroy the therapeutic alliance with the other partner. If there are trust issues in the relationship, the therapist may either default to offering only conjoint sessions or the therapist may take the position that she has no secrets from the individual sessions and will speak freely in the couple sessions. A refusal to keep secrets might mean that some material never comes to light, but it will reduce the likelihood that one partner can break the other partner's alliance with the therapist.

Contraindications for addressing intimacy problems in therapy. Some relationship problems exert such a pervasive effect on the functioning of the relationship and the individual partners that intimacy-focused therapy is counter-indicated until these have been at least partially resolved. Some of these so violate the trust of the partners that partners must work on rebuilding

Table 3.2 Contraindications for focusing on intimacy problems

Relationship Crisis	*Steps Required before Focusing Therapy on Intimacy*
Affairs	Partners must decide if they want to rebuild the relationship and provide some security for each other. Partners must make trust-building arrangements. Partners should deal with issues of guilt, betrayal, punishment, and forgiveness along with intimacy.
Abuse and/or violence	The abused partner must develop plans for protecting his or her physical safety. The abusive partner must work on anger management, control issues, jealousy, and so forth. The abused partner must feel sufficiently safe to express him- or herself freely to the partner before conjoint therapy begins.
Partner is ready to leave relationship	A contract in which the partners promise not to threaten to leave or to begin divorce proceedings for a set period of time. The contract creates sufficient trust for risking intimate relating.
Other trust violations (stealing money, lying)	Partners must make trust-building arrangements.
Substance abuse	While influenced by a mind-altering substance, the individual cannot engage his or her partner in genuinely intimate interactions. The substance abusing partner most likely needs to stop using the substance before intimacy-oriented work is possible.

trust before they can begin to take the emotional risks necessary for enhancing intimacy. Contraindications are presented in a checklist in Appendix A in the Intimacy Signature Basic Intake section and listed here in Table 3.2.

These counter-indications are the minimum requirements for focusing therapy on intimacy issues:

1 Absence of major trust violations. Most distressed couples will have multiple reasons, in their minds, for mistrusting one another, but affairs, stealing or transferring funds, chronic lying, and especially abuse and violence create crises of mistrust, and couples will need to cope with the crisis before they can think about the day-to-day functioning of their relationship. Trust violations are especially problematic for taking risks with intimacy, as these interventions involve taking emotional risks even under favorable conditions.

2 Absence of fear: Partners cannot be intimate if they are afraid for their own safety in the presence of the other. Victims of domestic violence often report that their partners will not seem to be overreacting to what they say within the time frame of the therapy session, but may "punish" the partner later for challenging them. Conjoint couple therapy is counter-indicated when one partner fears for his or her safety.
3 Both partners are at least temporarily committed to improving the relationship. Many couples do not seek therapy until one of the partners is ready to leave the relationship. The therapist may make the assumption that if the partner is in therapy, then there is a minimal commitment to see it through, and can therefore ask the leaving partner to commit to however much time they can in order to give the therapy a chance to make a difference. The goal here is for the leaving partner to have some hope that the relationship can be more gratifying; promising major changes in a short time is likely to backfire.
4 Absence of substance abuse: The mind-altering characteristics of alcohol and recreational drugs make genuine intimacy impossible because one partner is wearing a chemical disguise. To gain an intimate connection, partners must be willing to encounter each other without depending upon the influence of these drugs. That said, I acknowledge that some couples will report that sharing substances (e.g., drinking together, getting high together) has been a primary commonality that they have shared over the years. For these couples, confronting the decision whether to stay together or separate will depend upon whether they can find commonalities other than their use of substances to hold them together.

Signs of Success or Improvement

It is my experience that couple therapy does not end when the partners stop having troubles (because there are always troubles), or even when the same old troubles morph into new, more manageable troubles. Further, it seems that individual personalities do not change dramatically as a result of couple therapy. What does change are the partners' ways of thinking about themselves, their partners, their interactions and their responses to the new way of thinking. Along with changes in thinking and behavior, partners learn to manage their emotions. They especially become more adept at soothing themselves when their partner is unavailable to fulfill their needs. Conversely, they also feel sufficiently entitled to ask for what they want, and at times, insist upon it. Each individual's self-efficacy with respect to interactions with the partner has been strengthened when therapy is successful. Increased self-efficacy, in turn, opens the door to intimacy. At the end of therapy, partners should report more intimacy in at least one domain (e.g., in conversation, touching, shared recreation, sexuality, or shared spiritual activity).

Partners who are winding down their therapy report some of the following:

1 More frequent experiences of sharing joy and of appreciating one another and their life together.
2 More frequent experiences of relaxing their public personas together increased permission to be "off-line" with one another without having to be vigilant about the partner's response.
3 More relaxed around the house, less vigilant and nervous about how the other will react to whatever they say or do or fail to do.
4 Going through some of the same problematic interactions as in the past, but less upset over them. Certain previously devastating interactions pass over lightly, and they are able to be open to intimate connection later.
5 Partners are more "philosophical," or accepting, of the particular brand of frustrations they encounter with one another, because many of these are functions of the pairing of their particular, individual personalities.
6 Therapists will notice partners expressing or demonstrating more empathy with one another than they may have before therapy.
7 Finally, partners will more readily acknowledge the fundamental intimacy challenge: Enjoying quality intimacy requires that they balance relaxing and putting their feet up with one another while each simultaneously maintains certain levels of respect and attentiveness for the other.

Conclusion

This cognitive-behavioral therapy translates intimacy dilemmas into specific treatment goals and strategies. Goals for treatment, consistent with the cognitive-behavioral therapy tradition, are specific with regards to domain (i.e., behavioral, cognitive, and affective goals) and are used to set agendas for therapy sessions. I place particular emphasis on individual partners taking responsibility for changing their own contributions to couple problems by combining conjoint and individual treatment and by ensuring that there are couple goals and individual partner goals for each couple. To establish and maintain a therapeutic alliance, the therapist offers him- or herself as a source of need-fulfillment, an affirming, validating partner in treatment, an instructor, facilitator, guide, and taskmaster to individuals and couples who want to enjoy the benefits of intimate relating and create long-lasting and rewarding relationships.

4

BEHAVIORAL INTERVENTIONS

For therapy focused on intimacy problems, behavioral interventions serve the purpose of helping couples change intimacy-sabotaging patterns of behavior into behavior that permits or enhances intimacy. These interventions are also useful for teaching skills to individuals who have trouble establishing or maintaining intimate relationships.

Those familiar with classic behavioral couples therapy (Jacobson & Margolin, 1979) remember that training in communication and problem-solving skills has been the cornerstone of behavioral approaches to treating distressed couples. More recent approaches (e.g., Baucom & Epstein, 1990; Datillo, 2010; Epstein & Baucom, 2003; Jacobson & Christensen, 1996) have expanded classic behavioral couple therapy to include interventions aimed at changing dysfunctional thinking patterns and associated affect as well. The next three chapters show how these three types of interventions can work together to reduce couples' intimacy-related problems.

Behavioral interventions are especially useful early in therapy. They function both as diagnostic and as therapeutic tools. They can be diagnostic when used early in treatment to determine if couple problems can be fixed with straightforward information and skill training, or if skill training's limited benefits make it apparent that the couple's problems have more complex underpinnings. For example, it may seem to the therapist at first blush that a couple's repetitive, irresolvable conflict results from deficits in communication skills. However, if the therapist begins therapy with communication training, it often becomes apparent that one or both partners already possess the skills in question and are failing to use those skills in the marriage. The failure of skills training to ameliorate the couple's presenting problem tells the therapist that he or she must also explore the cognitive and affective aspects of the couple's intimacy dilemma.

Even when they are not sufficient in and of themselves, behavioral interventions are very useful. They help to establish the therapeutic alliance by offering hope in the form of positive reinforcement for making small changes. Couples who are threatening to separate, for example, are often pleased to discover that a behavioral contract that postpones talk of separation for a specified time period reduces their anxiety and gives them the freedom to take more risks with one another. Further, communication skills training can help the couple to break ingrained negative and destructive communication habits that they have developed over many years. In their excellent manual

Table 4.1 Behavioral interventions

Type	*Phase of Therapy*	*Intervention*
Behavioral	Early	Behavioral guidance
Behavioral	Early	Behavioral contracting Specific, concrete, and collaborative agreement about how compromises will be carried out
Behavioral	Early	Increase positive behavior Behavioral exchange, caring or giving days
Behavioral	Early	Encourage effective self-expression
Behavioral	Middle	Identify behavior-outcome connections and respond effectively
Behavioral	Middle	Teach intimate communication skills Self-expression skills Listening skills, including listening to difficult messages
Behavioral	Middle to Late	Social skills training/behavior rehearsal Behavioral guidance about appropriate social or relationship behavior Graded task assignment—break skills and actions into steps and tackle them one at a time Behavioral rehearsal—client practices what he or she will do or say to cope with an upcoming challenge Client practices to become more skillful
Behavioral	Late	Reverse roles role play Helps partners see the wisdom in both sides of a polarized conflict Teach partners about polarization Each partner verbalizes the middle ground of the dilemma, with special attention to articulating the partner's pole Each partner articulates a compromise, including the partner's perspective Once compromise is reached, move to acceptance of differences and not getting everything that you want

Expanded Cognitive-Behavioral Therapy for couples, Epstein and Baucom (2003) suggest that "distressed couples often need a series of interventions to help them begin to interact with each other in more constructive ways—to break a negative pattern that may have become ingrained. Therefore, we do not assume that they will necessarily continue using all of these behavioral strategies . . . instead . . . once the couple becomes effective at no longer interrupting and each person truly listens to what the other person says, then [for example, using reflective listening in each and every conversation] may be less important" (p. 297). Epstein and Baucom's perspective on behavioral interventions with couples mirrors the findings of outcome research on behavioral couples therapy (see review by Snyder, Castellani, & Whisman, 2006), which shows that behavioral interventions are very helpful in the short-term but may not create habits that can be sustained over the long term.

Table 4.1 summarizes the behavioral interventions that are discussed in this chapter. Some of these interventions are adapted from classical and contemporary systems for conducting behavioral couple therapy (Baucom & Epstein, 1990; Datillo, 2010; Epstein & Baucom, 2003; Jacobson & Christensen, 1996; Jacobson & Margolin, 1979). This chapter demonstrates how they may be implemented to relieve problems associated with intimacy dilemmas.

Behavioral Guidance

Oftentimes it may seem to couple therapists that partners behave in the self-defeating ways that they do because it has not occurred to them to behave differently. Partners engage in disruptive behavior because that is the kind of behavior that they observed growing up with their parents or because they otherwise lacked role models who communicated effectively. Many couple partners have had little or no exposure to psychological concepts. Under these conditions, it can be very helpful for the therapist to suggest alternative ways of behaving to one or both partners. In partners who are otherwise interpersonally skilled, the alternative behavior may already be in their repertoire, but it hasn't occurred to them to use it in the situation at hand.

For example, Carla's therapist suggested some ways she could more effectively encourage Doug to self-disclose vulnerable aspects of himself, thereby increasing the likelihood that they would have the kind of intimate conversation that she wanted them to have.

Therapist: You know, Carla, you all have told me about several instances in which you had arguments that distressed you both, and it has occurred to me that these were instances that could have turned into the kind of intimate conversations that you like to have with Doug. And I think that there are some things you could do to turn them in the direction you want.

Carla: Well you know, he does tend to be wrapped up in himself quite a lot! When I want him to be thinking about what needs to be done around here, or what Jeremy [our son] needs, he's thinking about work or about that damn lawsuit.

Therapist: And I'll bet when you told him that, he stopped talking pretty fast! Consider how that conversation might have gone. What would have happened if you had expressed some sympathy or concern? I mean, you've acknowledged in here quite a few times that you feel so bad for Doug having to go through all that. What if you had said, "Doug, I am so sorry that you have to go through all of that. You are such a conscientious businessman, you don't deserve this. Maybe we can do something fun with Jeremy today to help take your mind off of it." . . . This is really for you, though; you want more intimate conversation and fun times with him. This could open some doors.

In this example, the therapist gives Carla behavioral guidance on responding to Doug's disclosures about his emotional upsets. To facilitate Carla's learning, the therapist can set up role play rehearsals (described later in this chapter) to give her the opportunity to practice the new behavior. The therapist can also encourage Doug to give Carla feedback about how the new response affects him.

Behavioral Contracting

In couple therapy, behavioral contracting refers to a specific, concrete, mutually endorsed agreement that each makes with the other for a specified period of time. Behavioral contracting is an intervention that has been with us for many years (Jacobson & Margolin, 1979; Stuart, 1980) and is a very effective way of beginning intimacy-focused couple therapy.

Reduce anxiety about ambivalent commitments. First, behavioral contracting can be used to reduce partners' anxiety about their relationship's uncertain future and can permit them to take the inevitable emotional risks that are associated with trying new ways of relating intimately. When one or both partners are poised to leave the relationship, a behavioral contract can specify a period of time during which the couple will refrain from planning, discussing, or even thinking about ending their relationship, in order that they feel freer to concentrate on improving it. In this case, the behavioral contract functions as a crucible of relationship stability that permits the partners to risk new behavior. If the contract is successful, partners should feel freer to let down their defenses and interact more intimately because they know they will not be abandoned for the duration of the contract. As one young woman put it, "I had no idea how much better it could feel once he stopped talking about ending it all the time."

Collaborative compromises that work. A second use of the behavioral contract is to establish concrete and specific agreements for carrying out compromises. For example, couples who are having problems with Dilemma #2, I versus we and whose relationship is not meeting one partner's needs, can benefit from a behavioral contract that specifies a course of action that can potentially meet both of their needs. Behavioral contracting involves four steps, as follows:

1. *Problem clarification:* In the first step, the therapist helps the partners clarify their problems to themselves and one another. If the couple is dealing with Dilemma #2, the therapist helps each partner to see that although theirs is a couple problem, each of them is troubled by a different aspect of it.

For problem clarification, the therapist explains the usefulness of describing problems in specific, behavioral terms. She also uses behavioral guidance and feedback to help each partner communicate what he or she is wanting, using specific, nonblaming concrete language.

2. *Translate problems into agreements:* The therapist explains to the couple how behavioral contracts work. The therapist teaches the partners how to transform specific requests into a mutually agreeable behavioral contract.

3. *Establish a time line:* The therapist guides the couple toward finalizing the contract by helping the couple agree upon how long it should be in effect and when its effectiveness should be reevaluated.

4. *Reevaluate the contract:* On a mutually agreed-upon date, the therapist and couple reassess the contract from each person's perspective and revise for the future. At the reevaluation session, it is useful for the therapist to remind the couple that, although it is very nice to be more relaxed about the issue because of the contract, they should remember that the issue is still important to them and that they are only relaxed because they trust the other person (and themselves) to follow through.

Behavioral exchange and giving days. A third use for behavioral contracting is for increasing reciprocity of positive actions in the relationship. A behavior therapy intervention for accomplishing this purpose that is very useful for treating intimacy problems is contracting for behavioral exchanges (Jacobson & Margolin, 1979; Stuart, 1980), or as Jacobson and Christensen (1996) reconceptualized this intervention, *Giving Days.*

Giving Days is a helpful intervention for couples that lack intimacy because they lack times of enjoyable companionship in which to experience it. These low-intimacy couples spend little time in shared leisure or cannot find pastimes that both enjoy. As a result, partners lack positively reinforcing interactions and experience their relationships as less rewarding than when they first became a couple. Couples who lack positively reinforcing interactions can feel discouraged about the future of their relationship. Giving Days can increase the amount of positive reinforcement each partner experiences in the relationship.

Giving Days, introduced by Jacobson and Christensen (1996) as an updated version of behavioral exchange (Jacobson & Margolin, 1979) differs from the original behavior exchange technique in that the partners communicate what they would like to do for the other instead of each telling the other what they want the other to do for them. The partner then chooses which actions, among the things that the other would like to do, that would please him or her the most. Giving Days allows partners to experience giving acts from one another that they know the other truly wants to give.

A useful variation on Giving Days simultaneously emphasizes each partner's responsibility to do things just to please the other and the importance of demonstrating appreciation for what the other does. To introduce Giving Days, I ask them what they can do this week to be a better partner and to focus on making that effort. The other partner communicates about the amount of reinforcement he or she would experience as a result of the various things the first partner is willing to do. An additional emphasis is on each partner monitoring only their own part and not monitoring the partner's contribution. This division of responsibilities conveys the message that blaming the other for relationship problems is not constructive whereas focusing on improving one's own relationship behavior is helpful. They are asked to do the exercise daily as homework and report back the following week. The receiving partner's assignment is to express or show appreciation for the giving act. The Giving Days Set-Up Sheet in Appendix C—Therapist Worksheets helps get the process going in the session.

Assigning Giving Days early in therapy often gives the couple a boost in hope and positive feeling for one another. These feelings of hope and positive sentiment set the stage for commitment to therapy and to making more enduring changes. In my experience, Giving Days tend to decrease in frequency over the long term. Even when I check with the couple diligently week after week to find out how well they are doing with the giving behaviors, partners will tend to slack off after awhile. Further, the receiving partner has a tendency to habituate to the positive behaviors so that those behaviors do not elicit the same positive emotions as in the beginning. Giving Days are effective, nonetheless, for lifting the spirits of the partners in the early stages of therapy and pave the way for the efforts required to make longer-term changes.

Effective intimacy-distance regulation. Behavioral contracting can also be used to help the couple experiment with changes in the way they regulate intimacy and distance. Recall from Chapter 1 that intimacy-distance regulation encompasses those processes of initiating, reciprocating, and declining intimacy that maintain the homeostatic balance between intimacy and separateness in a couple's relationship. A common complaint, especially from husbands about wives, is that wives fail to initiate sexual activity or to show enthusiasm for sex beyond complying with their husband's initiations.

If the wife has not expressed objections to having sex with her husband, but instead has complained of lack of time or energy, the therapist can help the couple make a behavioral contract that will increase the wife's interest in initiating sex. For example, the therapist can encourage the wife to commit to setting aside a time during the week when she will initiate sex with her husband. For wives who complain that husbands ask for sex without doing anything to set the proper mood, the contract can provide her with the opportunity to set the mood however she wants. When wives initiate, they are less dependent upon their husbands to set the mood because they are creating their own optimum time to have sex. Husbands are encouraged to back off from initiating in order that they give their wives a chance to initiate. This backing off is necessary for the husband who may otherwise preempt his opportunity to enjoy being asked by his wife. It might also be necessary for the husband to agree to take on more responsibility for managing the children or the house in order to lessen his wife's burden (or they may need to hire help if they can afford it). This intervention amounts to a contract between the husband and wife regarding the initiation and reciprocation of sexual activity for the following week.

In my experience, there are significant short-term benefits from this intervention. Husbands will enjoy being asked, and wives often report that they enjoyed taking charge of a sexual encounter with their husbands. However, it is often the case that after a couple of tries, the couple gets distracted and goes back to husband-initiated sex, about which the husband (or whoever is the initiating partner) will eventually complain. In this case, I will often give them a choice: to continue to work with me to change their pattern or to accept and even enjoy the pattern that comes naturally for them given their two personalities. I then offer some relationship education, telling them that informal roles often emerge in relationships as a result of two different personalities. I suggest that it would be more realistic for the husband to expect occasional initiations from his wife than it would be for him to expect a strictly equal sharing of sex initiations between the two of them.[1]

Teach Message-Focused Communication

When partners must communicate challenging material that requires a response from the other, they can benefit from traditional communication skill

1 Traditional sex role attitudes can also predetermine a couple's pattern of intimacy-distance regulation.

training. Challenging communication refers to messages that can be blaming and punitive unless conveyed with care and forethought. Punitive communication can be minimized when partners learn how to bring up concerns without attacking, how to express needs, how to ask for wants without demanding or giving ultimatums, and how to demonstrate respect for partner's needs without backing off on one's own (see Baucom & Epstein, 1990; Jacobson & Margolin, 1979). Communication skill training helps couples get their messages across while minimizing the emotional cost of that communication to individual partners and the relationship.

Traditional behavioral couple therapy provides a list of constructive communication skills that is frequently missing from distressed couples' communication and encourages clinicians to offer couples step-by-step training in the use of those skills (e.g., see Baucom & Epstein, 1990). As others have noted (e.g., Epstein & Baucom, 2003), lock-step behavioral communication training can meet with resistance from clients who are loathe to sound "unnatural" or "artificial" using rule-bound communication. The artificiality of traditional communication skills training is especially salient when couples are working on intimate communication, which by definition is a relatively spontaneous outpouring of hearts with public facades and defenses down. Both Jacobson and Christensen (1996) and Epstein and Baucom (2003) have developed alternative models for communication training that are less rule-bound than traditional behavioral couples therapy, although still allowing couples to avoid the pitfalls of their old communication habits.

The message-focused communication training described here has as its goal to teach clients to critically evaluate their own (but not their partner's) communication and to revise what they say as they go via the application of general principles of good communication. The desired outcome of message-focused communication training is for each partner to be aware of the impact of his or her speech on the partner, whether of the messages that he or she wishes to convey or of the way that those messages are communicated. It further aims to help partners maintain a willingness to evaluate and alter their communication in order to convey messages as constructively as possible.

Message-focused communication training is especially useful for couples who present with conflict over intimacy or repetitive, unresolved conflict. Helping the couple refocus on the messages that they wish to convey interrupts cycles of blame and fault-finding, among other destructive habits. What follows is a description of each of the five therapist interventions that together constitute message-focused communication training. The first two steps allow the therapist to meet each partner's needs to be understood and accepted, which alleviates some of the anger and frustration and prepares the partners for the next steps in the process.

1. *Acknowledge the feelings.* The therapist should acknowledge the emotions that accompany self-defeating communication and the validity of what the communicating partner wants (e.g., "I can hear in your voice how frustrating

it must be to ask him this time after time and to have it appear that he's never really understood what you are asking him to do").

2. *Convey understanding*. Let the client know that you understand the message, as above (or clarify it if not, e.g., "OK, now I think I understand. It's not just that you want him to put his arm around you, but you want a smile from him from across the room, or to see him turn to you in a welcoming way when you walk up to him at a party, and other things that communicate to you that he's glad you're his date").

The third step should be somewhat stimulating and intriguing to the partners, as it helps them to see the interaction from another perspective. That perspective in turn helps them to see another way to approach the communication problem.

3. *Offer an alternative perspective*. Communication training gets difficult when partners get upset about what the other is saying and overreact. Alternative perspectives can help partners each value what the other has to say even when it's something they don't want to hear by considering the greater disadvantage of letting too much go unspoken.

Here the therapist helps the client see both sides of her failure to communicate, from her partner's as well as from her own perspective (e.g., "You know, I think this seems like a simple request that someone as intelligent and perceptive as your husband can surely understand. But I think there's more going on here. It may be that emotionally, because he's struggling so much with his own anger, that he finds it difficult (when you're making demands) to get to his warm feelings for you. It's ironic too, because part of the criticism that he gets from you is that he doesn't understand you, and part of his inability to follow through with what you ask of him is because of his reaction to your criticism. Once he's mad, it's hard to find it in his heart to smile at you"). Although the client is frustrated because she thinks her husband is ignoring what she's asking of him, the therapist helps her to see that his lack of compliance is due to his own emotional struggle and, further, her way of communicating what she wants may be preventing her from getting what she wants.

The therapist may also offer an alternative perspective to the partner in the listening role. Listening partners often relax when they realize that acknowledging communication is not the same as agreeing with it or as acquiescing to a demand. The therapist can suggest, "You can encourage her to be briefer with her complaints if you acknowledge at the outset that you understand what she's asking for. It doesn't necessarily mean that you agree with her."

The therapist can encourage couples who are ambivalent about intimate communication to discuss with one another the potential conflict between intimacy and openness on the one hand and harmony on the other. High levels of openness increase intimacy but also increase the potential for conflict. High levels of harmony require tact and selective sharing that reduces mutual knowledge and risks letting important issues go underground, where they affect the relationship in unexpected ways. Both openness and tact have their place in a good relationship; the challenge for couples is finding the best balance for their individual personalities and their relationship.

4. *Help clients devise realistic communication goals.* Couple partners commonly argue about who is right and get caught in cycles of blame and self-defense. The role of the therapist in Step 4 is to help partners connect faulty communication goals and the frustrating fruit of their conversations. First, the therapist can help couple partners consider whether pursuing their short-term goals will lead to long-term losses. He or she can ask whether winning the argument, forcing the partner to see their own point of view, or convincing the partner of the correctness of their own position will encourage intimacy for either one of them. A second approach is to help couples understand the difference between talking and communication: Talking can involve partners trying to outmaneuver each other whereas communication is for conveying and receiving messages. The therapist can help couple partners maintain their message-focus (i.e., maintain a focus on conveying and receiving messages instead of on being right) by interrupting them when they argue and encouraging them to refocus their attention on achieving their goals. By helping the couple maintain this focus, the therapist can prevent a merry-go-round of argument that never leads to a resolution. The therapist is also modeling for the couple what they will eventually need to do for themselves.

5. *Suggest behavior rehearsal as a method for partners to learn alternative communication behaviors when their old behavior obstructs their goals.* To help couple partners decrease the frequency of behavior that obstructs their communication goals, the therapist has two options. First, the therapist may suggest specific behavioral changes to the client (e.g., "I think you had his attention and then lost it, with the loudness and the accusation. Would you like to try it again, this time without raising the decibels?").

Second, the therapist can model more effective communication by role-playing with one of the partners while the other one observes. In this case, the therapist suggests that the frustrated partner watch the therapist demonstrate a different way and then afterward talk about how the partner liked the approach. If the partner sees value in the modeled behavior, the therapist can then talk the client through the process of trying it him- or herself.

Couple partners' communication is derailed when they get distracted by efforts to manipulate or compete with their partner and thereby lose their message in the process. Message-focused communication training is a five-step sequence for helping partners increase the effectiveness of their self-expressions and disclosures, with the goal of maximizing partner cooperation and minimizing defensiveness.

Help Clients Identify Behavior-Outcome Connections

Intimacy depends upon goodwill between relationship partners. Goodwill is difficult to sustain, however, in the face of fruitless arguments that leave partners feeling misunderstood, unappreciated, and ineffective. Couples can learn to reduce the number of these frustrating interactions when the therapist teaches them to make logical connections between their behavior and the reactions of their partners. Repetitive interaction patterns occur, in part, because partners fail to make these connections and modify their behavior accordingly.

Behavior-outcome connections take the form of if—then statements connecting one's own behavior to one's partner's reaction. They are acquired through repeated interactions with the partner, assuming that the individual is paying attention and attempting to learn from experience. Examples include, "If I criticize my partner, she will get defensive; if I express my appreciation to my partner, she will smile proudly and look happy."

Clients are especially likely to need help identifying behavior-outcome connections when they are operating out of idealized scenarios in which certain behavior *should* lead to certain outcomes. In their efforts to make these idealized scenarios come true, partners repeat the same behaviors over and over, each time looking for the same outcome that never comes and failing to make the connection between the actual, undesirable outcome and the behavior (Haley, 1987).

The pursuer-distancer relationship pattern exemplifies this process (Boszormenyi-Nagy & Spark, 1973). In this pattern, the two partners *polarize* around the issue of intimacy versus separateness or distance: One partner pushes for more intimacy whereas the other distances from the pursuing partner and avoids addressing his or her demands. Each person's response reinforces the other's negative behavior, causing a mutual influence cycle that has no end point. For example, the longer Michael maintains his pursuit of more intimacy with Owen, the more likely it is that Owen will relent and spend time with him, because he will notice that "it really has been a long time;" similarly, the more distant Owen's behavior, the more likely Michael's unmet needs will drive him to pursue. By maintaining their respective behaviors, Mike and Owen are "shooting themselves in the foot," as McCullough (2006) describes it, because neither has constructed a realistic behavior-outcome script.

In sum, training clients to make behavior-outcome connections helps them to more accurately perceive what works and what does not work, and thereby prevents them from repeating interaction cycles that have never paid off.

There are five steps involved in helping couple partners identify behavior-outcome contingencies:

1. *Therapist listens for partners' complaints about each other's behavior.* The behaviors that are best targeted by this intervention are those that meet three conditions: (1) They elicit undesirable behavior from the spouse or partner, (2) they are repetitive, and (3) they appear to be repeated without regard for the consequences. To demonstrate the use of this intervention, I am drawing on Tim's and Paula's treatment. In Tim's idealized notion of marriage, the way that Paula should react to his withdrawals was as real as the way she had actually behaved for the 10 years of their marriage. Tim did not see his behavior

as contributing to the frequency of Paula's complaints nor did it occur to him that he could behave differently. To complete the first step, the therapist reflected Tim's complaint that Paula's pressuring him to share himself was distressing and unpleasant for him. The therapist then suggested that Tim could do something about it.

2. *The therapist points out the connection between Paula's undesirable behavior and Tim's own behavior.* The second step involves the therapist sharing his or her own perception of the if-then connection between Tim's withdrawing and Paula's complaining. The therapist said, "You tend to keep your thoughts to yourself, Tim, and that prompts Paula to complain. Paula wants you to confide in her. She's not a live-and-let-live kind of woman. You didn't marry a woman like that, you chose Paula. Something about this appeals to you."

3. *Identify alternative responses.* For the third step, the therapist engages Tim in a discussion of alternative responses. What prompted him to withdraw? What else could he do instead of withdraw? How could he withdraw in a way that would not elicit the undesirable behaviors from Paula? The goal for this step in the intervention is for Tim to experience himself as having more behavioral choices than he perceives himself to have right now.

4. *Rehearse the new response in the session with the partner.* This is the role-playing step, which requires that the client practice alternative behaviors as a way to fully integrate them into his or her repertoire. The therapist serves as a coach and a source of feedback for the partner trying to make the change.

5. *Explore the client's perception of his or her behavior in the role-play practice.* As with other role-play practice interventions, it is important to elicit the client's thoughts and feelings about the practice and give the client an opportunity to critique his or her own work.

6. *Explore the client's perception of the outcome of the new behavior.* In this last step, the therapist queries the client making the change about how the client liked the alternative outcome that came with the alternative behavior. This gives Tim an opportunity to explore his feelings about Paula's response. If Tim perceives that his behavior can make a difference in how he and Paula interact with each other, then he is more likely to repeat this process and generalize it to other behavior-outcome connections. The intervention concludes with the couple's homework, which is to experiment with the new practice and monitor their feelings about it.

Teaching clients to notice and respond to behavior-outcome sequences has a cognitive outcome: It helps clients to think in terms of behavior and outcomes rather than in terms of "right versus wrong" or "who's to blame." By thinking more about their goals, by keeping their eyes on their desired outcomes, they can learn to minimize the undesirable behavior that they provoke in one another.[2]

2 I do not recommend this intervention for victims of domestic violence or other kinds of abuse.

Intimate Communication Training: Appropriate Self-Expression and Listening Skills

Sometimes clients will need additional communication skills to effectively deepen their interactions with others. Couple partners who want more intimacy can benefit from intimate communication training. Lonely individuals who have chronic problems with forming romantic relationships often require it. Intimate communication training teaches effective self-expression and good listening skills. Each of these is necessary for intimate communication.

Appropriate self-expression Among those who seek therapy because they have been unable to attract a romantic partner are individuals who fail because they do not share themselves with the people they meet. Without self-disclosure, lonely people fail to create a connection with potential partners (Rotenberg, 1997).

People who do not share themselves often say that they were not "raised that way," meaning that they rarely heard people in their families talk about personal, private things that they had on their mind to an empathic, caring listener. These individuals have no model for verbally intimate interactions. As a result, they feel (and are) clumsy when it comes to expressing tender feelings or giving others the gift of attentive listening.

The therapist may have to persuade the shy client that it is worthwhile to learn to be more open with others. The reticent, uncoupled client should hear that failing to talk about oneself in a meaningful, intimate way is likely to continue being a barrier to forming romantic relationships and that the client will need to increase his or her skill and comfort with intimate communication in order to achieve this goal (Prager, 1995). Therapists may also reassure such clients that intimate communication can result in one or both participants feeling accepted, affirmed, validated, and cared for (Reis & Patrick, 1996; Reis & Shaver, 1988). The therapist's role in training individuals in effective, gratifying intimate communication skills is to teach the skills and also to provide an experience for them, if possible, in which they experience the benefits of intimate communication first hand (Johnson, 2004).

Intimate communication skill training involves five steps. The steps in the training process are as follows:

1. *Therapist models good intimate communication skills.* The therapist may begin by modeling appropriate self-disclosure, positive involvement, and empathic understanding. Examples of the specific skills that go into these components of intimate interaction include self-disclosure, verbal validation of the client's perspective, communication of acceptance, affirmations of the client's positive qualities, and reassurances. Also important for intimate communication are listening skills such as open-ended questions, paraphrasing, and reflecting feelings, all of which show that the listener is tracking the other's speech and understands what the other is saying.

2. *Therapist explains the skills.* After modeling the skills, the therapist explains the skills didactically and gives reasons why each is important.

3. *Therapist structures behavior rehearsal of the skills.* The therapist next sets up role-play practices to give the client a chance to practice some of the skills. Therapist structuring begins with a description of role-playing, a rationale for using it, and instructions for carrying it out. Structuring continues during the role-play when the therapist breaks from his or her role and coaches the client on what to do at different points. The therapist involves the client in the setting up of the role-play and provides feedback during the role-play as well (if the latter creates confusion, the therapist can postpone the feedback until after the role-play).

4. *Reflect, offer feedback, and repeat.* In this final step, the therapist elicits the client's personal reflections on the role-plays and offers feedback in the form of suggestions for alternative ways of approaching the role-play. Then, the therapist encourages the client to repeat the practice as a way of refining the skills and incorporating the feedback. The therapist collaborates with the client by asking the client to evaluate his or her own performance before the therapist gives feedback. In this way, the therapist encourages the client to self-correct, building the client's independence and self-confidence. Whatever the client doesn't pick up, the therapist can share with the client.

It is a good idea to rehearse one skill at a time, as too much at once will cause the client to feel overwhelmed and risks reinforcing a sense of incompetence instead of ameliorating it.

Table 4.2 offers some additional therapist prompts that can be used when intervening with couples who require intimate communication training and includes giving the couple the repeat-practice for homework. Chapter 10 illustrates the use of behavior rehearsal with clients who struggle with Dilemma #3, the past lives in the present.

Listening skills. In order for therapy sessions to be productive, partners need to be able to sit quietly and listen to each other without reactively defending themselves or verbally attacking the partner. Being able to sit quietly and listen to the partner often requires multiple psychological skills. Baucom and Epstein (1990) note that "listening is an active process in which an individual must concentrate his or her attention on incoming verbal and nonverbal messages, interpret the meaning of those messages . . . and determine what would be an appropriate response to the partner . . . good listening cannot be taken for granted" (p. 105). Listening skills often include on-the-spot self-soothing (discussed in Chapter 5), the monitoring of one's own emotionally arousing interpretations of the partner's statements, and the ability to stop oneself from jumping to conclusions or engaging in emotional reasoning (both are discussed in Chapter 6). The behavioral component of listening skills can be taught in the following order, from the simplest to most complex component, depending upon whether the simpler approach is sufficient.

Table 4.2 Sample therapist interventions for teaching intimate communication skills

Intervention	*Examples*
Therapist models good intimate communication	*Self-disclosure:* "Sometimes I too find myself repeating the same thing over and over if I think I'm not being heard. Frustration can make you do that." *Verbal validation:* "The feelings you're having are quite normal; I see a lot of people in my practice who say that they want the things that you want." *Acceptance:* "Being intimate with words may not be your best strength, but you clearly have other ways of expressing yourself. We need to teach your partner how to read you better." *Affirmation:* "You are really working hard here today. You both deserve a lot of credit for hanging in there." *Reassurance:* "It's hard for anyone to change old habits. It will get easier as you practice."
Therapist explains intimate communication skills didactically	*Why skill is important:* "There is more to communication than simply talking and listening. How you say things can be just as important as what you say. There are a few key skills that can make communication go more smoothly. You are doing one of them now. It is called active listening." *Acknowledge the other's perspective:* "Your impulse is to jump in with your own thoughts, but try doing this first: Say to him, 'Let me make sure I understand what you're saying. You want . . . Is that right?' This way, before you respond, you reassure yourself that you know exactly what he means." *How to validate:* "Validating each other is something we can do without having to agree or give in to what they want from us. Validation conveys that we understand how or why the partner came to feel as he or she does; it allows you to go to discussing your different ideas instead of forcing each other to repeat endlessly because you don't think the other person has understood."
Therapist structures role-play practice	*Setting up:* "Let's spend about 10 minutes practicing how to explain to one another how you feel about your problem with intimacy. I'd like you to take turns stating the problem from your point of view. After the first speaker has finished, I'd like the listener to summarize what you think you've heard. If the message wasn't clear, we'll give it another try. I'll interrupt you occasionally to give you a few pointers. Who would like to go first?"

(*Continued*)

Table 4.2 (*Continued*)

Intervention	*Examples*
	Structuring communication in process: "Try this and you might reach her more effectively: Before you say what you want to say, check with her to make sure you understand what she just said. Then [to female partner] you tell him, yes or no; if he didn't get it totally you can clarify. Then it will be your turn to sit back and let him have his say." "You know, he just acknowledged one of your points. Before you push on past that, you could affirm him for doing that: Let him know you appreciate his effort to understand and acknowledge you. The affirming moment gives you both a chance to pause before you continue with your conversation."
Therapist elicits reflections on the practice and recommends repeating	Questions for eliciting reflections can include: "How do you think that went?" "How similar is this to how these conversations go at home?" "Before we go on, tell me how it felt to you to pause and acknowledge what she just said to you before you spoke. . ." "How was this different than before?" "What did you like about the way you communicated?" "How did it feel to hear acknowledgment from your partner?" "Learning to communicate effectively is like learning any other new skill. The more you practice, the better you get at it. It would be good if you two could set aside 10 minutes of each day to practice what we covered here today. Audiotaping the conversation and listening to yourselves can help you improve your skills. Try to be a better speaker and better listener each time."

1. *Teach the client to listen quietly without interrupting the partner.* The first step in listening skills training involves simple behavioral guidance, in which the therapist directs the client to listen until his or her partner has finished speaking and then they will get a turn to speak. This instruction usually comes during the assessment sessions. During an intervention, this behavioral guidance might come in this form, "Right now, I'm working with Althea to see if she might be willing to move closer to some of the things that you want, Romon. Under these circumstances, it is best if you can sit quietly and listen. By doing so, you will likely understand Althea better, because you will hear what Althea struggles with within herself in order to give you what you want from her."

2. *Teach the partner to use active listening skills to demonstrate understanding.* Especially useful for increasing intimacy in couple relationships are listening

skills that demonstrate understanding and empathy for the partner's perspective. The more difficult the message the partner is trying to assimilate, the more difficult it will be to demonstrate either understanding or empathy. It is possible to teach partners to demonstrate understanding using reflective listening, a classic behavioral couple therapy technique (Baucom & Epstein, 1990; Jacobson & Margolin, 1979).

3. *Teach the partners self-soothing techniques to prevent themselves from having emotional overreactions.* Reflective listening is especially difficult when partners are experiencing emotional overreactions to what the other is saying. Self-soothing techniques help partners calm themselves down during difficult exchanges, improving their ability to use the skills that they know. I find that I frequently must begin by working with these skills (Chapter 5 has a detailed discussion) and then move on to listening skills.

4. *If necessary, help the client to monitor his or her own interpretations of the partner's communication if these are negatively arousing and unrealistic.* Partners who overreact to one another's messages have often endorsed unrealistic and dysfunctional intimacy-related automatic thoughts or schemas. When they listen to their partner's message, they are confronted with a cascade of unwanted, automatic thoughts that cause them intense anxiety or anger. Under these circumstances, they may find that they cannot make use of self-soothing techniques because their own interpretations demand their overreaction. The therapist can then take this opportunity to teach them how to change their thinking pattern, using techniques discussed in Chapter 6.

Table 4.3 gives examples of effective and ineffective communication that therapists can give to their clients. The examples in the table are paired with the goals of interaction and the reasons why some communication brings the speaker closer to his or her goal whereas other communication is ineffective.

Reverse roles role-plays. Reverse roles role-plays proceed in much the same way as other role-play interventions but have additional purposes. The role-play rehearsal interventions described above aim to teach clients specific communication skills to help them to become more effective communicators and listeners. Reverse roles role-plays encourage clients who lack empathy for another person's perspective to get inside of that perspective and thereby increase their understanding of it. Second, they help polarized couples (i.e., those who unreasonably take oversimplified opposite positions on a complex issue) see a middle ground that is wiser than either of their extreme positions.

Implementation of the reverse roles role-play technique requires four steps. Please note that using this technique presumes a good alliance with the therapist and a comfort with trying new and difficult things in therapy on the part of the couple. It is not recommended for couples who are still stuck in a pattern of repetitive, irresolvable conflict. These couples may be unable to implement this technique.

Table 4.3 Examples of effective and ineffective communication

Goal	*Ineffective*	*Effective*
Bring up concerns	"You don't pay attention to me unless you want sex." *Why? The "you" characterization is an attack and is an overgeneralization that will elicit defensiveness.*	"I want to spend more time together. I enjoy our sex life, but I want to do other things together too. How about you?" *Why? The speaker speaks for him- or herself only and tells the partner about his or her personal experience. The speaker then demonstrates interest in the partner by asking him or her to talk about him- or herself.*
Express needs	"Can't you see that I'm lonely? I need to feel needed and wanted. If you can't do that, I'll just have to look for it somewhere else." *Why? The threat of leaving increases anxiety or angers the partner, thus defeating the speaker's effort to gain sympathy and concern and to teach the partner what he or she wants.*	"Even though I see you and the kids each day sometimes I feel lonely I don't feel needed anymore. I want to feel like I matter to you. Would you be willing to talk with me about this to see if we can fix it?" *Why? With this statement, the speaker speaks for him- or herself and shows an interest in hearing what the partner has to say.*
Ask for specific wants without criticizing	"You need to give me as much attention as you give to your computer." *Why? The speaker adds an irrelevant criticism to a simple request for more attention. The criticism is likely to arouse defensiveness (e.g., "I do not spend that much time on my computer") and distract the partner from the speaker's request. In addition, the request is vague and may be seen as overly demanding because of that.*	"I'd like to set aside time after dinner to do something together even if it's just watching TV for a little while." *Why? This request is specific and doesn't criticize the partner.*

(*Continued*)

Table 4.3 (Continued)

Goal	*Ineffective*	*Effective*
Demonstrate respect	"You don't know what you're talking about. You have no idea what's going on." *Why? This statement puts the partner down and questions his or her knowledge or intelligence.*	"I'm not sure I understand what you mean. Explain it again." *Why? This request gives the speaker the benefit of the doubt, implies that he or she is capable of making a statement worth hearing.*
Stand for one's own values	"I don't care what you think. I'm not going to give in on this. You're going to have to deal with it." *Why? The ultimatum is uncooperative at best and conveys lack of caring or respect for partner's needs and feelings at worst.*	"I see your point, but I feel very strongly about this. Can we find a compromise?" *Why? The statement acknowledges different wants and invites the partner to engage in cooperative problem solving. It skips criticism about the partner's wants or point of view.*

1 *Therapist gives rationale for the role-play.* The therapist explains that reverse roles role-plays have as their purpose to increase the partners' understanding of each other.
2 *Therapist sets up the role-play, collaborating with the couple to fill in as many details as possible.* The therapist uses a question and answer process to elicit from the couple a vivid and realistic scenario for the role-play. As part of setting up the role-play, the therapist articulates what he or she perceives to be the perceptions and feelings of each partner and encourages the couple to keep those in mind as they role-play. This is likely a necessary step, because the partners may be unable at this point to craft their own sympathetic portrayal of the other's point of view. In order for the reverse roles role-play to accomplish the objectives, the clients must have access to a sympathetic framing of the other's perspective.
3 *Begin role-play.* The therapist sits back quietly here and lets the couple experience the reverse roles role-play.
4 *Discuss the role-play, check feelings.* This step gives each partner a chance to tell the other how they felt in the other's shoes. It encourages empathic expression from each of them and increases mutual understanding.

Reverse roles role-play can be an effective method for increasing empathy and cooperation between partners, especially when they are polarized around an issue. It is best used when partners have learned to control their repetitive, irresolvable conflicts and have moved past blaming each other for the problems in their relationship. For this reason, it is best used in the middle or toward the end of therapy. It is also useful with individual clients to help reduce their anxiety about meeting, deepening, and sustaining relationships.

Some Caveats on Behavioral Interventions

Therapists should use caution when applying behavioral interventions because of some well-known risks that have emerged from research on behavioral couple therapy (Epstein & Baucom, 2003). First, therapists should beware of applying behavioral interventions too mechanically because couples may perceive this as a failure to adapt interventions to their unique problems. Behavioral interventions are most effective when they are treated as lenses that help increase a couple's awareness and ability to focus on behaviors that have heretofore been automatic and unexamined. When couples deliberately try to change their behavior patterns, they become much more aware of the problematic patterns and are more effective in their efforts to change.

Second, Epstein and Baucom (2003) suggest that therapists shy away from focusing on microlevel components of communication at the expense of addressing couples' presenting concerns. Fortunately, there are behavioral interventions that can be immediately applied to couples' presenting concerns (e.g., behavioral contracting can be used to help couples make needed time for themselves as a couple). Third, therapists would be wise to avoid pushing couples to maintain specific behavioral skills practiced in therapy over the long run. This recommendation stems from research on the long-term effects of behavioral couple therapy in which couples were found not to maintain specific behaviors practiced in therapy for long past the end of therapy.

Conclusion

Classical behavioral techniques such as communication skill training and behavioral contracting, and the intimate communication training described here, can teach couples techniques for reducing defensiveness and increasing intimacy in their relationship. Because these interventions often foster immediate behavioral change, they are especially useful for instilling hope and goodwill early in therapy. Because they require changes from both partners, they remind couples that both have to make an effort in order to see change in their relationship. Behavioral interventions are also specific enough to give to couples as homework, even when the sessions are devoted to cognitive change. Couples who have unresolved intimacy dilemmas also struggle with overreactive affect and self-defeating thinking patterns along with problematic behavior. Interventions that target these problems are the subject of the next two chapters.

5

AFFECTIVE INTERVENTIONS

The expression of affect is both a source of intimacy and a problem. When negative affect, particularly anger, is not managed effectively and is displayed rather than expressed responsibly, it derails couple communication, damages trust, and drives partners apart. In contrast, the expression of what Johnson and her colleagues call "soft emotions" (2004; see also Jacobson & Christensen, 1996) can invite partners to share them, in the case of joy, happiness, or excitement, or they can invite partners to offer comfort and physical closeness, as with sadness or fear.

Overly reactive emotionality on the part of couples in therapy reflects, at least in part, the individual partners' inability to self-soothe in the face of negatively arousing interactions with the spouse. When relationship partners can control the intensity of their negative affect during interactions with their partners, they can improve their ability to think through and cope effectively with their relationship dilemmas. They can also better communicate their needs and wants to their partners in a way that is most likely to be heard and to be experienced as intimate. Further, individuals who can soothe their own emotional upsets are personally empowered to take more risks with intimacy because they know that they can handle the outcome.

Affect is also problematic when partners' own emotions are not accessible to conscious thought. If overly reactive emotionality makes it difficult for partners to resolve their intimacy dilemmas, then partners' lack of sensitivity to their own emotions makes it difficult for partners to share their feelings with their partners and thereby limits intimacy. Under these conditions, one or both partners may feel shut out of the other's inner life. Further, a partner who lacks awareness of his or her own day-to-day feelings and emotions may fail to respond to them constructively, until they build to an intensity that is no longer easily managed or communicated.

Problems coping with emotions and sharing them with one's partner require therapeutic interventions that directly target affect. This chapter presents affectively oriented interventions that can help partners with their intimacy dilemmas.

Most of the time, in cognitive-behavioral approaches to therapy, disturbed affect is addressed by altering the thinking processes that elicit, sustain, and

Table 5.1 Affect-oriented interventions

Type	*Phase of Therapy*	*Intervention*
Affective	Early	Therapist soothes anxious or angry affect
Affective	Early	Teach self-soothing
Affective	Middle	Emotion-regulation training
Affective	Middle	Increase emotion tolerance
Affective	Middle	Pause before speaking
Affective	Early to Middle	Dual monitoring
Affective	Early to Middle	Self-awareness training

intensify it (Epstein & Baucom, 2003). However, sometimes it is helpful to intervene directly with affect by altering its autonomic concomitants. These direct affective interventions often yield more rapid results than cognitive interventions, but because these techniques require constant attention, their effects decay over time. They can be replaced eventually with longer-lasting cognitive interventions that change affect via changes in attitudes and thinking patterns. Affective interventions are especially useful from the early to the middle phases of therapy because rapid results solidify the therapeutic alliance and build hopes for the future of treatment and the relationship.

The affective interventions discussed in this chapter are listed in Table 5.1. Some of these interventions are best when paired with cognitive interventions whereas others stand well on their own. The goals of these interventions overlap because there is considerable individual variation in the effectiveness of the various techniques. This chapter's presentation of affect-oriented interventions begins with some brief one-to-two session interventions with client affect and concludes with multistep interventions aimed at longer term change.

Therapist Soothes Angry or Anxious Affect

Using the techniques described in Chapter 3 for building the therapeutic alliance, the therapist can soothe partners' anxious or angry feelings early in therapy when partners are unable to do so themselves. The therapist soothes by using listening skills to demonstrate understanding, which validates and affirms each partner's experience and conveys acceptance. In other words, the therapist becomes an intimate partner and offers the provisions of intimacy to the partners at a time when they are in crisis.

As the therapy progresses, the therapist will become more selective regarding the circumstances under which he or she provides soothing to the couple. Soothing from the therapist is most useful later in therapy when one or both partners are taking risks and trying new behavior. However, when the therapist is in an educational role, the therapist is less of a soothing influence than a stimulating one. Here is an example of a therapist articulating this shift in the role with a client:

Therapist: I feel as sympathetic now as I did when you first came in about the sacrifices that you have made and the small amount of return you believe you have gotten for them. I see you as someone who is now stepping up and asking for more of what you want. It impresses me that you are doing this; it is a courageous change for you. Now you are ready for the next step—to learn to calm yourself down when you are upset. As you feel more competent to care for yourself, you may find that you are happy if he comes to soothe or support you but that you don't have to crash bottom if he doesn't.

Teach Self-Soothing Techniques

Self-soothing is a process of calming oneself down and thereby decreasing emotional agitation. It is crucial to any successful couple therapy practice, as intensity of anxiety or anger is closely linked to impulsive behavior (Weitzman, McHugh, & Otto, 2011), which in turn is often destructive to fostering a safe climate for intimate relating. Self-soothing training is useful for several intimacy-related problems. First, self-soothing techniques are helpful to individuals who are averse to taking emotional risks to enhance relational intimacy with their partners. A reluctance to try new behavior often stems from the individual's concern about how he or she will feel if the risky behavior does not pay off the way it is hoped. Rather than have to cope with negative affect afterward, some clients will get stuck in a rut of defensive behavior that reduces negative affect in the short term but is ineffective in the long run. Second, self-soothing training is useful for individuals who depend too much on their partners for soothing. An individual can appear to depend too much on the partner if he or she demands soothing from the other regardless of what is going on. Self-soothing helps people soothe their own hurt or angry emotions independently and helps them to better weather the normal negative emotions that come and go in intimate relationships. Third, self-soothing is helpful for relationship partners who believe they cannot tolerate the emotional vulnerability that comes with intimate relating. These individuals often withdraw when intimacy increases or push the other away with negative behavior. Self-soothing skills empower these individuals to stop dysfunctional behaviors that have as their unstated purpose to alleviate the individual's uncomfortable emotions. Fourth, self-soothing is a kind of self empowering technique for clients whose struggle with Dilemma #2, I versus we, results in their feeling overwhelmed by the influence of their partner (see Chapters 8 and 9). These individuals often overreact, either with intense anxiety or anger, to the things that their partners say. Self-soothing techniques can help them to calm themselves when they feel an overreaction coming on.

Progressive relaxation. There are as many self-soothing techniques as there are diverse individuals. The most widely used technique from behavior therapy is progressive relaxation (Jacobson, 1938). Progressive relaxation involves deliberate relaxing of muscles via a two-step process. First, the client deliberately tenses certain muscle groups, usually proceeding in order from the head to the feet. Second, the client releases the tension and is instructed to notice the difference between the tensed and relaxed muscles. The role of the therapist is to talk the person through the alternating tension and relaxation. Jacobson's instructions for progressive relaxation are reproduced at http://www.anxietybc.com/sites/default/files/MuscleRelaxation.pdf.

Three-part breathing. Three-part breathing is a yoga practice designed to calm the mind. It can be done sitting or lying down and involves the following steps: (1) close the eyes, (2) focus attention on the natural inhalation and exhalation of the breath without altering it, (3) shift breathing to inhale deeply through the nose, (4) ensure that each deep breath fills the abdomen, causing it to expand, (5) upon exhalation, empty the abdomen of air, causing it to flatten against the backbone, (6) continue abdominal breathing for five to six more breaths, (7) increase inhalation until the breath expands the rib cage, (8) exhale the air first from the rib cage followed by abdominal exhalation, (9) repeat abdominal-to-rib cage breathing for five to six breaths, (10) continue inhaling after filling the abdomen and the rib cage until the upper chest area is filled with air, (11) exhale the breath in order, starting with the upper chest, then the rib cage, and finally the abdomen, and (12) continue three-part breathing for another 10 breaths. This yoga practice focuses the attention, quiets the mind, and relaxes the body.

Ujjayi breathing. Ujjayi (pronounced *oo-jai)* is breathing through both nostrils with the glottis held partially closed. The closing of the glottis causes the breath to make a windy sound in the throat. Concentrating on maintaining the ujjayi breathing and listening to the sound is soothing and the controlled breathing relaxes the body. More detailed instructions for ujjayi breathing can be found at http://www.yogajournal.com/poses/2485.

Self-soothing with the five senses. Marcia Linehan (1993) organizes self-soothing techniques according to their appeal to the senses. The sensory input that produces the best self-soothing effect will vary from individual to individual. The therapist should encourage the client to experiment with different sensory modalities until the client identifies the one that works best. According to Linehan (1993), a person can soothe him- or herself visually with a flower or a beautiful painting, auditorily with beautiful music or a wind chime, kinesthetically through yoga or jogging, or can enjoy olfactory soothing with incense, flowers, or perfume. One can self-soothe with touch by using comfortable clothing, comforters, massages, and pets.

Soothing self-talk. A popular and effective method for soothing uncomfortable emotions is through the use of soothing self-talk. With this intervention, the individual and therapist together come up with statements that the client can say to him- or herself that are calming and thereby reduce the intensity of negative emotions. The self-statement is used consciously and deliberately to comfort the self, in contrast to most emotion-generating cognitions that occur automatically.

The therapist usually has to help the client come up with soothing self-statements. On their own, clients will often come up with statements like, "Relax already!," "Don't be an idiot. This isn't that big of a deal," and so forth. It is best if the therapist takes an active role in collaboration with the client to formulate self-statements that are effectively soothing. For example, instead of saying "Relax already" when he or she feels anxious and pressured, the client can say to him- or herself, "I can take my time and think about what I want I do."

A useful way to help the client distinguish between his or her usual and possibly punitive self-statements and those that have the effect that he or she is seeking is to call the first the "bad coach" and the second the "good coach." The bad coach had good intentions and tries to soothe but instead agitates. The good coach is more skillful and can offer effective soothing.

Matching self-soothing techniques with individuals. Some individuals can readily learn and utilize self-soothing techniques effectively whereas others require more assistance. Some people will already know what works for them (e.g., working out, taking walks, or calling a friend). These individuals can apply existing self-soothing skills to their efforts to cope with intimacy dilemmas.

The therapist can help couple partners identify those activities that already work for them if they are not aware of them. Leading questions will help them recall: When do they remember feeling serene and at peace? When do they remember that they were upset and then did something that made them feel better? Was there something that worked when they were children, in the military service, or in graduate school? Once they identify some possibilities, the therapist can collaborate with them to set up an experiment to see if the activity effectively soothes them after a difficult interaction with their partner.

For those clients who do not already have a method of self-soothing, the therapist can teach one of the self-soothing skills listed above. Therapists can also take the cognitive approach discussed in the next chapter and teach partners to identify and transform the negative automatic thoughts and beliefs that fuel overblown negative emotions (see Chapter 6 for procedures). By recognizing that they need self-soothing and finding activities that allow them to do just that, clients are learning to observe and communicate their emotions rather than simply reacting to them.

Self-soothing for a low intimacy couple struggling with Dilemma #1, joy versus protection from pain. Having self-soothing skills means that, whether the partner is available or not, one has the wherewithal to soothe one's own hurts. Self-soothing skills should increase one's confidence in one's ability to withstand the risks of intimate relating and can be used as a step toward taking more risks for a person who has been risk averse.

According to Schnarch (1991), relationship partners need to be able to self-soothe because sometimes intimacy requires partners to disclose aspects of self to the other that the other does not want to hear. Under these circumstances, the partner's message is the cause of hurt and the individual must rely on him- or herself for soothing. Partners who are afraid of the negative emotions that their disclosures will cause the other or that their partner's response will cause themselves are often averse to taking the risk of sharing their thoughts and feelings. Ultimately, these risk-avoiding individuals will find themselves with less intimacy in their relationships unless they become more adept at self-soothing. In contrast, individuals who develop self-soothing skills will come to believe in their own ability to weather negative outcomes from emotional risks. Jessica's therapist encouraged her to soothe herself rather than avoid communicating with her partner Ann.

Therapist: Ann's pretty stubborn, and you worry about how she'll react if you tell her that you don't really enjoy the games.

Jessica: I'm a girly-girl deep inside, you know. She thinks that because I'm gay, I'll like all the stuff she likes, but I'm actually into fashion shows and romance novels and other girly stuff.

Therapist: Are you afraid she'll do something drastic, like fall out of love with you or break up with you?

Jessica: No, not that. But whenever she's mad at me, I feel so guilty. Also, I hate times when we're not close. I get depressed even if she's not doing anything to me. So I end up not telling her things that make her mad.

Therapist: And in the meantime, she's spending a fortune on season's tickets, box seats, and all.

Jessica: Yeah, I feel guilty about all that. I'm afraid I'll just blurt the truth out some time and cause even more trouble.

Therapist: How would you feel about our devising some strategies that would help you to speak up honestly to her—strategies that would give you more confidence that you wouldn't get too depressed if she's upset?

Jessica: I just picture the look on her face when I tell her and I feel awful. But I know being honest is the right thing to do. It's not like she doesn't have other friends who would go with her.

Therapist: In general, what do you do to feel better when you're feeling awful?

Jessica: Well, I'm not very good at it. When I was a little girl, I used to color in my coloring books. Whenever I think about calming myself down, I remember those days.

Therapist: Is there anything like coloring books that you do now that has the same effect?

Jessica: I've wondered about that, actually. Like whether I wouldn't enjoy painting or pastels, or even making one of those kits you can buy.

Therapist: Would you be willing to make an investment in one of those crafts?

Jessica: It's worth a try.

Therapist: The idea behind the investment is that you would have something that soothes you when you're feeling unhappy, which in turn might help you with speaking honestly with Ann. But first things first—experiment first with one of your crafts—pick one, try it—and let's see how it works.

Once Jessica has identified a self-soothing craft that works for her, she and her therapist can also work to change her upsetting thinking pattern (e.g., her automatic thoughts that occur when she sees hurt or anger on Ann's face) so that she is better able to take risks without getting overly depressed about Ann's reactions.

Soothing and emotional support is one of the benefits that relationship partners expect from each other, and it is highly correlated with partners' reports of satisfaction with their relationship (Cordova, Gee, & Warren, 2005; Gable, Gonzaga, & Strachman, 2006; Kirby, Baucom, & Peterman, 2005; Lippert & Prager, 2001; Prager & Buhrmester, 1998; Sprecher & Hendrick, 2004). Yet, it is a mistake for people to expect relationship partners to prop them up with affirmations and validations and soothing that individuals may not be able to provide themselves (Schnarch, 1991). Enjoying these benefits of intimacy is appropriate and is best distinguished from demanding that one's partner always be available with these provisions.

The therapist's emphasis on partners learning to self-soothe helps clients to appreciate what they do already to soothe themselves. Through the therapist's valuing of their self-soothing activity, clients can also learn to value the healthy things that they do already. Further, paradoxically, once relationship partners have been given "permission" by the therapist to be imperfect providers of nurturing to one another, they are often more prepared to extend themselves for the other.

Emotion regulation training. Clients who do not readily learn self-soothing skills can benefit from a more structured intervention, called emotion regulation training. The goal of emotion regulation training is to help individuals reduce their emotional overreactivity, particularly their feelings of anxiety and anger. Individuals who can benefit from emotion regulation training feel panicky or enraged by conflicts between their own personal goals and desires and their partner's goals or behaviors (i.e., they often have difficulty coping with Intimacy Dilemma #2, I versus we). Emotion regulation training can be used by relationship partners when they are in the heat of a negatively arousing interaction. Emotion regulation training requires five steps.

1. *Empower the client—frame this training as a way to reach client's self-stated goals.* The first step of the treatment, as always, is presenting it to the client, which in this case includes a promise of self-empowerment. The goal of the first step is to get the client to buy into the notion that self-empowerment is a desirable goal with desirable consequences. For example, here is how Jack and Alicia's therapist described self-empowerment for Alicia.

Therapist: I've begun to see you, Alicia, as struggling with two problems. The first is with the lack of respect, attention, and consideration to your wants and needs that you perceive coming from Jack. The second, though, is how upset you get—sad and angry all at once, putting all your energy into persuading Jack to give you respect and attention in the form that you want it . . . . It's those moments when you think you want a divorce. Jack, if you want your wife to be happier, then no doubt we'll have to work on some more effective ways that you can convey to her that her feelings and perspective are important to you. As for that desperate feeling that you get, Alicia, I hope you won't have to feel that awful feeling over and over until Jack's behavior changes, which could take some time. Waiting for Jack to change so that you can stop feeling so desperate gives Jack an awful lot of power over the way that you feel. I'd love to see you feel more empowered within yourself to take care of yourself emotionally even if Jack's behavior is frustrating. Self-soothing training will help you to feel less impatient and desperate about him changing."

By framing the emotion management training as a step toward feeling better herself and being less emotionally dependent upon Jack, the therapist opens the door to Alicia's gaining self-empowerment through her ability to self-soothe, an attractive alternative to either passively accepting or bluntly attacking Jack's inconsiderate behavior.

2. *Identify the emotion that is most troubling as focus of training.* The second step of emotion management training is to identify the specific emotion that the client would like to manage more effectively. The target emotion is the one that is most likely to escalate rapidly in intensity, with the result that the client (1) changes his or her ordinarily reasonable way of thinking and goes into "do or die" mode and (2) engages in behavior that sabotages the partners' intimate connection.

3. *Identify and validate healthy goals associated with current functioning.* The third step validates whatever the client is feeling and doing as a brand of intimacy-distance regulation. The therapist reassures the client that intimacy-distance regulation is a normal relationship process. The message to the client is that the impulse to avoid more intimacy than he or she feels comfortable with is healthy self- and relationship-protective when it is working well. For example, Bruce is setting intimacy boundaries and communicating to his partner Sharon when he wants time to be separate and pursue individual activities. It is important for Bruce to know that the therapist will not try to stop him from "regulating his intimacy boundary," but that the work will focus on increasing his repertoire of intimacy responses so that he is not setting boundaries so often that he leaves Sharon out in the cold. Sharon has already tried to persuade him to stop his boundary-setting; there is no point in the therapist repeating this failed strategy. If the therapist did take this route, the therapist could be seen as siding with Sharon against Bruce, which could disrupt the therapist's alliance with Bruce.

4. *Identify more adaptive strategies for managing difficult emotions.* The fourth step involves brainstorming alternative ways of being with the other person. For example, a client who desires more alone-time and rejects his or her partner's overtures frequently as a result could (1) initiate more touching or sexual contact to demonstrate affection; (2) communicate more clearly to the partner when he or she was likely to be more versus less open to the overtures as a way to simultaneously be more responsive and feel more control over the circumstances under which he or she is responsive; or (3) continue working with the therapist to fully explore any family of origin issues that might be contaminating his or her reaction to the partner's overtures.

5. *Experiment with alternative strategies.* The fifth step is the testing step, in which the client tries out one or more of the strategies that he or she has worked out with the therapist. Depending upon how much individual work the client needs in order to take the risk of putting some of the strategies into motion, this work can be done in successive couple sessions in which the client reports on how he or she felt about the strategies, and the partner provides feedback about how it was working from his or her perspective. For one couple who successfully applied emotion management training, the husband found that simply knowing that he would have his separate time, knowing that his wife would not be approaching him during those times, helped him to relax and enjoy her company more at other times.

Table 5.2 Emotion management training

Step 1:	Empower the client—frame it as a way to reach client's self-stated goals.
Step 2:	Identify the emotion that is most troubling as focus of training.
Step 3:	Identify and validate healthy goals associated with current functioning.
Step 4:	Identify alternative, more adaptive strategies for managing emotions.
Step 5:	Experiment with new strategies: Evaluate them for self, and partner also evaluates their impact.

Emotion management training is a process that targets maladaptive emotional responses with the goal of reducing the intensity of those responses, increasing the client's tolerance for the emotions, and empowering the client to cope with the negative emotion. Table 5.2 summarizes the steps involved in emotion management training.

Increase Emotion Tolerance

One way to help individuals who struggle with Dilemma #1, joy versus protection from pain, to have more rewarding intimate relationships is to encourage them to tolerate negative emotions. It is often the case that individuals who dread having negative emotions actually put themselves into more enduring negative mood states, such as depression, through their efforts to avoid feeling sad, anxious, angry, or even just emotionally vulnerable with their partner. Defenses whose purpose is to help individuals suppress or repress their negative emotions require emotional energy that could better be used to enjoy life and humor and to experience loving feelings. This intervention is for overly defended individuals; it helps them to better tolerate their own feelings and to learn through experience that emotions run a natural course. This intervention works best in an individual session.

Increasing emotion tolerance requires the client to experience his or her here-and-now emotions as they occur, label them, and accept them. The process of experiencing, labeling, and accepting an emotion functions to prevent the habitual defensive response and thereby prevents the undesirable consequences of the habitual defensive response. The role of the therapist is to guide the client toward consciously experiencing, labeling, and accepting his or her current emotional state. The therapist uses this intervention when he or she perceives the client is blocking emotions by talking or engaging other distracting behavior.

Increasing emotion tolerance requires the following steps:

1. *Stop defensive behavior and encourage internal focus.* Defensive behavior is so effective at maintaining emotional responses outside of awareness that most therapy clients will not be aware of it. The therapist will have a hunch

that the client is doing just that through observing emotion cues in the client's behavior, such as clenching the jaw, trembling around the mouth, tone of voice, or shallow breathing, to give some examples.

The best way to call the client's attention to this distracting behavior is to suggest that the client pause and turn his or her attention inward to see if he or she can become aware of any feelings. The therapist should then sit quietly and give the client a chance to focus and become aware of the feelings. The therapist can help the client become aware by suggesting that the client notice any sensations in his or her body.

2. *Encourage the client to label and stay with the emotion.* The role of the therapist in the next step is to encourage the client to describe the feeling as precisely as possible. For most clients, this will involve describing physical sensations that they then associate with an emotional label. Once the individual has described the feelings precisely, encourage the client to "let the feelings remain within you and observe them as they shift and change." The purpose of the self-focus and the suggestion that the feelings will change is to increase the client's emotional self-awareness and to teach the client through experience that emotions are transitory and change as they are experienced. Knowing that emotions are short-term phenomena can help the client accept their presence and engage in less defensive behavior to avoid them.

Therapist:	Now stay with that anxious scary feeling. Let it be inside of you. Where do you feel it most?
Client (eyes closed):	In my stomach, it's tight.
Therapist (slowly, quietly):	Stay with that tight feeling, keep your focus on it, let it be there. It's OK to have this feeling, nothing bad will happen. Pay attention to it and see if it shifts or moves.
Client:	It's still there, in my stomach.
Therapist:	Notice anything else about it? It's tight and . . . .
Client:	I have a kind of fluttery feeling, too.
Therapist:	Stay with those feelings, let them be.
Quiet pause.	
Therapist:	Where is the feeling now?
Client:	It's in my throat now. My throat is tight.
Therapist:	Stay with that tightness in your throat. Let it be, don't fight it.
Quiet pause.	
Client (starts to tear up).	
Quiet pause.	
Therapist:	What are you feeling now?
Client:	I feel sad.
Therapist:	Take your time, let yourself be sad.
Quiet pause.	

Client: Amazing how all those feelings are connected together—the anxious feeling, my sadness.

Therapist: You can learn things about yourself when you let yourself have your feelings and don't fight them . . .

Client: You were right; the anxious feeling kind of peaked and then went away.

Therapist: Feelings do that. They come in waves. If you let the wave peak and come down, you don't need to waste energy pushing it away. You can talk about the feeling too, if you want to.

The therapist's effectiveness with this step depends upon the therapist using a quiet, calming voice tone and moving slowly through the exercise (pausing frequently as noted). The purpose is for the client to fully experience and accept the emotions in the here and now, a first step toward learning to tolerate them (and eventually communicate them to the partner in an intimate moment).

3. *Encourage the client to tolerate and accept the emotion.* The final step involves the therapist encouraging the client to tolerate the emotion and accept that they will experience the emotion periodically. The final step actually encourages the client to think differently about him- or herself and his or her emotional experience. The therapist is encouraging the client to witness him- or herself having and surviving the emotional experience and to thereby change his or her self-schema to one of empowerment: "I am someone who is strong and capable enough to put up with a negative emotion here and there. I have just witnessed this through my own experience."

Increasing emotional tolerance encourages the individual to tolerate his or her own negative emotions. Tolerating an emotion is a necessary if not sufficient precursor to other skills such as self-soothing, effective communication of the emotion, and effective problem solving with the partner. It also increases the potential for intimate communication between the partners. Finally, it is likely a helpful precondition for successful implementation of emotional acceptance through building tolerance, an intervention aimed at couple partners accepting one another's periodically undesirable behavior.

Pausing to Reflect before Speaking

Pausing before speaking is an especially important intervention for couple partners who habitually engage in uncontrolled and destructive arguing and attacking in response to their frustration and anger. Pausing targets the impulsiveness and emotional reactivity that drives the behavior. It helps couple partners to focus on what they want out of their interaction and to think about how to respond rather than simply reacting.

Pausing before speaking not only allows partners a moment to calm down, but it also allows them to think about what the other has said and consider their own reaction without responding impulsively. If one pauses before speaking or acting, one can also predict how the other will respond to what one might say in response and can choose a response conscious of one's own goal. Pausing before speaking is a useful way to prevent one's own impulsive, emotion-driven behavior. It gives one a minute to let the emotion crest and subside before one attempts to communicate.

The steps in pausing before speaking are as follows:

1 *Think about what the other person has said.* Pausing and thinking stops impulsive, emotion-driven behavior and gives the client a chance to self-soothe.
2 *Label the emotion.* Labeling makes the emotion understandable and allows the client to match the specific emotion with the best strategy for managing and understanding it.
3 *Decide what you want.* The client thinks of what he or she wants to gain before speaking, in order to connect his or her behavior with the goal. Pausing and thinking about the goal improves the client's chances of being effective.
4 *Speak so as to achieve your goal.* The client draws on prior experience with his or her partner to think about how to communicate the message so that the interaction will go well. The client has some pretty good ideas about how the partner is likely to respond and pausing before speaking allows him or her to draw on that experience to increase the chances of getting what the client wants.

Teach couple partners to experience mutual appreciation. Intimate interactions are important sources of emotional support, confidence-building, and soothing (Laurenceau, Barrett, & Rovine, 2005). Nevertheless, as Berscheid (1983) has argued, many years of an intimate relationship can result in partners' losing appreciation for how much affirmation and support the other partner provides. When they first meet, and do not have such a ready source for intimate relating, people's reactions to their newly found intimacy is often gleeful, with each partner appreciating the good feelings they get from their interactions with each other. Once they get accustomed to their partner's need-fulfilling provisions, however, they stop noticing how much the partner gives to them. They then stop expressing appreciation and may even stop relating intimately.

The therapist can increase the couples' conscious appreciation of one another by inducing them to remember feelings of loneliness, their desire to share a future, and other feelings that they had before they met or became involved with the other. To find out what works for them, the therapist can ask about hugging ("how often do you two hug each other? Can you "hug until you relax?"[1]), listening to each other talk about the events of their day, hugging until they fall asleep, giving each other compliments or expressing appreciation about the partner's appearance, meals cooked, errands run, chores accomplished, children cared for, good sex, and so forth.

Another way to encourage the partners to appreciate what they already have is to ask the couple how they have managed, with all their distress, to maintain this particular source of mutual validation and soothing (e.g., one couple who fought frequently and brutally with one another, nevertheless, had sex three to four times per week, and both were positive about their sexual relationship). The purpose of this exercise in remembering is to cause a shift in perspective that helps to reduce the intensity of negative emotion partners experience when their needs are not being met. A useful homework assignment for following up involves each partner noticing the positives that he or she has previously taken for granted and expressing appreciation to the partner at least once during the week (or even every day).

Dual Monitoring

The goal of dual monitoring is to help partners acquire the ability to simultaneously monitor their own emotional reactions while also listening to and demonstrating respect for the partner's perspective. Through this exercise, partners can learn that they are capable of staying in touch with what they want while also listening to and acknowledging the other partner. Dual monitoring has affective and cognitive steps.

This exercise is best done with both partners present, but with one partner taking the role of the "working partner." The steps of dual monitoring are as follows (variation in the order of the steps works well, too):

1 *Identify one partner as working and one as assisting.* As this exercise requires the partner to evaluate his or her emotional reactions and think about how to respond to them, it is best if the partners learn this skill one at a time. The therapist can use a whiteboard to keep track of the working partner's responses to the exercise.
2 *The assisting partner repeats the primary message he or she wants the other to understand.* The message should be from a conflict that the couple struggles to resolve, one that elicits emotion from the working partner.
3 *The working partner identifies the emotion aroused by the assisting partner's message and rates the strength of the emotion.* Before he or she digs into an argument, the partner is encouraged to pause and identify the emotion.
4 *Identify the thought that accompanies the emotion.* The therapist asks the working partner to identify the thought elicited by the assisting partner's message and to make a connection between the thought and the emotion.

1 Schnarch (1997) uses this phrase when describing intimate contact.

5 *Encourage the client to consider a more emotionally neutral thought or offer one for the client.* If the client is experienced with automatic thought evaluation, the client may be able to come up with a neutral alternative. Otherwise, the therapist can offer one.
6 *The therapist works with the client's automatic thoughts, as described in Chapter 6.* The therapist helps the client to articulate the automatic thoughts, including any fear scenarios that are evoked by the partner's message.
7 *The therapist uses the chart to show connections between thoughts—interpretations—and emotions* (see Appendix F Therapist Worksheets for chart).
8 *The therapist helps the client identify the communication goals associated with the emotion, the thought, and/or the message.* The therapist asks what the working partner hopes to accomplish with his or her response to the partner. The therapist asks the client to consider how the interpretation of the partner's response, the goal, and the client's response all feed into each other.
9 *The perception check.* Last, the therapist encourages the working client to check out his or her perceptions by asking the assisting partner directly what he or she means by what was just said. The working client then checks his or her interpretations against what the partner said and considers whether the interpretations were accurate.

An example of the use of dual monitoring is found in Chapter 9, with Carla and Doug's dilemma.

Self-Awareness Training

Self-awareness training is distinct from the other interventions discussed in this chapter in that it is not focused on soothing and calming but rather on increasing an individual's sensitivity to his or her own affect and helping him or her to more effectively share his or her inner life with the partner. These interventions have as their purpose to encourage couple partners to notice subtle variations in their own feelings and emotions. As their ability to notice these subtle gradations in emotion increases, they will then have the choice to share them with their partners or not, and to consider the advantages and disadvantages of sharing.

Feeling-finding mission. The feeling-finding mission can be used for two different purposes. The first is to increase the individual's awareness of lower intensity feelings and emotions with the idea of increasing his or her problem-solving choices. An individual who is more self-aware can make better-informed decisions about whether to communicate or otherwise act on his or her feelings or not. Clients who are not accustomed to paying attention to their feelings often wait until a mild irritation becomes an outrage or a mild nervous feeling becomes panic before they communicate or act upon the feeling. The result of delayed problem solving is well-known to experienced therapists: The subsequent reactions are often overreactions, and the subsequent decisions are often impulsive. The second purpose is to help people who have low levels of psychological mindedness to become more aware of their day-to-day internal experiences and thereby share them with their partner in the interest of increasing relational intimacy.

The intervention is given as a homework assignment, in which the client is asked to monitor any low-intensity feelings that he or she might have throughout the week and notice when they occurred. It is useful to monitor both negative and positive feelings for purposes of this exercise. Clients who are inclined to write benefit from keeping a journal of their thoughts and feelings. The client then reports on what he or she has noticed at the next therapy session and talks about what it was like to notice these mild feelings. Depending upon the overall purpose of the exercise, the therapist can then move from this intervention to intimate communication training or problem solving.

Zones of awareness exercise. This intervention, derived from Gestalt therapy (Perls, 1969), works best in an individual therapy session. It offers in-session instruction on how to tune into feelings and emotions. Some individuals will say that they never have any feelings or emotions, and this exercise will help them learn how to discover them. It is useful for people who report that they feel nothing but numb or that they don't have feelings like other people. It is important because people who are unable to access their feelings will likely have difficulty with intimacy (Prager & Roberts, 2004). The zones of awareness are the inner zone, the outer zone, and the middle zone. Most useful for self-awareness training is in-session work that helps the client become more aware of the inner zone. According to Joyce and Sills (2001), the inner zone includes visceral sensations such as heartbeat, respiration rate, and muscular tension, and feelings that correspond to emotions, such as a tightness in the head, throat, chest, or abdomen, a pressure behind the eyes, or butterflies in the stomach.

The therapist can teach a client to access the inner zone by encouraging the client to focus inward and to "imagine that your attention is like a beam of light, a searchlight that is scanning your body for feelings. I encourage you to scan your body beginning with the top of your head. Focus the beam of your searchlight on the top of your head and move it slowly down to your forehead . . . now around to your temples . . . now down the back of your head . . . do you notice any sensations, any feelings? . . . OK, next move the beam of light to your face. Start with your eyebrows and eyes . . . check behind your eyes" and so forth. After the exercise, it is useful to ask the client, "How was that for you?," which is likely to bring out attitudes about emotions that affect the expression and even the experience of emotion. Zones of awareness training can enhance intimate communication in the couple session when the client is encouraged to talk about his or her experience with the exercise with the partner.

Guided fantasy. Guided fantasy is another intervention that is useful for helping clients gain access to their inner experiences. Guided fantasy has been used to help people identify feelings and emotions that they do not ordinarily access. It can also be used to help people accommodate new information about themselves with their self-concepts, particularly aspects of the self that are apparent to others but outside of their own awareness (Perls, 1969).

In guided fantasy, the therapist guides the individual through a fantasy that is specifically designed to increase his or her awareness of some aspect of him- or herself. Frederick Perls was famous for using dreams as the subject matter for guided fantasy (1969), whereas my own teacher, Earl Koile, taught me to develop the fantasy content from my own hypotheses about what would be most compelling for the particular client. Guided fantasy works best when the therapist takes no stand on what the outcome should be, but rather encourages the client to notice whatever inner experience is waiting to be discovered. The therapist encourages the client to use the material that the fantasy brings up to accept him- or herself as he or she is, while he or she simultaneously sets goals to improve if that is what he or she desires.

The steps for implementing guided fantasy, used by the therapist in the example below, are as follows.

1 *Link the guided fantasy to the client's goals for him- or herself.* The therapist explains how the guided fantasy will further the client's own goals, couched in language of personal growth, self-expansion, or enhanced effectiveness.
2 *Induction.* Like hypnotherapy, the guided fantasy works best after an induction that helps the client relax and focus inward. The therapist directs the client to get comfortable, to close his or her eyes, to focus on any tension in the body and relax that tension, to focus on breathing, or to imagine that he or she is floating. The therapist may check with the client to find out if he or she is in a state of relaxation and weightlessness when the therapist suspects that the client is.
3 *Begin the guided fantasy.* The therapist sketches out a scene in broad outline for the client to imagine. As much as possible, the therapist lets the client fill in the details of the scene, as it is counterproductive for the therapist to insert details that will interfere with the image that the client is creating in his or her mind. As the therapist guides the client to the point at which the therapist expects him or her to discover something new about him- or herself, the therapist is actually letting the client guide. The therapist's role is to come up with a metaphor for self-exploration. In the example below, the corridor with doors was a metaphor for a particular point in the client's past from which the client might learn something about him- or herself in the present.
4 *Deepen the guided fantasy.* The therapist asks the client each step of the way what is present in his or her mind's eye and uses the "props" in the

scene to encourage the client to explore further. In the example below, the corridor and doors were props that could be used to encourage the client to look more closely at some aspect of his or her inner life.

It is important that the therapist stay in touch with the client throughout the guided fantasy practice. One way is to ask, "How are you feeling right now? Where are you now? What do you see/hear?" This helps the therapist follow the client in the fantasy; otherwise, the therapist is at risk for interrupting the client's self-exploration process.

5 *Leave the fantasy.* It is important that the therapist offer the client a fantasy pathway for leaving the fantasy and returning his or her attention to the present and the therapist's office. In the example below, the therapist simply instructs the client to return the same way he or she arrived. The therapist will guide the client in the example as he or she goes back down the corridor, finds the elevator, walks out of the lobby onto the street, and so forth.
6 *Debrief.* In the last step, the therapist and client talk together about what the client learned from the fantasy, helping the client to integrate the experience by putting it into words and relating it to the work he or she has been doing in therapy. Below is an example of how guided fantasy proceeds. The symbol " . . . " indicates a pause of a minute or so, during which the therapist gives Jeff time to fix the fantasy in his mind.

Therapist: You know, I can't help but wonder if that aspect of her personality—her warmth and emotionality—was part of what attracted you to her, even part of why you chose to marry her out of all of the women that you might have met along the way.

Jeff: I'd never thought of it that way, but that might be right.

Therapist: I mean, she can do the very thing that is so difficult for you.

Jeff: I've admired it about her, and it was great for our kids while they were growing up.

Therapist: So you could use her good qualities as a guide, to help you expand your own repertoire of relationship behavior and increase your ability to enjoy being intimate with her.

Jeff: She gives me such a hard time, though. I don't think I deserve it.

Therapist: When she's in session and this comes up, which I'm sure it will, that will be something we can work with her on. But now, as it's just you and me, let's work on your personal growth. Would that interest you?

Jeff: What do you mean?

Therapist: *[Link the guided fantasy to the client's goals for himself.]* I mean, you've said you don't feel things, like love, warmth, and so forth. We could try an exercise that would help you tune into some of your more subtle, less intense feelings, feelings that fly under your radar right now but might be very important to you.

Jeff: OK. How do we do that?

Therapist: *[Induction-slowly, at an even pace, minimal inflection.]* OK, start by getting comfortable in your chair. Move around a bit until you feel relaxed and can stay in position for a while. Now focus on your breathing, concentrate on breathing evenly and completely . . . . and as you get more relaxed, close your eyes . . . . *[Begin the guided fantasy.]* I want you to imagine that you are on a street that you've never seen before, any kind of street . . . Now walk down the street at a comfortable pace—tell me when you've got that street in your mind's eye . . .

Jeff: OK, I see it.

Therapist: What do you see as you look around?

Jeff: I see some buildings, old ones . . . like I'm walking downtown.

Therapist: How do you feel being on that street?

Jeff: Like this is a safe place somehow—

Therapist: OK, what I'd like you to do is keep walking on your street until you come to a building that looks inviting to enter and stop in front of it.

Jeff: OK . . . [a few seconds pass] . . . OK I'm in front of a big stone building with one of those big entryways from the 1950s, with a revolving door.

Therapist: OK, when you're ready walk inside . . . if you were to travel to the upper floors how would you do that? Are there elevators, stairs?

Jeff: A row of elevators in the lobby.

Therapist: When you're ready, take one up . . . Are you in the elevator?

Jeff: Yes, going up.

Therapist: Let the elevator take you to whatever floor it likes and let you out.

Jeff: OK, the eighth floor.

Therapist: What do you see as you get out of the elevator?

Jeff: A corridor, like an office building or maybe a hotel.

Therapist: *[Deepen the guided fantasy.]* Imagine that this corridor is an important time period in your past. Can you? Take a minute . . .

Jeff: OK. . . .

Therapist: Do you know what period you are in?

Jeff: I guess age seven or eight.

Therapist: OK, are you ready to walk down this corridor of your life when you were seven or eight?

Jeff: OK.

Therapist: Start walking down the corridor slowly and as you walk, I'd like you to try the doors. Find the one that is open for you to go through.

Jeff: I think they're all open.

Therapist: Great. Tell me when you've tried one that opens.

Jeff: OK, the first one.

Therapist: Can you see inside?

Jeff: It looks like an office and a hotel room all at once.

Therapist: Is there anything for you to learn in there? Any reason to go in?

Jeff: No, I don't think so—well, I take it back. I'm going in.

Therapist: . . . OK, tell me about the room: What do you see? . . . What do you hear? . . .

Jeff: There's a fat notebook with writing on the desk.

Therapist: How do you feel about looking at it?

Jeff: Very curious.

Therapist: OK . . . What do you see in it?

Jeff: Somebody's written a story about my mom and me . . . . It's got beautiful pictures with gold leaf on it. They're kind of old-fashioned, drawings, with color, they're really beautiful and give me this incredibly nostalgic feeling.

Therapist: Stay with that feeling a minute, let yourself be with it . . . What's happening as you do that?

Jeff: There's a lot to appreciate about my mother, even though I'm angry with her. She's a link to something important in me, a part of who I am . . . Something beautiful that's captured in these pictures.

Therapist: Stay with that, see what comes up for you. Take your time.

Jeff (tearing up): . . . I'm not sure what it is, but I wish I could ask her.

Therapist: You feel sad?

Jeff: Yes, I wouldn't know what to ask her even if she was still here.

Therapist: Can you make it OK for now, not to know? Accept that?

Jeff: Yes, but I want to come back and find out.

Therapist: OK, well take a minute now and see if anything comes up.

Jeff: . . . No, I already know I won't get an answer today. At least I know about this beautiful book, these pictures.

Therapist: You have a beautiful gift that she's given you? Not yet opened? Inside of you?

Jeff (tearing up): I think so.

Therapist: *[Leave the fantasy.]* Are you ready to leave the room with the book?

Jeff: Yes.

Therapist: OK, keep your eyes closed and retrace your steps. Do you want to take the book with you or leave it there?

Jeff: Leave it here—it's a part of this room, this building.

Therapist: OK, great. Now begin to retrace your steps, return the way you came . . . back down the corridor to the elevators . . . when you've completed your journey, come back to this room . . . let yourself sit quietly for a moment before you open your eyes . . . and whenever you're ready, open them . . . now take a look around and get yourself reacquainted with the present moment! *[Debrief.]* And when you're ready, please share any additional thoughts or feelings you have about your journey.

Jeff: . . . That was not what I expected! But it was nice. I've been angry with my mother for so long; it was amazing to discover that there is this whole beautiful part of what my mother gave me . . . I'll have to think about what that is.

Therapist: Why don't you focus on that during the week? Keep a journal if you like, and we can talk when we get together again, about any insights that you gain.

Guided fantasy allows a client to explore affect without having to intellectualize about it or even understand it fully. It is the first step toward a more complete self-awareness and understanding and gives the client some words with which to express what may have been inexpressible in the past. It may also give clients new affective experience, as it did for Jeff in the example.

Conclusion

Affective interventions aim to help individuals negotiate their unresolved intimacy dilemmas by directly targeting overreactive or problematic affects. Affective interventions help individuals soothe themselves when they experience intense, negative emotions in interactions with their partners. They also help individuals to become more aware of their own affect, as a step toward helping them think through their problems, identify what it is that they want, and maximize their effectiveness in obtaining it. Finally, affective interventions increase individual self-awareness and foster personal growth and self-acceptance, and thereby enhance partners' capacities for intimate relating.

Because intimacy-related problems are usually multidetermined, affective interventions alone will not usually resolve them. They can, nevertheless, be used early in therapy with rapid results, offering hope to discouraged relationship partners. They may also be prerequisite for cognitive or behavioral interventions that rely on a person's being able to think through their dilemmas and choose among potentially effective responses to those dilemmas.

1 Schnarch (1997) uses this phrase when describing intimate contact.

6

COGNITIVE INTERVENTIONS

Problems with intimacy arise out of unspoken beliefs, expectations, and assumptions about oneself, one's partner, and intimate relationships. Beliefs provide maps or guides for creating and sustaining intimate relationships. Distorted or unrealistic beliefs complicate people's efforts to cope with the dilemmas of intimacy. Further, beliefs about intimate relating are tied to people's fondest hopes and greatest fears for the future, and when activated, can elicit strong emotions. Intense negative affect and the defensive behaviors used to control it drive negative interaction cycles that preclude more intimate relating. Moreover, because no two partners are carrying exactly the same set of beliefs, partners' cognitive maps for intimacy can clash.

The close association between thinking and emotion that inspired the cognitive therapies (e.g., Beck, 1976; Ellis, 1962; Baucom & Epstein, 1990) is used in intimacy-focused couple therapy for helping partners to soften negative affect. Couple partners are continuously interpreting and evaluating one another's behavior. These interpretations and evaluations elicit emotional reactions, as much or more than what the other actually says. Therapeutic intervention that changes thinking patterns may well produce the most robust and enduring changes in affect and behavior for individuals and couples struggling with intimacy-related problems.

I conceptualize intimacy problems as products of intimacy dilemmas that are normal and that do not reflect character flaws in either partner. A benign framework is one of the most powerful tools the therapist has and is itself a cognitive intervention (Datillo, 2005; Jacobson & Christensen, 1996). Ideally, the therapist teaches the framework in a way that allows clients to (1) see their problems in a new light and (2) use that new light to illuminate new courses of action. Cognitive interventions that target mistaken thinking patterns aim to help clients think more realistically about themselves, their partners, and their relationships.

In the last 20 years, couple partners' cognitions about each other and the events in their relationships have taken on a major role in the theory and practice of couple therapy (Baucom & Epstein, 1990; Epstein, 2006). Efforts are being made to expand the scope of cognitive behavioral couple therapy to include problems with infidelity (Baucom, Gordon, Snyder, Atkins, & Christensen, 2006), substance abuse (O'Farrell & Fals-Stewart, 2000), and trauma (Johnson & Williams-Keeler, 1998), to name three. This treatment continues in this vein by applying a cognitively oriented approach to intimacy problems. Table 6.1 summarizes the cognitive interventions that are presented in this chapter.

Table 6.1 Cognitive interventions

Type	*Phase of Therapy*	*Intervention*
Cognitive	Early	Develop realistic expectations and goals Of intimacy and intimate relationships Of how much people can change People are "packages" Normalize
Cognitive	Early	Provide a benign alternative framework Therapist can provide alternative interpretations of events before the client has developed the skills to do so
Cognitive	Throughout	Teach identification of automatic thoughts Evaluate automatic thoughts in couple sessions using "perception check" Teach modification of automatic negative thoughts in individual sessions Dual monitoring
Cognitive	Middle	Teach identification of problematic intimacy schemas Therapist articulates schemas Therapist keeps a list of each client's schemas
Cognitive	Middle to Late	Intimacy schema evaluation and modification Therapist brainstorms with the couple Helps them evaluate advantages and disadvantages and make rules that work
Cognitive	Middle to Late	Cognitive rehearsal Client identifies negative automatic thoughts and thinking errors that might hamper his or her coping with an upcoming challenge and creates rational alternatives
Cognitive	Middle	Teach partners to talk in relational rather than right-wrong terms Reduce polarization through education and a relational perspective

(*Continued*)

Table 6.1 (Continued)

Type	*Phase of Therapy*	*Intervention*
		Work with the couple to demonstrate advantages and disadvantages of each pole Help them identify the golden mean, the optimum balance between two poles
Cognitive	Middle	Self-empowerment training: Teach the client to think of him- or herself and behave as a potent adult in a relationship with the partner
Cognitive	Middle	Acceptance training Partners identify thoughts (and emotions) that make it more difficult to accept partner differences Partners generate alternative attitudes that make it easier to accept the other and simultaneously soothe individual fears, unmet needs

Intimacy Schemas

Anxiety- or anger-saturated expectations about self, partner, potential partner, intimacy, or relationships drive irresolvable intimacy dilemmas and the ensuing problems associated with them (i.e., lack of intimacy, conflict over intimacy, repetitive, irreconcilable conflict, and lost love). From self-psychology and research on social cognition (e.g., Markus, 1977), *schemas* have been identified as the building blocks of habitual thinking patterns. Schemas are "broad, pervasive themes . . . " or beliefs that are connected to "memories, emotions, thoughts, and bodily sensations regarding oneself and one's relationships with others" (Young, Klosko, & Weishaar, 2003, p. 7). Schemas help us to organize our experiences, understand what is happening to us and why, and predict what will happen next. Schemas function like networks of related cognitions. We use them when we are trying to understand what our partner says and does, to interpret what is going on "behind the words." We draw on them when we make inferences about others' intentions. They are overlearned beliefs and belief systems that are activated by relationship events and usually exist outside of our awareness. Intimacy-oriented therapy understands schemas to be emotionally charged beliefs that are continuously referenced during couple interactions, for the good or detriment of the relationship.

Schemas are organized hierarchically, with more specific, directly experienced concepts nested within more general, abstract concepts (e.g., Jordan's experience with his marriage, in which he and his wife Merrianne have sex once a month, is nested within conventional notions about marriage within the culture, in which couples are supposed to have sex once a week or more frequently). Figure 6.1 displays the hierarchical organization of schemas.

Schemas can be adaptive or maladaptive. Repeating patterns of change-resistant, relationship-sabotaging behavior signal the presence of problematic intimacy schemas.

Intimacy schemas are organized according to whether their content focuses on the self, the partner, or the relationship (or, partners in general or relationships in general). Nevertheless, attachment theory proposes that each schema that defines an aspect of the self also, conversely, defines an aspect of the partner (Bowlby, 1969). Similarly, each intimacy schema that defines an aspect of the partner also defines an aspect of the self. Intimacy schemas, because of their relational content, have this multisided aspect. With a partner schema of "My partner is indifferent" there is a corresponding self-schema that says "I am a victim" or "I am unlovable." For heuristic purposes, I will refer to self, partner, or relationship schemas in this book, but at times, it will be apparent that the mirror image of any partner schema is a self-schema.

Self-schemas. Self-schemas are beliefs that we hold about ourselves. Significant for intimacy-oriented therapy are our beliefs about ourselves in relation to intimate others; most of us has a set of "lover/husband/wife" schemas that

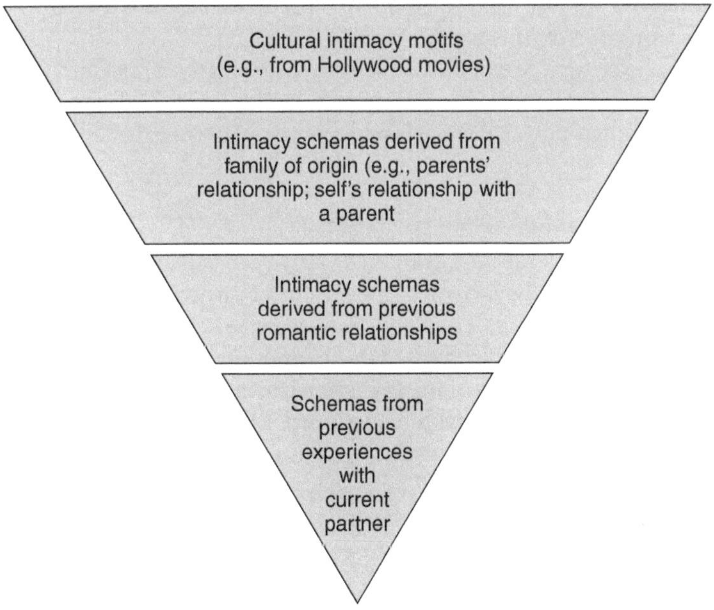

Figure 6.1 Hierarchical organization of schemas

constitute our conceptions of ourselves as romantic and life partners. Because self-schemas are the flip side of partner schemas (Bowlby, 1969), when we believe our partner to be withholding, we may believe that we ourselves are insatiable. If we believe our partner to be overpowering and domineering, we may believe that we ourselves are easily victimized and helpless.

Challenging relationship dilemmas activate concerns about the self and concerns about the self create relationship dilemmas. Individuals can have problems with intimacy because one or more of the three intimacy dilemmas activates a negative self-schema, which in turn causes the person to be flooded with negative automatic thoughts. This flood of negative thinking may make the intimacy dilemma appear to be insurmountable. Intimacy-activated negative self-schemas are often childish, out-of-date self-schemas. Because they are childish, they are accompanied by feelings of helplessness and impotence. For the same reason, however, they may be amenable to change.

Self-empowerment. Self-empowerment is an aspect of the self-schema. Self-empowerment refers to our belief that we can act competently in our own behalf. When we perceive ourselves to be empowered, we expect to be able to identify desirable yet realistic goals for ourselves and our relationships, and we expect to be able to make progress toward obtaining those goals. We perceive ourselves as having as much power and influence over our relationship as our partners do, and therefore rarely feel victimized by our partners. When self-empowered, we do not need to attack our partners nor do we need to defend ourselves from our partner's presumed attack.

Self-empowerment leaves us with less intense negative affect and with fewer defensive, dysfunctional relationship behaviors. Empowered partners do not abdicate their own power in order to blame their partners for all of their ills.

Fear scenarios. Intimacy schemas are beliefs about self, partners, or intimate relationships, or they are fear scenarios. Fear scenarios are a particular type of intimacy schema. They involve projections about the individual's life that have catastrophic endings. They are projected consequences that the person believes will come to pass in his or her life and relationship if certain conditions are not met. By definition, fear scenarios are emotionally charged, so that when events seem to be taking us toward a feared scenario, we react with anxiety. When confronting an intimacy dilemma elicits intense emotions, the confrontation has likely activated an anxiety-provoking fear scenario.

Fear scenarios are activated in several ways: by certain partner behaviors, by types of interactions with the partner, and even by fantasies in which the partner's response to the individual's entreaties propels the individual toward a frightening conclusion. Fear scenarios stem from universal human fears (e.g., of a painful death), from cultural themes (e.g., in America, people worry about being old and lonely without sufficient funds to live on), from gender scripts (i.e., women in many cultures will have nowhere to live unless they have a husband), or from people's own personal histories (e.g., Renata fears being stuck in a loveless marriage like her mother was).

Fear scenarios are associated with anxiety by definition, but we can become furious at a relationship partner for behaving in a way that activates the fear scenario. Someone who is prone to overblown anger is blaming his or her partner for activating a fear scenario and the anxiety that goes with it. Individuals who expend energy pushing each other to change and adapt perceive their partners as being powerful enough to "drag them through the mud" to the conclusion of a fear scenario, and conversely, perceive themselves as helplessly observing a catastrophe in the making. The anger is an expression of powerlessness and all of the frustration that goes with it. Table 6.2 lists definitions of schemas associated with intimacy-related problems.

Table 6.2 Descriptions of problematic intimacy schemas

Schema	*Variations*	*Description*
Self-schemas		
I am unappealing.	I am undesirable. I am unattractive. I am socially inept.	*The assumption that potential partners will not want to get to know you because of something about the first impressions that you make—lack of physical beauty, lack of charm or conversational skill, or excessive shyness.
I am unlovable.	I am flawed. I can't have needs. No one would want to stay with me.	*A fear, if not conviction, that no one could love you if they knew your true self. *Finds ways to play it safe, to hide behind a facade to assure that the partner does not have a chance to reject what he or she cannot see. *Behavior is inflexible because it is reactive to the anxiety associated with "being discovered."
I am fragile.	I can't stand it. I need to avoid. I need protection. I need to be taken care of.	*The assumption that you will not be able to handle the consequences of taking emotional risks. *Expectation: Experiencing negative emotions will be catastrophic (Ellis, 1962). *Paralyzed by the fear that the partner will reject or humiliate you, and you believe you "cannot stand" it.

(*Continued*)

Table 6.2 (Continued)

Schema	*Variations*	*Description*
I am the victim.	I am helpless. I am hopeless. I am abused. My intentions are always good, but I am still misunderstood.	*The assumption that, if your partner has hurt you, he or she deserves to be punished, and it is up to you to do the punishing. Believes that partner could avoid causing hurt but doesn't and therefore causes hurt on purpose. *Activated by negative emotion; justifies cruel, punitive behavior.
I am Mr./Ms. Fix-It.	I'm a caretaker. I'm not worthy unless I'm doing for someone else. I can't stand someone else's pain, anger, etc.	*The assumption that you are at fault for, or you are responsible for fixing, any malady, negative emotion, or problem of your partner's or of the relationship. You believe you are responsible for your partner. *Anxious about anyone being hurt.
Partner-schemas		
Partner has the power.	Partner is inconsiderate, abusing, or a bully. My partner makes me do X. If my partner does X, I must do Y.	*Partner can call all the shots in the relationship. Partner's wants, needs, and goals overwhelm one's own. Partner can choose to fulfill one's needs or not, and partner determines whether needs are met. Often accompanies the assumption that you must change your partner if you hope to get your needs met. Also often accompanies the belief that you can change your partner if you are clever or persuasive enough.
Partner is indifferent.	He doesn't care about me. She'll never listen to me. She doesn't pitch in or doesn't care about the family.	*The assumption that your partner has negative intentions toward, lack of interest in, or lack of love toward you. You believe if you "mind-read" your partner's motives, you'll find your partner to be sinister or indifferent. *You interpret much of your partner's behavior as directed toward or having to do with you. You place yourself at the center of your partner's motivational world and lack empathy for your partner's concerns. *Belief that if your partner's efforts aren't directed toward fulfilling your needs, your partner must be indifferent.

Table 6.2 (*Continued*)

Schema	*Variations*	*Description*
Partner is fragile.	I can't tell him; he'll have a break down. I can't burden her with X.	*You assume that your partner can't know about or can't handle certain information. You expect that your partner will be hurt or crushed, and you will feel guilty or ashamed as a result.
Partner must compensate for self's pain and losses.	She could do it for me, but she refuses. He never remembers what I tell him to do.	*You hope that your marriage/relationship will contain everything good that you missed in childhood. When your partner's behavior fails to compensate you, you interpret this as a willful withholding of your entitlement, a repeat of your childhood experience, and/or a punitive desire to see you suffer.
Relationship-Schemas		
Things should always go right.	If you do X, we'll split up, ruin the relationship, stop loving each other, ruin the intimacy, or never have sex again.	*You hold onto a high standard for yourself, your partner, and for intimacy. The assumption that, if you demand enough from your partner, you can make your standards a reality.
Intimacy should be easy.	If you just relax and let it happen, everything will be good.	*The assumption that intimacy should be spontaneous and natural rather than requiring effort. Intimacy that requires effort such as asking for what one wants is discounted or devalued. If sex must be scheduled, it's ruined beforehand.
Pleasure-seeking is shameful.	All she thinks about is having fun, spending money, vacations, etc. There is so much to do, and he won't help.	*You believe that self-indulgence is shameful. You dare not pursue pleasure for its own sake lest you feel ashamed. Hyper-responsible and dutiful, you may frustrate your partner's needs for intimacy if not your own. Sit in judgment when others want to be happy and enjoy themselves.
Women and men must be different.	A man who won't support the family financially is not a real man.	*The assumption that, in order to be a "real" man or "real" woman, you must restrict your behavior to conform to cultural ideals and requirements (as should your partner).

Table 6.2 (*Continued*)

Schema	*Variations*	*Description*
	I expect a woman to keep my house clean for me if I support her.	
Fear scenario		
My future is predetermined.	If I let him X, then Y will happen. If she doesn't stop X, then Y.	*You fear that, if you do not or your partner/your relationship does not proceed as you planned, a calamity will happen.

Automatic Thoughts

As has been well-documented by cognitive therapy researchers (Beck, Rush, Shaw, & Emery, 1979; Clark & Steer, 1996; Dobson & Breiter, 1983; Sookman, Pinard, & Beauchemin, 1994; Young, Klosko, & Weishaar, 2003), problematic schemas are often revealed via negative automatic thoughts. Automatic thoughts are those that spontaneously pop into the mind without one's taking the time to fully evaluate a situation or event. They are the thoughts that occur to us when we make no effort to consider our interpretation of an event. Automatic thoughts can be positive or negative, but the focus here is on the negative ones that are associated with intimacy problems. Intimacy-related automatic thoughts are exemplified by, "It's stupid to care about that, so I won't mention it," or "He didn't initiate sex; he must not think I'm sexy." Baucom and Epstein (1990) catalogued five different types of automatic thoughts that are relevant to couple relationships: (1) assumptions and expectations about the self, the partner, or the relationship, (2) standards for self, partner, or relationships, (3) expectations of self, partner, or relationship, (4) specific inferences about a partner's motives, and (5) attributions about who or what is responsible for couple problems.

Automatic thoughts are logical conclusions drawn from intimacy schemas. Some are generated by self-schemas such as "I am fragile" (e.g., "If I'm rejected, I'll be devastated," "If I'm vulnerable, I'll be totally ashamed"). Other negative automatic thoughts stem from a partner schema such as, "My partner is fragile" (e.g., "my partner will never recover" from anger, sadness, or embarrassment, or "my partner will become mentally unstable if . . . "). Still other automatic negative thoughts may emerge simultaneously from two or more problematic intimacy schemas, such as "I am a victim" and "my partner is indifferent" and contain thoughts about both self and other (e.g., "Why bother to ask for what I want when I know he will never give it to me" or "She won't show up on time, I'll be totally embarrassed, and she won't even care").

Some automatic thoughts distort reality (e.g., "If she rejects me, I will never love again"). Others may contain a kernel of truth (e.g., "She has hurt me before") followed by a self-defeating conclusion (e.g., "I'll show her; I'll protect myself from now on"). Epstein and Baucom (2003) underscore the importance of distinguishing between cognitive distortions, which are demonstrably false, and negative cognitions, which may have a kernel of truth. These two different kinds of automatic thoughts may require different interventions, as will be discussed later in this chapter.

Automatic thoughts are not the same as intimacy schemas. Automatic thoughts are focused on a particular situation, whereas intimacy schemas are generalized beliefs that can be applied to multiple situations. Intimacy schemas affect the way we interpret relationship events. Negative automatic thoughts are conscious or easily accessible, whereas intimacy schemas operate outside of our awareness and are not so easily accessed. Intimacy schemas are often revealed only via themes that are shared by successive series of automatic negative thoughts. The theme that ties the thoughts together is the schema.

Intimacy schemas determine the content of intimacy-related automatic thoughts. For example, intimacy schemas generate inferences about our partner's intentions. Inferences are automatic thoughts that pop into our minds within the time frame of an interaction (although they can also emerge from imagined conversations that individual partners play out in their heads, such as worst case scenarios). Inferences answer the question, "why did he do that?" or "why did he say that?" Inferences can either calm or intensify our emotional reactions to a partner's behavior. Intimacy schemas affect the way we interpret our partner's behavior unconsciously, because these assumptions about self, partner, intimacy, and relationship are like the air that we breathe: inhaled, depended upon, but rarely articulated or examined in the light of day. When our schemas are open to examination and revision, they can be adjusted to better fit the information that we encounter every day in ourselves and our partners and are then very useful cognitive shortcuts that help us process what goes on in our relationships.

When intimacy schemas are inflexible or out-of-date, they can generate automatic thoughts that intensify our negative emotions unnecessarily. This occurs because schemas function as shortcuts for recognizing familiar scenarios and for coding how we should feel and behave in response to those scenarios. In order for schemas to be useful, we must generalize from earlier, specific experiences to later experiences, and we will sometimes overgeneralize.

Cognitive Interventions

Develop Realistic Expectations and Goals

When therapy is focused on intimacy problems, the therapist will often take on the role of "intimacy expert," in which the therapist's primary role is educating clients about intimacy and intimate relationships. The goal of this psycho-education is to help clients develop more realistic expectations about intimate relationships, about themselves, and about their partners. Realistic expectations are needed when clients come to therapy and their stated goals are not achievable or when their goals are not in their own power to achieve, as when one partner's goal is that the other partner should change.

Normalizing. I discussed normalizing in Chapter 3 as a form of reassurance and comfort for distressed clients. Normalizing is also a cognitive intervention that fosters realistic expectations. Basic intimacy dilemmas are inevitable as they are defined here and can be understood as normal challenges of couple relationships. Once couples understand that they are coping with a normal, even inevitable intimacy dilemma, they are liable to stop blaming one another and to start solving their problems.

Behavior change, yes; personality change, no. One of the most common problems couple therapists face is that of helping clients to see when they are asking their partners to change aspects of themselves that are not ordinarily subject to willful efforts at change. I call this intervention behavior change versus personality change, because experience (and research) suggest that people can change specific behaviors (to an extent, under the right environmental conditions), but rarely change heretofore stable, consistent patterns of behavior that we call personality. The following is an example of a therapist's educating clients about the difference between behavior change and personality change.

Therapist: Nancy, you said you want a partner who will keep an eye on the state of your house and yard, who will help you monitor what needs to be done and do it. You see that something needs to be done on Wednesday, let's say. And each day after that, you walk around the house and there it is, it's not done. So he finally gets to it on Sunday night. And by then you're furious and frustrated and wondering why you had to endure looking at it for all that time.

Nancy: That's how I feel. And I wonder why he lets things go like that.

Therapist: And it seems to you, Nancy, that Lance is procrastinating or doesn't care about you or the house because he can put it off for so long.

Nancy: I don't know how else to understand it.

Therapist: I think I see where your frustration comes from—you are waiting for Lance to see what you see and get frustrated when he doesn't. You don't just want him to do his share, you want him to see when his share needs doing.

Nancy: I get so tired of nagging him, I just want to shut up and see when he finally gets around to it.

Therapist: The one thing you can't give him, though, are your eyes. Have you noticed that you consistently see things long before he does? By the time it's intolerable to you, it's still flying under his radar . . .

Nancy: Why doesn't he see it? Why can't you see it, Lance?

Therapist: We each have our level of tolerance for household order or lack thereof. Lance's tolerance is higher than yours. Because his tolerance is higher, he doesn't see it. You don't see things either when they are within your tolerance. It's only when they get intolerable that you see them.

Nancy: But he can tolerate so much—I can't ever live with what he tolerates.

Lance: C'mon Nancy, I'm not that bad.

Therapist: Before you get to arguing about whose tolerance is worse or better, what do you say we try working with the tolerance that you each have and figure out how you can live together with this difference. What this means is that you accept that you have different eyes for disorder, and then you decide how to make that work for you instead of against you.

Nancy: You know, his dad's the same way. . . .

Therapist: Great! Nancy, what you're noticing in the similarity of Lance and his dad is that easygoing, high tolerance level. And it sounds like a quality that you like. You know, psychologists are discovering that there is an inherited component to personality. Lance possibly inherited a tendency to be easygoing like his dad. Then, being raised by his dad, he got that tendency reinforced through observing his dad. So this characteristic is really a part of Lance. . . . So what's a fair way for each of you to accept that you have different eyes for disorder? Yet still keep the house a bit more orderly than Lance would have it if left on his own?

The therapist in this dialogue educated Nancy about her unrealistic expectation that Lance would see what needed to be done just when Nancy saw it. As soon as the therapist pointed out that this was unrealistic, Nancy and Lance started arguing about something different (i.e., who is more tolerant). Although this in itself was not a desirable outcome, it demonstrates how potent therapist education about realistic expectations can be in couple therapy. This therapist wisely stopped the nonproductive competition about who tolerates what and steered them into problem-solving mode. The issue of partner personality and unrealistic expectations becomes especially salient when partners are coping with differences in their intimacy needs (Dilemma #2; discussed in Chapter 9).

Irritating things come in attractive packages. Sometimes two personality traits seem to go together. Nancy's problem with Lance, described above, could also be understood as the result of irritating personality traits that sometimes come bundled in with desirable and attractive personality traits. This notion was first articulated by Murray Bowen (1978), who noted that couples often quarrel about the downsides of the very traits that attracted them to one another in the first place. The therapist can instruct couples to accept "personality packages" when they find themselves trying to change a characteristic that has become irritating to them in the partner. Here is an example of another way to intervene with Nancy's unrealistic expectations of Lance.

Therapist: What is likely to happen if you divorced Lance tomorrow and went out to find another guy who would see these problems the way that you do? What would it be like to marry a guy who would be on top of things, very organized, and efficient?

Nancy: I dated someone like that once but didn't stay with him.

Therapist: What happened between you?

Nancy: He was pretty serious and focused, and finicky about being tidy. I ended up not being that attracted to him, and we broke up.

Therapist: So you didn't want to marry him? Even though he was organized and neat and did his share?

Nancy: No, I just couldn't get that attracted to him. He actually drove me a little crazy with his neatness.

Therapist: His combination of qualities didn't work for you then. It happens that way. Things that you really like—like being easygoing—go along with other things that you don't like as much. So what do you value most? A guy whose easygoing nature means that you will see what needs to be done first and will probably have to tell him when it's starting to bug you? Or do you value more a guy who's not easygoing, but who has high standards for how your house looks and would not only chip in but would insist that you do more than you're doing now? Both are viable personality packages, right? What does it mean that you chose Lance?

Nancy: I was more attracted to him and enjoyed his company more from the beginning. So I guess I've made my decision, haven't I.

This therapist paints a picture of what being married to someone who is more vigilant and organized might be like as a way of helping Nancy to be realistic about what she expects from Lance and from marriage. She is helping Nancy to see that no matter to whom she is married, she will be making accommodations to another person's personality and that some of those accommodations will require effort on her part.

When partners accept that sometimes negative emotions occur in intimate relationships, their emotions will be less overwhelming. Realistic expectations can prevent couple partners from exacerbating their negative emotions with provocative and unrealistic thoughts (e.g., "She's in a bad mood. I'll leave her alone for awhile" versus "We have an important problem to resolve, but she won't talk to me. I must pursue her until I can make her talk about it").

Catching Automatic Thoughts in Conjoint Couple Sessions

It is when couple partners are talking with each other that the therapist is most likely to catch their automatic thoughts. This is because couple partners are engaging in habitual behavior when they are talking with each other. What they are doing is so overpracticed that they do much of it without planning or considering it. In conjunction with automatic interaction behavior, clients are likely to verbalize their automatic thoughts. The role of the therapist is to help partners notice the thoughts as they speak them and to reflect on the impact of the thoughts on their intimate connection. In the example below, the therapist helped Carla catch and identify an automatic thought.

Therapist:	When I hear you talking about that, sometimes I can hear you making a connection between what Doug says and what you have to do, as though he were the dictator of your relationship. That is, he makes some comment, critical, about you, and you feel you have to do something about it, like he was a dictator.
Carla (quiet, thinking):	Hmmmm. But you know, I'm done with that; I'm not doing that any more. He acts so dominant, and I used to, you know, tow the line, go along, be silent. But no more.
Therapist:	Hmmm this sounds better—you caught yourself thinking you should "shut up," and you immediately decided, no, I'm not doing that any more.
Carla (laughing):	I did, didn't I? You know how determined I am, that I will not ever go back there! . . .
Therapist:	This conversation between one thought and another that you have—those are your thoughts, much more than they are Doug giving you commands, so to speak.

In this example, the therapist heard Carla telling herself she had to stop talking if Doug criticized what she said. So the therapist reflected this automatic thought back to her as a way of putting the thought itself at the center of attention where it could be examined for its validity.

In couple sessions, the therapist can help partners catch and identify their automatic negative thoughts by stopping the action, pointing them out, and expressing curiosity about them. The fact that the therapist notices the thought and is curious about it starts a process whereby the client can also become curious and examine the thought itself rather than simply reacting to it. This is the first step in modifying automatic negative thoughts in couple therapy.

Evaluating Negative Automatic Thoughts in Couples Therapy

Couple therapists can offer their clients in vivo evaluations of the validity of their thoughts and hypotheses by encouraging each partner to check things out with the other. Individuals can learn to evaluate evidence that their beliefs about the partner and the partner's motives are supported by their own or their partner's experience. The goal is to reduce the emotional impact of unrealistic, distorted thinking about themselves, the partner, and the relationship, and replace it with more realistic, discriminating thinking patterns. When this technique of evaluating the validity of assumptions is used in a conjoint couple session, with the partner as a source of reality-testing, it becomes a couple-level intervention that can change the way individual partners think about the relationship and the way the couple talks about intimacy.

Negative mind reading is a common form of negative automatic thinking about the relationship partner. The individual assumes that he or she knows what the other was thinking and reacts to it negatively as though the other person had actually voiced the negative thought. For example, Jordan would assume that when Merrianne seemed to be distant from him she must not be interested in how his day went, so he avoided initiating contact with her. He would not consider alternative explanations for her preoccupied look. Further, Jordan's avoidance of her gives the impression that he wants to be left alone, so she leaves him alone.

In session, when the therapist hears mind reading between spouses, this thinking error should be pointed out and each provided with an opportunity to check out the validity of his or her assumption. In pointing out a thinking error, the therapist can soften the observation by normalizing the error as a common mistake that spouses make. He can explore with the mind reader the false assumption that if you know someone well enough, then you can intuit what they think or feel. When conclusions are based on nonverbal behaviors such as facial expressions or body posture rather than words, the error rate can be high.

After getting an agreement from the couple that it would be worthwhile to do so, the therapist should stop the conversation when mind reading occurs to suggest a perception check, meaning the client gives the other partner a chance to verify its accuracy.

Modify negative thoughts about partner differences. Below is an example of how a therapist might help a client modify negative automatic thoughts by encouraging the client to consider alternative explanations for an upsetting event. In this case, the automatic thoughts are upsetting interpretations of partner behaviors that reflect their different needs and wants. Modifying negative thoughts involves the following steps:

1. The therapist frames the problem in a way that is consistent with the way the partners understand it.
2. The couple identifies the precipitating event or situation.
3. Each partner names the emotions experienced at that time and rates the intensity of those emotions.
4. Each states the thoughts that went through his or her mind that led to these emotions. This can include interpretations or perceptions of the event or other automatic thoughts that popped into the person's mind.
5. The automatic thoughts can then be evaluated for accuracy, or the therapist can encourage the person to come up with less upsetting alternative explanations, as in the following dialogue. This dialogue also provides an example of how a therapist can introduce cognitive therapy and the use of worksheets into a couple's therapy.

Therapist: I see two goals for the two of you around this issue. One we've already worked on, which involves getting Sam to hear your concerns, Gina, and to respond to them constructively. There's another goal, though, and that's how to make this issue less painful for you, Gina. Would you be willing to work on this with me? *[Therapist frames the problem as Gina understands it.]*

Gina: OK.

Therapist: I'm going to show you a way of managing your negative emotions by taking more control of how you interpret each other's behavior. One thing that we have learned from research on negative emotions in relationships is that a partner's behavior that might be just irritating, but not the end of the world, becomes something that is totally upsetting and disrupts a relationship because of the way that we interpret it. A good example is the issue we've been working on. Sam said that he was hoping to do something today that didn't involve Gina. Gina, you interpreted that as an indication that he doesn't enjoy your company or doesn't respect your wishes. The thought that he doesn't enjoy your company is actually more upsetting than the fact that he wants to "play by himself" one day. Do you see what I mean? . . . That thought, "He doesn't enjoy spending time with me anymore" is truly upsetting. I would find it upsetting if I thought that about my husband. So one way of managing your emotions is to reevaluate your interpretation of what Sam's behavior means. Like, what if you interpreted it the way we've been talking about, that Sam is different than you and needs more time to himself than you do? Or, he has interests that you don't share and he really wants to pursue them because they're fun for him? See, you have the same behavior here, but two different interpretations. Moreover, once you have an alternative interpretation, you can check that interpretation out with him and see if he agrees with it. *[Therapist gives Gina time to do this.]*

Gina: OK so is it true?

Sam: It's what I've been trying to tell you! Sometimes I just want to do my own thing. It has nothing to do with you or how much I love you.

Gina: *[Sits quietly and refuses to look at Sam. Therapist gives her time to think.]*

Therapist: I'd like to share a couple of cognitive therapy techniques with both of you. This chart shows you how to expand beyond your usual interpretations of each other's behavior and consider alternatives. Maybe we'll have time to fill one out for each of you, but for now, let's start with Gina. Gina, I'd like to show you how to use it for this situation that we've just worked on, and then I'll give you one to take home and fill out for another situation and bring in next week. Sam, if you'll follow along, I hope you'll get the idea. This chart gets you into your head, thinking about what's going on between you, and helps you to think rationally and reasonably about how you want to handle it.

Now, to begin, you make a note of what happened between you. In this case, you'd write down that you wanted to spend time with Sam, but he wanted to go to the baseball game with his guy friends, OK? So write that down first. . . . *[Gina identifies the precipitating event.]* This clarifies the situation and encourages you to be descriptive rather than putting Sam down. See how that works? You're like a newspaper reporter who's trying to report the news without editorializing.

In the second column, write down each emotion that you felt when this happened, for example, angry, sad, and lonely. OK, what do you have there? *[Gina identifies the emotion.]*

Gina: Angry and lonely.

Therapist: The next step is to rate the strength of each emotion you felt on a 1–100 scale, where 100 is the strongest emotion that it's possible to feel and 0 is like being asleep, OK? This will be important later when you test out the effectiveness of your alternative interpretations. OK, so how strong were the emotions in this incident?

Gina: Well, the anger was 90; the loneliness maybe 80.

Therapist: OK, great, so we've got a fix on how strong those emotions were. You're rating them as extremely strong, am I right?

Gina: Yes, the anger was stronger than the loneliness, I suppose, but the loneliness was pretty strong, too.

Therapist: OK, the next step is to put the thought or interpretation with the emotion. First, just list every thought that comes to mind when you think of Sam going to the game with his friends instead of spending the day with you . . .

Gina: Here's a couple, I can't remember what else.

Therapist: OK, we're doing this together, so let me tell you one or two that I remember from a couple of weeks ago, and you let me know if they're relevant . . . Next, put "A" next to the thoughts that make you angry and "L" next to the thoughts that make you feel lonely. *[Gina identifies the thoughts that go with the emotions.]*

Gina: All of these thoughts make me angry.

Therapist: OK, this is important. You've just had an important realization that comes from learning this technique. All of your interpretations go with your anger, but you have a feeling of loneliness that's not associated with your interpretations. Could the loneliness be a result of the situation? You want to spend time with Sam, but he's going to the game with his friends?

Gina: Definitely.

Therapist: OK, so what that means is that the anger and the loneliness may come from different causes. I'd like to work on the causes of the anger in this session, OK? And then work on the causes of the loneliness in a later session. I'm suggesting that for two reasons: One, you two came into therapy because you wanted to stop this fighting, and I'm assuming that anger leads to fighting. Correct?

[Gina and Sam nod in agreement.]

Therapist: Second, we've got the causes of the anger right in front of us, so I want to go with the momentum. OK, the last step is coming up with alternative interpretations. One sure way to get some of these is to ask Sam how you should interpret his plans to go to the game, whether they are any indication of how much he enjoys being with you. I call this your "perception check." Want to try a perception check with Sam?

Gina: OK, what does it mean that you're going to the game instead of doing something with me?

Sam: It's because I love baseball, Gina, and you don't. You could go to the games with us if you wanted, but you don't enjoy it. So please let me enjoy my games.

Therapist: I like the nice, straightforward way you answered her, Sam. If you did that with a neutral or even a tender, loving voice tone, you might even persuade her that you like her while you're saying it! And accomplish two things at once. Just something to keep in mind, OK? But for now I want to finish working with Gina. Gina, what are you thinking about Sam's explanation?

Gina: I believe it partly. I know he likes baseball; I don't question that. I just wonder why baseball always comes first.

Sam: It doesn't always come first, only when there's a game. Otherwise, I'm home. It's not like I run around with the guys all the time and am never here.

Therapist: OK, so what just happened here is that Sam got defensive when you said that. Usually, people get defensive when they believe they're not being perceived accurately. We can talk later about how to avoid getting into defensiveness, but for now, let's work on finishing this exercise. So Gina, for the sake of our finishing this exercise, will you write the explanation Sam just gave you into your "alternative interpretation" column? And then, add "baseball always seems to come first" into the "My Interpretation" column. I encourage you to change "always" to "very often" to make it closer to how you actually perceive it. Now Gina is there any other interpretation in the third column that you'd like to check out with Sam.

Gina: Yes, I want to ask Sam how he thinks we can have a good marriage when he always—I mean, often—chooses going to baseball games over being with me.

Therapist: OK, good, you're finding out how Sam thinks about this. Try asking this in another form, so that you're actually checking out your interpretation. Go back to your list. Which interpretation are you checking out with him with this question?

Gina: Well, the second one, that he'd rather be with his friends but mostly, that he doesn't care enough about me to make plans with me.

Therapist: OK, so phrase it like you're checking out your interpretation. Is it true that . . . ?

Gina: Is it true that you don't care enough about me to make plans with me? Why don't you make plans with me?

Sam: I do make plans with you.

Therapist: OK, Sam, let me stop you here. Gina's working very hard here, and she deserves a thought-out answer from you, and this would be a good time to say something that isn't defensive. One way to get around defending yourself and getting into that pattern that you both hate so much of attack-defend is for you, Sam, to assume for a minute that she's at least partially right, that perhaps you don't make plans with her that frequently. Is it possible that she's partially right?

Sam: Well, we're married, she's always there, I guess. So when I don't have a baseball game or something else, I assume we're doing something.

Therapist: OK, let me work with you a minute. Would you be willing to acknowledge to Gina that she has a point? Without totally giving in to what she wants, without being a doormat?

Sam: OK, Gina, you do have a point. We tend to do things spontaneously, at the last minute instead of having plans.

Gina: So you see how that's a problem for me? I never know when you're going to be free to do something with me, so I end up waiting and getting mad at you because I'm waiting.

Therapist: This is great, now you're problem solving again. Now you're in a position to change the way you do business—to start making plans together, so that Gina can know and look forward to things that you do together and not wait around when you're not free. I'm going to make a note for us to get back to this next time, because, Gina, I want to review your initial interpretations and your alternative ones. What do you have for alternative interpretations? Notice that one of your interpretations was valid while the rest needed modification to be valid or weren't valid at all. Your interpretations are now closer to Sam's feelings and reasons. . . .

Therapist: Now that you've checked out your interpretations with Sam and have some accurate alternatives, the final step is to evaluate your emotions. So write angry and lonely down in the last column and rate how much you feel them now, after this exercise, on a 1–100 scale.

If the alternative interpretations are effective, the emotions (in this case, anger) should be rated as less intense even if just a little. Less intense anger means that the client is making progress replacing unrealistically negative automatic thoughts with more measured, realistic thoughts.

Usually, the introduction to cognitive modification in the couple session, particularly when combined with interactions in which partners check interpretations with each other and partner responses to these perception checks are modified, takes a whole session.

Evaluating negative automatic thoughts in individual sessions. Another strategy is to work individually with the partner who seems to have the most negative automatic thoughts about his or her partner. For example, even when things had been going well for a while, Nancy found herself criticizing Lance frequently for his lapses, resulting in Lance's feeling on edge a lot of the time. From Nancy's perspective, she had to learn to accept Lance's bad habits with more equanimity and stop taking responsibility for them. Lance's office, for example, was a disorderly mess, but Nancy wanted to accept that as long as the door was closed it didn't affect anyone's life except his.

Nancy's next step was to "catch herself" the next time she had the irritable feeling toward Lance and then pause and examine it and its source before she acted on it. With the help of the therapist, who used Socratic questioning to help her identify her thoughts, Nancy determined what thoughts were contributing to her irritability. In an individual session, the therapist helped Nancy to systematically identify the event-thought connections using a version of Beck and colleagues (1979) Daily Record of Dysfunctional Thoughts, shown in Table 6.3. Nancy and her therapist then collaborated to develop some alternative thoughts that Nancy could use to replace the old thoughts (and calm herself).

Negative automatic thoughts about sexuality. A couple's sexual relationship can be sabotaged if one of the partners believes that his or her body will never pass muster with the partner. Clearly, the broader society with its ubiquitous focus on female bodies and physical attractiveness and its punitive messages toward women who do not live up to high standards affects women's participation in sexual intimacy. Women are at risk for standing outside of themselves and looking in. Rather than undergo this kind of painful, negative self-evaluation, they may withdraw from sex. It is also too easy for women's relationship partners to punish them by commenting negatively on their bodies.

Men are vulnerable to negative self-scrutiny as well. Men tend to judge themselves by how their erections function: how quickly do they get one, how long does it last, and so forth. Sex therapists McCarthy and McCarthy (2003) argue that men are especially vulnerable to this sort of negative vigilance about themselves after they pass 35 or 40, and their sexual functioning noticeably changes.

Clients who avoid sex because they cannot shut off the negative litany in their heads about themselves may need individual work. Negative internal

Table 6.3 Nancy's automatic thought monitor

What Happened?	*My Feeling*	*My Interpretation*	*Another Interpretation*	*My Feeling*
Lance threw his briefcase down on the dining room table where I had just cleaned and straightened.	Irritable, angry 60	He doesn't remember anything that I ask him to do (keep his stuff off the table). He doesn't care how our house looks.	Lance's ideal is not identical to mine. He's just not thinking about what he's doing. It's a habit—I can help him break it.	Irritable, angry 25

litanies inhibit desire, so that the individual no longer even feels that he or she wants to have sex. In my experience, negative thinking about body and sexuality are best handled with a combination of interventions, including (1) lifestyle changes that involve body-friendly eating, grooming, and exercise habits; (2) self-affirming, positive self-talk that recasts negatively labeled aspects of the self in a positive light; (3) changes in the environment that elicit the new, positive self-talk; (4) traditional cognitive therapy techniques, including automatic thought and schema change strategies; and (5) traditional sex therapy techniques.

Clients with sexual inhibitions due to excessive self-criticalness may benefit from lifestyle changes, such as relaxation and yoga breathing training, self-touching and pleasuring exercises, and a more body-affirming lifestyle. In addition to assisting individual partners in evaluating negative thoughts about their own bodies and sexuality, the therapist can help clients decide on steps they want to take toward changing the things about themselves they find unacceptable. When change is desired, therapists can assist partners in developing a body-affirming lifestyle through healthy eating, exercise, attractive, stylish clothing, and/or participation in sports. Compliance with medication regimes may also be a part of this lifestyle. The challenge for the therapist here, as it is with any program that requires self-discipline and client compliance, is to collaborate with the client in the identification of small steps and intermittent rewards in order that clients receive sufficient reinforcement along the way to be motivated to sustain the healthy behavior.

Clients who criticize their bodies can change negative self-statements about their bodies to more positive ones. Therapists can help clients avoid comparing themselves unrealistically with idealized groups. For example, women who compare themselves with the airbrushed images in magazines are bound to believe that they come up short. A client who is overweight can learn to replace a litany of negative thoughts about her weight with positive thoughts about her curves, for example. She can use her environment to elicit and reinforce these thoughts by posting photographs of attractive, curvy women like Queen Latifa and Kirstie Alley in accessible places in her home.

When clients' thoughts about their bodies or their sexuality are unrealistic or are accessible to problem solving, therapists can help them identify and evaluate their automatic thoughts. Clients can learn to replace negative, unrealistic thoughts about their bodies for more realistic ones.

Identify Problematic Intimacy Schemas and Their Associations with Emotion and Behavior

When working with intimacy problems, it is important that the therapist listen for themes underlying the automatic thoughts that clients verbalize in the session with one another and with the therapist. As couples bring in various problems from one session to the next, thematic commonalities in the complaints become apparent to the therapist who is listening closely for them. These thematic commonalities stem from the problematic intimacy schemas that have been activated by the partner's behavior and that have thereby generated the complaints. Figure 6.2 shows how several automatic thoughts can be generated by a single schema.

To determine when couple interaction is activating intimacy schemas—when it activates basic assumptions about the self, about the partner, or about intimacy in general—the therapist's best indicator is the strength of the emotions aroused, emotions that may seem out of proportion to the stimulus from the therapist's perspective. Once these strong emotions are evident, the therapist can stop the interaction (e.g., "Ok, let's stop, let me see if we can all understand better what's going on here"), help the partners calm down (e.g., "take a deep breath with me, and if it's OK with you, Sarah, I'd like to talk with Adam for a few minutes and get a sense of what goes on with him when you two get into this kind of talk"), and then talk one-on-one with one of the partners about what they were thinking when they were having the strong emotions (e.g., "I thought I saw some tension in your face when Sarah said that, Adam, and wondered if what she said just then—about your relationship with your son—is the kind of thing that contributes to the feeling you

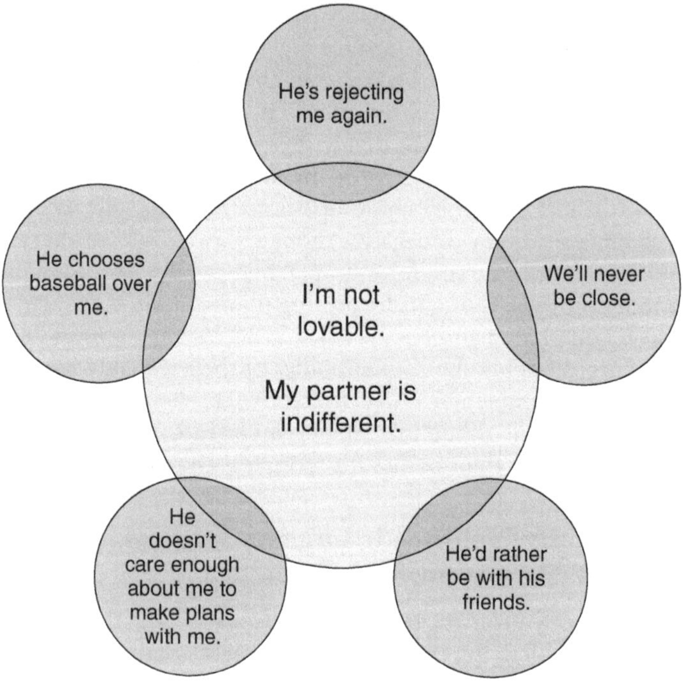

Figure 6.2 Connecting automatic thoughts to underlying schemas

were talking about last session, about Sarah not being tuned in to all that you do for the kids"). It is common to find that intimacy-related thinking patterns are not accessible to the individual partners until they are in the middle of an interaction with the other. Couple interaction, therefore, provides an optimum opportunity for partners to discover their own and their partner's intimacy schemas.

Because they are elicited in the context of interaction and because most people react to them rather than reflect upon them, many intimacy schemas generate emotions and motivate behavior and still exist outside of the individual's awareness. These not-yet-articulated schemas are the ones that the therapist's questions are most likely to uncover at the time that the couple interaction elicits them. Others are readily available and reported by the partners, whereas there are others still about which individuals know but are not ready to share with their partners. The latter type will likely emerge in the individual interviews.

As these themes come to light, the therapist should work with clients to identify and label them. Nonetheless, the therapist should not be tempted to identify schemas for the client too soon in therapy. Although the therapist may have identified the schema correctly, the therapist may describe it in a way that the client doesn't identify it as a belief over which he or she has ownership. Beck et al. (1979) offer the following caution, "If the therapist leaps prematurely to the identification of a basic belief, he runs the risk of confusing the patient . . . [this is because schemas] are not articulated by the patient without considerable introspection . . . therapists are particularly vulnerable to the risk of presenting their own biases—what they speculate the patient's beliefs are. If the therapist, however, will listen to and work with the patient, therapy is more likely to stay on target" (p. 247). In order for schema-focused interventions to work, the client must recognize the schema as his or her own.

Once automatic thoughts have been identified, and especially if the same automatic thoughts come up repeatedly, the therapist can ask the client to read through the thoughts he or she has listed on the automatic thought monitor and see if there is a theme that the thoughts have in common. When the client articulates a theme, the therapist can help him or her put it into words so that it sounds like a belief. For example, here is one way that Gina's therapist could work with her to identify her schema.

Therapist: It can be helpful to identify themes or beliefs that automatic thoughts share in common. Automatic negative thoughts, thoughts that upset you, may spring from a common belief that colors your way of understanding what happens in your relationship. Looking at your list of thoughts for this week, in the automatic thought column, do you see a theme that ties the thoughts together? Could they all share an assumption or belief about yourself or about Sam?

Gina: Well, it seems like I'm saying that he holds all the cards. He gets to decide whether to be with me or not, and whichever way he decides, he gets what he wants. Whereas I'm in the position, because I want to be with him, of being with him only if he feels like it or if he doesn't, scrounging around for a second-best option.

Therapist: It sounds like you're saying that Sam gets to call the shots.

Gina: I guess he does get to. That makes me mad.

Therapist: Why don't you write your theme at the top of this page, and I'll put it in your file for us to work on next time.

Gina: OK, let's see how would I say this?

Therapist: Try saying it out loud first.

Gina: It seems like he gets his way no matter what.

Therapist: That's fine—it's your theme, so you should name it! . . . When you monitor your thoughts this week using your chart, put a star next to each thought that seems to reflect that theme. Some probably will reflect the theme whereas others do not. Bring those in and we can talk about what you learned about the theme by doing the exercise.

The therapist has ensured that the theme is articulated in a way that makes sense to Gina. Then she gives Gina homework that will give her a chance to think about the theme as she reacts to relationship events during the week.

Over the next few sessions, the therapist can check with Gina when she thinks she hears the theme influencing Gina's thoughts as she communicates them. She can ask Gina if she again perceives that Sam has the power in this situation, and she has no choice. Repetitive identification of schemas gives clients the opportunity to increase their awareness of how these schemas affect their emotions and their behavior in various situations. It is useful for the therapist to keep a list of each client's most commonly activated intimacy schemas in his or her session notes to increase the likelihood that the therapist will use the same label each time he or she observes the schema operating. The list of intimacy schemas provided in the Intimacy Signature Basic Intake can be useful for the therapist in this regard. If the client is open to exploring the connection between the schema and his or her current reaction to the partner, the therapist can then proceed to help the client identify what it is that the partner does or says that is significant to the client.

Methods to evaluate schemas. Schemas are beliefs and may not necessarily be based on fact or objectively viewed experiences. Relationship schemas or self-schemas about how partners are supposed to behave in a relationship usually come from our early experiences in our families of origin. For example, children watch how parents interact and form ideas about how relationships should work and how people are supposed to behave toward one another. Sometimes parents also give direct instructions about how to behave in relationships with others, such as, "Be nice to each other. Share your toys. Say thank you." Adult experiences with a spouse, parent, or romantic partner can also lead to the development of schemas related to relationships. For example, the schema that "men can't be trusted" might stem from an experience with an unfaithful boyfriend.

The simplest strategy for dealing with problematic schemas is to get couples to state them out loud. Hearing themselves verbalize their internal rules for one another or for the relationship can be enough for them to realize that their ideas are impractical, inaccurate, or not really applicable to their current relationship. The therapist uses reflection and Socratic questioning to encourage verbalization of the schema such as in the example below.

Patty: I don't think he loves me.

Therapist: What do you mean by that?

Patty: He never buys me what I ask him to buy. He gets other people exactly what they want, but when it comes to me he is always off. He doesn't really know me.

Therapist: How is this connected to the idea that he doesn't love you?

Patty: If he loved me, he would get the present that I want. He would make the effort to listen and to find out what I really want.

Therapist: And he doesn't do that now?

Patty: Well he does it with small things. He brings me coffee when I'm putting on my makeup in the morning, or he rubs my feet when I've been on them all day at work. I know this sounds horrible, but I just want him to buy me the right present just like he does for his kids and his mom.

Therapist: And that would mean that he loves you?

Patty: I know he loves me. I really know he loves me. I don't know what I'm saying. I guess I think that if someone loves you they always know what you want and what to do for you.

Therapist: Always?

Patty: Well, not always. It sounds so stupid to hear myself say these things. I sound so spoiled. He does spoil me in a lot of ways. I guess my father was always so good at gift giving for me and for my mom. He died when I was a teenager, but I always remember how beautifully his gifts were wrapped and how happy my mother was when she opened them.

Therapist: So is that where you got the idea about love and gift giving?

Patty: I think so. I'm sure I did. But that was the only time he made my mother happy. He had a drinking problem and was gone a lot.

So I don't know why I am pushing the gift giving so much. I have a good and caring husband. He doesn't drink. He is kind, and he tries hard. I know he loves me.

Therapist: So what do you want to do with the idea that if he loved you he would always know what you wanted?

Patty: It's stupid. I know he loves me, and I know he tries. I just need to be grateful for what I have. I just hear my friends talk about the perfect gifts their husbands give them, and I want that too. My husband is good at lots of things, but he isn't that good when it comes to buying me gifts. It's not a big deal.

Patty in this example applied an "I am unlovable" schema to a situation in her marriage to which it did not apply, and through her work with the therapist, was able to see the errors in her logic.

Sometimes spouses' schemas are incompatible and can stress a marriage. For example, if one partner heard his or her parents show love by protecting each other from any bad news ("I am Mr./Ms. Fix-It"), he or she would form the belief that this was how couples are supposed to be. If the other partner was raised by parents who shared all their thoughts and feelings with one another, regardless of the emotional impact ("Intimacy is honesty"), he or she would think that was normal intimacy. The goal of evaluating schemas in couple therapy is not to determine which idea is correct and which is incorrect. The goal is to determine whether or not these schemas enhance intimacy in the current relationship, the advantages and disadvantages of retaining them or discarding them, and how the differing schemas of two partners can be reconciled.

The therapist can facilitate the schema evaluation process by helping the two partners to define their beliefs, such as the degree to which spouses should confide in one another. By listening to each partner's point of view, the therapist might be able to verbalize their schema such as in the following:

Therapist: Phil, it sounds like you believe that it's better if you don't share bad news or negative thoughts and fears with your wife. Donna, on the other hand, you seem to believe it is best for spouses to share all their intimate thoughts and feelings with one another even if they are negative. Did I get that right?

Donna: Well, not every thought and feeling. If he doesn't like what I'm wearing, I would rather he kept his opinion to himself.

Phil: I figured that one out the hard way. She asked me what I thought about this outfit she was wearing, and I told her the honest truth that I didn't really like it. It was definitely the wrong thing to say.

Therapist: So there are some things you both agree can be left unsaid, but there seem to be many other situations where it is unclear what should be shared and what shouldn't. In those cases, Donna leans toward more sharing, and Phil leans toward less sharing. Does that sound right?

Phil: Yes.

Donna: That sounds right.

Therapist: Instead of saying that sharing thoughts and feelings is right or wrong, let's try to come up with rules or schemas about sharing that are agreeable to you both. What are the options?

The therapist facilitates brainstorming of rules regarding sharing thoughts and feelings versus protecting the partner's presumed fragility and directs the couple to find a plan that they both find acceptable. The follow-up homework is to try out the new rule to see if it works.

Some schemas are shared by couples but are a source of problems in the relationship. Consider what would happen if both Donna and Phil shared the schema from the example above, that a truly loving spouse protects his or her partner from bad news or his or her dissatisfaction with something, and does not cause any negative feelings in the other. This one can be a problem when the mutual caretaking results in emotional distance between the partners because each is trying hard to protect the other from a negative feeling. To help this couple, the therapist can follow these schema evaluation steps.

1 *In-session evaluation of disadvantages and advantages of schema.* The therapist walks them through a discussion of the advantages and disadvantages of retaining their version of this schema ("We are Mr. and Ms. Fix-It for each other").
2 *Couple keeps the list of schema pros and cons identified in the session.*
3 *Follow-up observation and decision-making period.* The couple follows up with a period of observation between therapy sessions that would allow them to add to the list as they focus on how their schema plays out in their everyday lives. If there are more advantages, then the schema is retained, and if there are more disadvantages, the schema is replaced with a more useful or accurate schema.
4 *Identify and test an alternative schema.* A therapy session in which they brainstorm ideas is followed up with the selection of an alternative schema and pilot-testing between sessions.
5 *Evaluate the alternative schema with the therapist.* A follow-up session helps the couple to determine if their new schema works or needs to be modified to fit their marriage.

Couples should be warned that in times of stress, they will feel compelled to resurrect their old schemas. In the course of couple therapy, they will need to periodically discuss the progress they are making with implementation of the new schema and times when the old one seems to predominate. If the modified schema is to be retained, the couple must find ways to remind themselves of the new rule.

Using guided fantasy to work with schemas. Guided fantasy can be very useful for exploring schemas. Jeffrey Young and his colleagues (2003) argue that guided fantasy helps clients "identify schemas, understand childhood origins of schemas, and relate schemas to the patient's presenting problems" (p. 110–111). The advantage of guided fantasy is that it helps the client to emotionally revisit, in a vivid way, the situations in which they originally formed the relationship expectations that became their intimacy schemas. This revisiting allows them to feel the schema-associated emotions and thereby compare them with the emotions that they feel in their current relationships. This is an important step toward developing alternative explanations for the way that they feel in their romantic relationship. It also encourages them to look more closely at the events that elicit the schema-related emotions versus those events that do not and consider whether their current relationship is eliciting those schemas because of its similarities to early experiences or whether they need to develop alternative inferences about the current relationship that are not based on the intimacy schema.

The therapist who is using guided fantasy to explore a schema will want to use instructions relevant to discovering a possible source of the schema in the client's past. These instructions can work effectively for that purpose:

> "Now I'd like you to imagine that you can travel back in time. Imagine a magic carpet (or a time machine), something that can take you back, and imagine yourself getting in or on and beginning a journey into your past. . . . Now experience yourself going back and back, until your transportation slows down and stops. . . . Now you're getting out and you look around. Take a minute and absorb where you are. . . . How old are you? . . . Can you describe the place to me? . . . *[Prompts, if the client has trouble describing.]* What's the weather like? What color is the bedspread? What's on the wall to your right? *[etc.]* Who's at home now? . . . Where is he or she? . . . How do you feel about his or her being there? . . . What would happen if you went and joined him or her in the next room? . . . How do you feel about that?"

In my experience, it is important to get the details of the background fixed as this increases the vividness of the imagery and also helps the therapist determine whether the client is able to get into the image. It is helpful to talk in the present tense to increase the client's experience of being in the significant place with the significant people in the moment. The here-and-now focus increases the likelihood that the client will experience the schema-related emotions. It is also helpful for the therapist to avoid talking too much or filling in too many details, as the moments of quiet give the client the psychological space to picture the image, to suspend his or her awareness of the present moment and immerse him- or herself in the imagery experience.

Some questions to increase the vividness of the fantasy for the client:

> "How does it feel to be in your old neighborhood, there on your street, by the big willow tree at the end of the block? [or] How does it feel to be getting ready for bed, there in your childhood bedroom? . . . What's going to happen next? . . . Who will come and say good night to you? . . . Where's your big brother? . . . What do you notice about the bed? . . . Now that you're lying in bed, how do you feel about drifting off to sleep? Do you expect the night to be peaceful? . . . What will it be like in the morning?"

The questions the therapist asks the client will be guided by the therapist's hypotheses about what the client is struggling with in his or her current relationship.

When the client starts feeling the emotions associated with a schema-relevant event, it is helpful to encourage the client to explore the emotion itself. The advantage of staying with the emotion rather than pushing it away is the client learns that he or she can feel the emotion and nothing terrible will happen as a result.

The therapist should also give the client the opportunity to come slowly out of the guided fantasy. Instructing the client to take his or her time as he or she travels back to the present and to open his or her eyes when ready ensures that the transition is not too abrupt.

Working with negative intimacy-related self-schemas. Some clients who avoid intimacy do so because they assume that their partners agree with their own negative self-schemas. Intimacy avoidant individuals entertain thoughts such as those listed previously in Table 6.3, including, "My partner will reject or disapprove of me" or "Talking about that would make me appear weak to my partner," and "it is better to play it safe and save face than to risk humiliating rejection." Thoughts like these can reveal an underlying belief such as "I am unlovable." Individuals with these schemas are struggling with Dilemma #1 and may respond well to cognitive modification techniques.

Listed below are steps for applying Beck and colleagues' (1979) schema modification process to problems with intimacy. The therapist may use the steps that are most appropriate for a particular client and may not use all the steps.

1 *Educate the client in the cognitive model of emotions.* Schema modification work is most effective if the client understands the relationship between thinking patterns and negative emotions, and the way that ineffective, undesirable behavior can proceed from a particular set of thoughts or emotions.
2 *Educate the client about the connection between previous relationship experiences and current thinking patterns.* It can be beneficial for the therapist to explore previous relationship experiences with the client and for the therapist to formulate for him- or herself and with the client possible connections between those experiences and the client's expectations and fears about the current relationship.
3 *Teach clients to recognize and modify distortions in their thinking about themselves.* Clients who avoid intimacy because they believe themselves to be unlovable are jumping to conclusions about what others will think about them. They predict that they will experience rejection, disapproval, or humiliation as a result of others not finding them lovable and come to the conclusion that it is better to play it safe than risk feeling these emotions. People with negative self-schemas may stay so much within themselves that others think they are aloof; they therefore have difficulty making friends or being comfortable in social situations.

   Therapists can help clients identify errors in their thinking about themselves by asking them some of the following questions about their negative self-evaluations (or by asking clients to take the questions home and answer them for homework).

   a Is this thought overstating something negative about me? For example, Katherine had the automatic thought that, "I will never find a husband, men always leave me" which sprang from her self-schema, "I am unlovable." One way Katherine can evaluate whether the self-schema is accurate is to consider who has loved her and who has not loved her and whether it is valid to generalize from those who did not. If the schema, "I am unlovable" is not 100% true, Katherine could reasonably conclude that it is an overgeneralization based on some bad experiences.
   b *Do I have all the information I need to draw this conclusion about myself?* When Katherine tells herself, "I will never find a husband," she is *fortune-telling,* predicting a future that no one can know in advance. When Katherine tells herself, "It's fun now with Ben, but I don't think he's really crazy about me," she is *mind reading,* assuming she knows what Ben is thinking without checking it out with him.
   c *Am I assuming that something is true just because I'm feeling bad today?* This is a useful question to ask clients who are experiencing anger. If Gina believes that she is being mistreated by Lance when he spends a Saturday afternoon with his friends instead of with her, does this indicate that her self-schema "I am a victim" is true or does it only

indicate that she is disappointed that a hoped-for event did not come to pass. *Emotional reasoning,* believing that a feeling is proof that an idea is true, is a thinking error if there is no other indication that the thoughts are true.

d *Am I criticizing myself, my partner, or my relationship for not living up to a standard?* Is the standard my standard or someone else's? Is it a realistic standard? Am I putting myself (or my partner) down because I am not living up to a "should?" These questions are useful for individuals who endorse the intimacy schema, "Things must always go right," and then blame themselves (or their partners) when they do not. It can be useful to think back to the source of the schema (Where did I learn this? Who taught it to me? Would he or she still want me to hold onto that schema now?) and evaluate its usefulness in the present.

4 *Teach cognitive modification techniques.* When the therapist identifies these thinking patterns during couple therapy, it is helpful to set aside individual sessions to teach cognitive modification skills. I encourage clients to read Wright and Basco's *Getting Your Life Back* (2001), Burns's *Feeling Good* (1999), or Greenberger and Padesky's *Mind Over Mood* (1995) and teach them cognitive modification techniques. Instead of monitoring mood shifts, as is practiced in Beck's cognitive therapy, these individuals will monitor their interactions with their partners and notice connections between the decisions they make about when and how much to share of themselves, when to have sex, etc., and their thoughts about themselves.

5 *Teach clients to make the connection between their negative self-schemas and their problems with intimacy.* Clients should first learn to think realistically about what they disclose to their partners, entertaining the idea that what they have to say is interesting to the partner. Assuming that the partner is not extraordinarily rejecting, belittling, or likely to threaten abandonment, the therapist coaches these clients on how to see the connection between their negative assumptions about themselves and their avoidance of intimacy.

This technique is best implemented by (1) focusing the session on a specific incident (2) encouraging the client to examine the evidence for and against her schema-related automatic thoughts (3) returning to discuss the schema and whether the client's truth-detecting process supports its validity and (4) returning to the client's behavior during the incident use the same process to help him or her come up with a more reasonable belief and more constructive, accompanying behavior.

6 *Teach clients to identify alternative, realistic beliefs about themselves.* The therapist then further coaches the client on (1) identifying alternative,

more realistic views of themselves and (2) assigning as homework an experiment to test whether the alternative thinking patterns make it easier to share themselves with their partners. Follow-up sessions give clients the opportunity to talk about how the new view of themselves stacks up to their daily experience and to modify the schema as necessary.

Cognitive Training for Self-Empowerment

Self-empowerment is an especially important aspect of the self-schema that contributes significantly to partners' ability to address intimacy dilemmas and resolve them satisfactorily. Empowered partners can act effectively in their own behalf without distancing or denigrating their partners. An empowered person can manage conflict without becoming either a doormat or a selfish cad.

Cognitive training for self-empowerment is a useful intervention strategy for partners who blame one another for their relationship problems and fail to take responsibility for their own contributions. Partners who blame often operate out of "I am fragile" or "I am a victim" self-schemas. They may demand to be treated with kid gloves or fear that they will be irretrievably damaged by the partner's behavior. They may portray themselves as innocent sufferers and react defensively to the partner's communication instead of listening. They may also believe that "My partner has the power." They may remind therapists of a child whose will is overpowered by a stern, demanding parent. Cognitive training for self-empowerment can help partners alter these self-defeating schemas and the emotions and behavior that accompany them. In doing so, it also encourages them to take more responsibility for their own contribution to problems in the relationship.

Cognitive self-empowerment training is not a step-by-step intervention as are many of the others described in this book. Rather, it is a menu of micro-interventions from which the clinician may select, depending on the client's needs. Assuming that their partners are not verbally or physically abusive, increased self-empowerment leads clients to feel less helpless and paralyzed by their partner's behavior and thereby less likely to defend, blame, or attack in response.

Step 1: Set the Stage—Persuade the Client that Self-Empowerment Will Improve the Quality of Life

Self-empowerment training begins with the effort to persuade partners that working toward their own empowerment is a worthy goal. Partners who are focused on blaming one another tend to be resistant to acknowledging their own contributions to relationship problems. Self-empowerment training helps them see that acknowledging and fixing their own contributions to relationship problems can be beneficial for them. The therapist can use one or more of several persuasions to convince clients to engage in self-empowerment training rather than continuing the "blame game." Here are four persuasive communications from which the therapist can choose. With each persuasion, it is important that the therapist reassures the partners that he or she will be working with both of them to change their behavior. This is important for maintaining a therapeutic alliance with both partners. Once that commitment is made, the therapist may make one or more of the following points:

1. *While your partner is making changes, this will help you feel less upset in response to his or her behavior.* This persuasion covers four interrelated reasons for working toward one's own self-empowerment: (a) behavior change is gradual because old habits die hard and while your partner is working on changing, he or she may slip into old, upsetting behaviors; (b) after therapy is finished, it is likely that he or she will slip again under certain conditions (i.e., when tired or under stress); (c) you still get very upset by this behavior; and (d) it is worthwhile to work on being less upset.[1] Logically, this persuasive message leads to a contract for teaching the client to more effectively soothe him- or herself.

2. *There is a discrepancy here, between the many challenges that you handle successfully every day and the way that your partner can ruin your day with one rude remark or gesture.* This persuasion overlaps with the previous one and adds an affirmation from the therapist. Here, the therapist is providing an empowering message by pointing out the discrepancy between the client's competent adult self and the overreactions to provocations by the partner.

3. *Your partner's behavior comes as much from his or her personality as it does from anything you do. You seem to view your partner as larger than life when in fact, he or she is a traveler in life just like you.* The self-empowerment process can aim to change the individual's partner schema and help the client see the partner more clearly as a fellow human being with the same vulnerabilities as his or her own. Rather than taking everything the partner says as a reflection on self, the client practices seeing the partner's behavior as a predictable aspect of his or her personality. Demystifying the partner's power enhances self-empowerment.

4. *Working on changing yourself allows you to avoid the most frustrating position in the world: that of trying to make someone else change. If things don't work out between you, learning other ways to handle differences will be beneficial for your mental health.* This persuasion is useful for partners who are reluctant to make changes unless the partner makes changes. These individuals are overly vigilant of the partner's behavior and want a tit for tat trade in effort. Partners who are unsure of their commitment to remain

1 This instruction should not be used if partners are being unfaithful, abusing substances, or engaging in verbally abusive or physically violent acts against one another.

in the relationship also find this argument persuasive. In either case, the therapist motivates them to take responsibility for their own behavior by seeing the benefits of change for themselves as individuals. Partners often breathe a sigh of relief when they realize that they do not have to choose between leaving the relationship or futile efforts to manipulate the partner into change.

5. *Even if he or she deserves to suffer for what he or she does, you are in a bind because your focus on teaching your partner a lesson still leaves you feeling small and helpless.* Even if your sole purpose is to make your partner feel as bad as you do, you are still putting your energy into something over which you do not have control, which is how your partner feels. Maintaining that focus only reinforces your feeling that you have no power or control. Even if you succeed at punishing your partner, you don't feel successful or happy. Working on self-empowerment will help you to feel happier and more competent. It will help you to focus on what you can change and help you to accept what you cannot. Self-empowerment helps you to focus your attention on positive change.

Once one or both partners has bought into the notion that greater self-empowerment will allow them to acquire valued competencies and enjoy their relationship more fully, then the therapist can teach one or more of the following skills, depending upon the individual's needs.

Step 2: Teach Skills for Soothing Negative Emotional States

1. *Teach the individual to pause before speaking, to be less reactive.* Part of self-empowerment training is to teach the client to be less reactive by pausing before speaking (see Chapter 4 for a full description). The client can use the pause to calm him- or herself down and to think about what to do.

2. *Cognitive self-soothing.* Intense negative emotional reactions, especially feelings of helplessness and powerlessness in the relationship, can be soothed by changing thinking patterns. Self-talk counteracts self-schemas of fragility and victimization by reminding the individual that he or she is in fact robust and competent. For cognitive self-soothing, the therapist and client together generate possible self-soothing and schema-counteracting self-statements in the session. The most effective self-statements are those that the client believes and that he or she finds comforting and soothing. The therapist should monitor the client's reactions to self-statements closely and reword them to more effectively challenge negative self-schemas if necessary. Carla and her therapist, for example, came up with these self-soothing statements: (a) I will never be the submissive doormat I was then; (b) I am a successful, competent woman; (c) I am independent and resourceful; and (d) Doug says things on impulse, I don't have to worry about everything that he says. The client writes the self-statements down during the therapy session and then practices them

at home between sessions. She posts them in places where she will see them and be reminded of them. She then reports back on the effectiveness of the self-soothing statements to the therapist the following week.

Step 3: Teach Self-Empowering Thinking Processes

3. *Schema evaluation: Therapist affirms more empowered self-schema for client and creates cognitive dissonance for the client about the old, out-of-date schema.* As often as not, clients confront situations that overwhelm their new self-soothing skills or perhaps their compliance with the self-statement homework assignment slips as the weeks go by. Under these circumstances, it is useful for the therapist to affirm an updated self-schema for the client at critical points during treatment, particularly in conjoint sessions.

4. *Work to change the negative self-schema to encourage self-empowerment.* Often, evaluation and changing of the client's self-schema is the core of self-empowerment training. The goal is to reduce the client's overreactive emotions and/or ineffective responses to what the partner says or does by increasing the client's perception of him- or herself as a competent, potent person. Working with the negative self-schema is especially apropos when the client is aware of the schema and its negative impact on the intimate relationship. As described above, the therapist first teaches the client how to monitor his or her cognitions. The client maintains the automatic thought monitor, writing down his or her feelings and thoughts about him- or herself after any upsetting interaction with the partner. In the following therapy session, he or she then examines the event-associated automatic thoughts to determine if any are reflecting the old self-schema. If they are, the client and the therapist use the techniques described earlier in this chapter for evaluating the schema. Finally, the client identifies an alternative belief that more accurately represents the facts at hand than the old self-schema did.

5. *Use the "so-what" technique with clients who endorse an "I am fragile" self-schema.* With clients who avoid facing their dilemmas because they dread taking risks, the "so what" technique is useful for de-catastrophizing their worst case scenarios. Here is an example of a therapist using it with a young woman who was hiding her feelings from a young man she had been dating for several months:

Therapist: So you're being really careful with him, not rocking the boat.

Jennifer: That's really why I'm here. I've been trying really hard to just enjoy it for what it is, a really good time, but I'm getting so emotionally involved I'm afraid I'm just going to come out with something, you know, tell him I love him or ask him where it's going or whatever, and he'll freak out and then it'll be over.

Therapist: *[So-what technique.]* So what if it ended? What would that mean to you?
Jennifer: I can't even think of it. I've been so ready for a real relationship—I'm so ready to get married, I want to have children. I'm 33, and I feel like time is running out for me.
Therapist: You're hearing that biological clock ticking away.
Jennifer: I'm so afraid that he's my last chance.
Therapist: Wow, that's a lot to have riding on a relationship that you feel so uncertain about.
Jennifer: That's why I'm here; I want to relax about this.
Therapist: You want him to be *the one,* but you're hiding yourself from him.
Jennifer: I suppose that's true. If I'm going to tell him how I feel, I want the timing to be right.
Therapist: I worry that it's the caution itself that's tying you up in knots.
Jennifer: But losing him is worse.
Therapist: *[So-what technique.]* What if you lost him as a result of telling him how you feel?
Jennifer: I would kick myself! I would think that I lost him because I couldn't wait just a little while longer.
Therapist: It sounds like you're more afraid of kicking yourself than of losing him. If you didn't kick yourself and you lost him, what would that be like?
Jennifer: Uummmm. . . . I never thought of that! Well, even if I don't kick myself, I might be alone forever.
Therapist: *[So-what technique.]* What if you never meet the right man? What if?

In this session, Jennifer's therapist uses "so what?" and "what if" questions to help Jennifer face the fears that are preventing her from opening up with Brad and taking the consequences. The therapist's target is Jennifer's "I'm fragile" schema, which results in her believing that she cannot face the outcome of her conversation with Brad without being depressed and lonely. The therapist's use of the technique ultimately helped Jennifer to expand her self-awareness to include a part of herself that is goal-directed and resourceful.

6. *Work to change unrealistic partner schemas that undermine self-empowerment.* When self-empowerment is the goal, the therapist often works simultaneously with self- and partner-schemas. Individuals who imagine their partners to be more powerful are vulnerable to feeling intimidated by their partners and to blaming themselves when their partners are unhappy. Changing the partner schema relieves the unhappiness associated with the "My partner has the power" schema and also uses self-talk to help the client counteract the negative partner schema. For example, if the partner makes a disparaging remark, the client can tell him- or herself, "I know my partner

can be careless with words. Those words do not describe me." Changing the partner schema also affects the "I am a victim" self-schema indirectly. As the client learns to think differently about the partner's purported power over him or her, the client is also challenging his or her beliefs about him- or herself.

There is a risk that the client will simply reverse the victim-persecutor relationship schema and start to abuse the partner. The therapist can intervene by using the fifth persuasion technique above and letting the client know that abusive behavior is just the flip side of the same lack of self-empowerment. The therapist can encourage the client (and the partner) to see his or her reversal as a step along the way to a more long-lasting sense of self-empowerment that will allow him or her to feel sympathy for the partner's needs while simultaneously taking care of him- or herself.

7. *Acceptance training: Encourage self and partner acceptance.* Most individuals who can benefit from self-empowerment training will benefit from acceptance training. Jacobson and Christensen (1996) define acceptance as "pain plus accusation equals marital discord; pain minus accusation equals acceptance" (p. 104). In the likely event that the partners must accept aspects of one another that they don't like and that cause them pain, partners will benefit from learning how to soothe themselves in light of that pain. In this case, the therapist can combine self-soothing training with acceptance training and may find that one will not work without the other. Dis tressed partners who are trying to change undesirable personality traits in one another often behave in ways that cause more hurt. Acceptance eliminates the frustrating and usually fruitless efforts of one partner to "make the other change." It is useful when the therapist focuses acceptance training on a broad acceptance of the frailty of all human beings.

Step 4: Teach Empowered Communication Behavior

8. *The therapist models an empowered response.* For clients who have never seen an empowered response to a spouse's provocation (e.g., growing up, in prior relationships), it is useful for the therapist to demonstrate what such a response would look like. Once he or she has demonstrated the response, he or she can then work with the client to identify what he or she would have to be thinking to respond that way. Demonstrating is especially useful when a client cannot imagine another way to respond than what he or she is already doing. Demonstrating also offers a type of hypnotic suggestion, in which he or she pictures him- or herself being able to behave effectively. These kinds of suggestions can be repeated throughout self-empowerment work and function as interventions in themselves, enhancing the client's perception of him- or herself as competent to handle the partner's complaints.

9. *Notice behavior-outcome connections and use more effective self-expression and listening skills.* The empowered individual can tell his or her partner what he or she wants from the partner without putting down the partner or elaborately defending the self. This intervention is useful when partners fail to speak up because they believe they are undeserving or that their partners "should know" what they want because they've told them before (they think). Empowered communication accepts the partner's perspective and gets to the point to maximize the client's likelihood of attaining the desired outcome.

These nine self-empowerment techniques together are aimed toward helping clients overcome perceptions of themselves as fragile or victims and overcome perceptions of their partners as overwhelmingly powerful. Self-empowerment training is a schema altering process that involves a constellation of techniques that work together, flexibly combined to meet the client's needs.

Normalizing Is Not Always Appropriate

The use of cognitive interventions presumes that neither partner's behavior is abusive and is causing or could potentially cause physical or psychological harm to the other. I would not use normalization or self-empowerment cognitive strategies if either partner were afraid of the other's potential violence or if one or both partners habitually belittled, denigrated, or demeaned the other. Further, I do not normalize substance abuse, affairs, habitual lying, or other untrustworthy behavior. I also refuse to normalize stonewalling, a deliberate refusal to respond to genuine distress in the other partner that has, as its intention or its effect, the dismissing of the other's needs (Gottman, 1999). For clients in emotionally abusive relationships, I recommend Patricia Evans's (1996) book *The Verbally Abusive Relationship: How to Recognize It and How to Respond.* For helping clients cope with the aftermath of an affair, I recommend Janice Spring's (1993) *After the Affair* or Douglas Snyder, Donald Baucom, and Kristina Gordon's *Getting Past the Affair: A Program to Help You Cope, Heal, and Move On—Together or Apart* (2007).

Conclusion

Cognitive interventions play a central role in therapeutic work with intimacy dilemmas, because cognitions elicit the emotions of intimate relationships and because intimacy schemas provide "if-then" rules for behavior. Beliefs about the self, the partner, and intimate relationships are carried forward from earlier experience and shape subsequent relationships for good or ill. Intense emotional reactions to moderate provocations are signs that dysfunctional intimacy schemas may have been activated. Cognitive interventions can be used both in conjoint and individual therapy sessions and can target automatic thoughts or intimacy schemas or both. Cognitive interventions help couple partners acquire more realistic expectations of themselves and one another and help them see the connection between their own behavior and their partners' reactions. Even more, cognitive interventions help calm people's fears about the psychological risks of intimate relating and thereby open the door to more meaningful intimate relationships.

7

INTIMACY DILEMMA #1: JOY VERSUS PROTECTION FROM HURT

Joy versus Protection from Hurt

Even in the best of relationships, the possibility of a joyful and meaningful intimate encounter coexists with the risk of hurt. Intimacy Dilemma #1, joy versus protection from hurt, refers to the delicate balance that each intimate partner maintains between openness on the one hand and self-protection and concealment on the other.

When we are coping successfully with Dilemma #1, we are able to disclose when the time is right for ourselves and our partners, based on our previous experience in the relationship. Previous experience teaches us to recognize times when we are likely to get a warm, intimate response to a disclosure. If a relationship partner comes home feeling tired, preoccupied, overworked, or stressed, we may wisely postpone a discussion of delicate feelings because we are unlikely to get a sympathetic response under those conditions. Relationship partners who cope well learn to balance their desire for intimate relating with their desire to protect themselves from hurt.

Dilemma #1, joy versus protection from hurt, has three significant aspects, (1) a motivational and emotional aspect called intimacy ambivalence, (2) a behavioral aspect, which includes intimacy-distance regulation behaviors, and (3) a cognitive aspect, manifested as a stable set of beliefs and expectations for intimate relating called intimacy schemas (see Table 6.2 for a list of schemas). The most effective combination of interventions for couples struggling with Dilemma #1 targets the following: (1) ineffective attempts to regulate the ebb and flow of intimacy and distance that ultimately interfere with intimacy and (2) ways of understanding self, partner, and intimacy, ways of interpreting the significance of relationship events, that exacerbate negative emotions and decrease the pleasure partners glean from intimate relating.

This chapter addresses intimacy's core dilemma by offering a theoretical framework for understanding it, methods for assessing its presence as a relationship problem, and suggestions for helping people to cope more effectively with it. The goal of the interventions discussed in this chapter is not to help partners completely avoid a dilemma that is inherent in intimate relating. Rather, these interventions are designed to help partners repair relationship damage resulting from dysfunctional efforts to cope and to devise ways of coping that are uniquely suited to their needs and concerns.

Intimacy Ambivalence

Not everyone wants the same amount of intimacy in the same form, yet all human beings yearn for intimacy. Intimate time exists in contrast to our public lives. As we go about the business of life, at work and in our communities, we routinely protect our most vulnerable selves; we keep secrets, we hide our emotions, we assume public roles, and we maintain a cool public persona. In contrast, we drop much of our self-protective behavior in our most intimate relationships and assume that we can "be ourselves" and "put our feet up." When we are being ourselves we think, feel, say, and do things we would not when we are editing for public consumption.

The process of becoming more intimate with another is charged with fulfilled yearnings, excitement, and happiness and is one of our most powerful sources of *joie de vivre.* Because there is also the potential for hurt and disappointment, we are challenged to find the right balance between intimacy and self-protection.

The corresponding mix of emotions we feel about being intimate is called *intimacy ambivalence.* Intimacy ambivalence is our response to intimacy's approach-avoidance conflict, in which the same person or encounter simultaneously promises to fulfill our intimacy needs and positions us to be hurt. Intimacy ambivalence is built into intimate relationships. Everyone hopes for a pleasurable and validating experience in intimate relationships, and everyone has had the experience of netting something less pleasant.

Coping with Intimacy Ambivalence via Intimacy-Distance Regulation

People cope with intimacy ambivalence by regulating intimacy and distance. *Intimacy-distance regulation* refers to the processes by which the balance between intimacy and openness versus distance and self-protection is maintained in the couple relationship. Intimacy-distance regulation allows partners to sustain a level of intimacy that permits them to reap rewards and to avoid anxiety and hurt. When there is not enough intimacy, partners' satisfaction with the relationship deteriorates. If left unchecked, declining intimacy may ultimately lead to the relationship's demise (e.g., Gable, Gonzaga, & Strachman, 2006; Sprecher & Hendrick, 2004). Intimacy-distance regulation prevents the erosion of satisfaction by maintaining intimacy.

Intimacy-distance regulation is accomplished through behavioral sequences that help partners to balance their yearning for intimacy with their fear of intimacy. Intimacy-distance regulating sequences occur within a given interaction in the form of subtle (or not) "come closer" or "leave me alone" messages. Intimacy-distance regulation also refers to patterns of interactions over time by which partners signal their availability to one another. These sequences answer the questions, "How do we get close?, How do we separate?, and How do I say yes or no?"

Intimacy-distance regulation is also an individual, emotional signaling process. Most of us feel lonely, bored, or cut off when intimacy in a key relationship drops below or never reaches levels that fulfill our needs. If we haven't heard from a special person in awhile, or talked with that person at length, or received a hug or other sign of affection lately, we feel as though something is missing from our lives. Couple partners are no exception, and one or both will pursue the other when it seems that they are losing touch with the other's day-to-day thoughts and experiences. When intimacy is too high, however, we might also feel uncomfortable and anxious. When someone we don't know very well opens up and tells us about a heart-wrenching experience he or she is going through, we may feel uncomfortable because the person has created more intimacy between us than seems appropriate to the friendship (Prager, 1995). Even when a romantic partner wants to linger in bed when we are ready to get up, or wants to talk about love when we think that is "mushy," we may crack a joke to break the mood and get to less anxiety-provoking ground. In this way, we readjust the level of intimacy to match our intimacy needs of the moment. In couple relationships, exchanges that either increase or decrease the level of interaction intimacy become patterned as each partner adjusts interactional intimacy in response to his or her own intimacy needs in his or her own characteristic way, while also adjusting to the partner's behavior. These intimacy-distance regulation patterns determine a couple's level of relational intimacy.

Intimacy Homeostasis

The family systems concept of homeostasis (Jackson, 1957) is central to understanding intimacy-distance regulation in couple relationships. Jackson introduced the concept of "family homeostasis" to denote the observation that "the continuous interplay of dynamic forces within the family tends towards the maintenance of certain forms of equilibrium among family members" (Ferreira, 1963, p. 457). *Intimacy homeostasis* refers to the day-to-day adjustments couples make to keep variability in relational intimacy centered on a golden mean. The golden mean is that level of intimacy that permits the most relationship stability by maintaining the intimacy status quo in a relationship. The relationship can destabilize when intimacy is too high and creates more anxiety than can be easily managed. Defensive behavior may be overused in efforts to defend against perceived vulnerability. Relationships also destabilize when intimacy is too low and partners feel lonely and disconnected. The relationship between intimacy homeostasis and intimacy-distance regulation is shown in Figure 7.1.

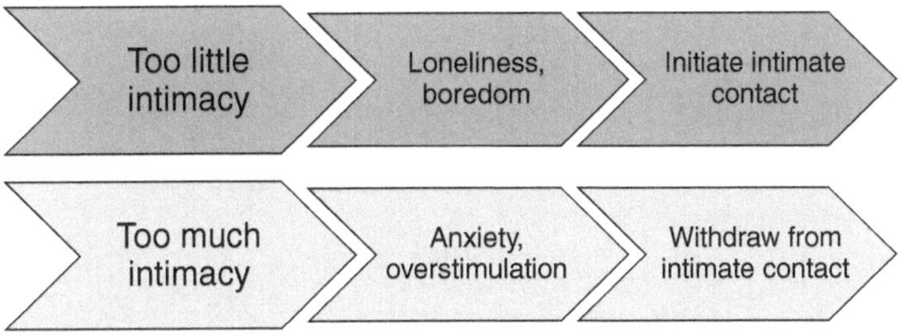

Figure 7.1 Individual intimacy-distance regulation

The pursuer-distancer pattern first observed by Boszormenyi-Nagy and Spark (1973) is a good example of intimacy-distance regulation. Partners caught in the pursuer-distancer pattern have achieved an intimacy homeostasis at a high price. Pursuing and distancing partners are each stuck in one role—either seeking more intimacy or seeking more separateness—and each has lost her perspective on the value of the other's role. Murray Bowen (1960) called couples who were stuck in opposite positions on important issues "polarized."

Intimacy-distance regulating interactions in intimate relationships maintain a continuous balance around the golden mean, although the pattern itself may not be fully apparent or rewarding to the partners. The golden mean for each couple will be different and can change over time.

Intimacy-Distance Regulation Requires Interpersonal Skill

How smoothly people regulate intimacy affects the overall level of relational intimacy by (1) determining how often and under what circumstances the couple will be intimate and (2) associating predictable consequences with intimate overtures or with a partner's need to postpone intimacy. Positive consequences will encourage people to engage in more intimate interactions whereas negative consequences will function to discourage people from intimate relating. Optimally, the skillfulness with which people initiate or refuse intimate overtures work together to keep the intimacy doors open while simultaneously protecting each partner's vulnerabilities.

Intimacy-distance regulation requires partners to be skillful in several communication areas: (1) initiating intimacy, (2) accepting or reciprocating partner initiatives, (3) declining partner initiatives, (4) withdrawing from intimate interactions, and (5) responding to a partner's declining or withdrawing—see Figure 7.2.

Initiating intimacy and reciprocating. When one partner initiates intimacy, the other can either reciprocate or decline. Partners take the initiative by

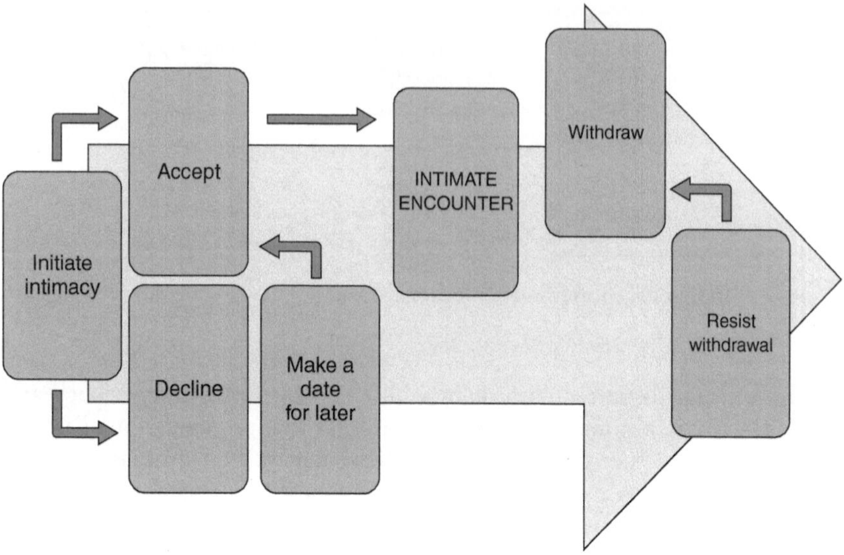

Figure 7.2 Intimacy-distance regulation process

signaling their availability for an intimate interaction. Skillful initiation of intimate interaction is inviting and elicits an expectation in the partner that the interaction will be rewarding. When reciprocating, the partner's behavior signals availability for intimacy using behaviors that are either parallel (e.g., one winks and the other winks back) or complementary (e.g., one starts talking and the other listens).

Declining intimacy. Declining intimacy includes any communication that conveys unavailability or lack of desire for intimate relating. Skillful declining can be quite simple, such as "I have a headache" or "I have a deadline" with no negative emotional consequences. Any implied rejection in declining intimacy can be softened either by verbal reassurances or by postponement, such as "you do look sexy, though" or "how about tomorrow night?" although postponement is only positive if there is a history of follow-through. A skillful response is matter-of-fact, leaving the door open for a later intimate interaction.

Withdrawing from an intimate interaction. Once engaged in intimate interaction, partners must at some time withdraw and either cease interacting or shift to another interaction mode. As an intimate interaction winds down, one partner will initiate withdrawal with either a verbal statement or a behavioral shift such as getting up out of bed or turning on the television, that results in the partners moving from an intimate interaction into mutual time alone or another type of interaction such as planning the day. In response, partners can either comply with or resist the other's withdrawal. In the first case, a partner might shift to his or her own individual activity or, in the second case, say, "Oh honey stay and talk a little longer." In the absence of significant intimacy problems in the relationship, withdrawal and compliance are unremarkable and even invisible to the partners.

Intimacy Schemas and Dilemma #1

Our willingness to risk hurt by being intimate along with our desire to avoid or escape hurt are due in part to our intimacy schemas. Table 7.1 shows the intimacy schemas most likely to contribute to problems with Dilemma #1. These schemas are problematic because they intensify affect associated with the negative pole of intimacy ambivalence and motivate avoidance, distancing, or withholding of self. When overused, these behaviors represent intimacy-sabotaging responses to the dilemma.

Summary

Because intimacy is rewarding and also entails risk, couple partners balance intimacy and its risks with defensive, self-protective behavior. Intimacy-distance regulation behavior, which results in couples moving in and out of intimate contact, ensures that a delicate homeostatic balance is maintained in the relationship. Although intimacy-distance regulation requires interpersonal skill on the part of the partners, many couples find ways to regulate intimacy without compromising relationship quality.

Intimacy ambivalence, intimacy-distance regulation behavior, and intimacy schemas together create each couple's intimacy homeostasis and their distinct response to Dilemma #1, joy versus protection from hurt (see Figure 7.3). Dilemma #1 begins when individuals bring ambivalence about intimacy with them into their relationships, yearning to move closer to their partners and yet holding back because they are averse to taking the risk of being hurt. Along with ambivalence, they bring behavioral habits that help to defend their vulnerable selves against hurt.

When they establish a relationship, the two partners together make behavioral adjustments until they stabilize an interaction pattern that balances, for each of them, opportunities for intimacy with sufficient autonomy, privacy, and separateness. Intimacy schemas function as maps or blueprints that guide their behavior and intensify or soothe their emotional reactions to relationship events (Reis & Patrick, 1996). The next section addresses dysfunctional patterns of coping with Dilemma #1.

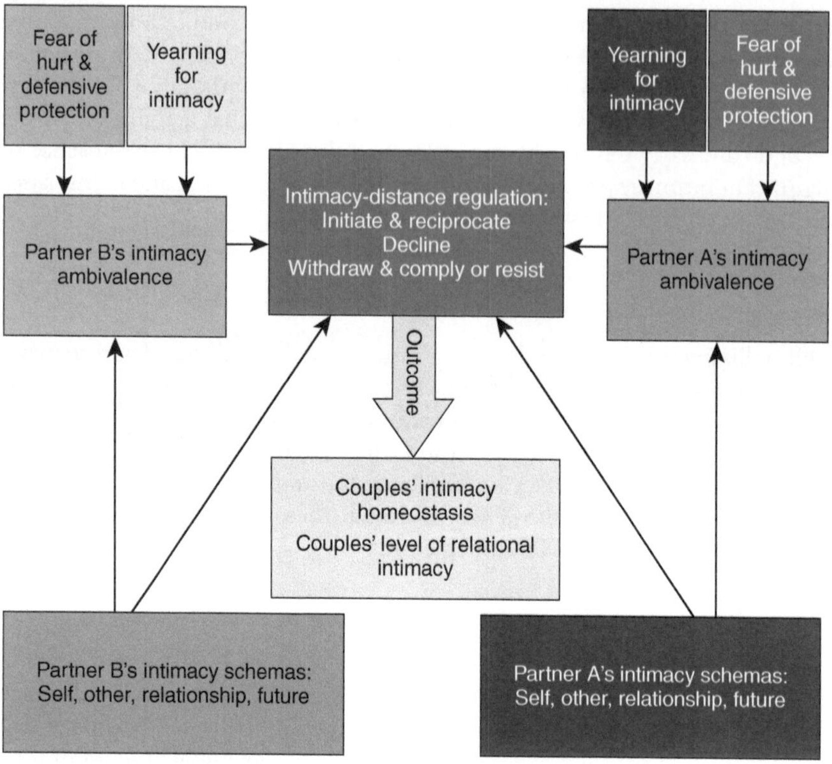

Figure 7.3 Intimacy-distance regulation process

Dysfunctional Coping with Dilemma #1

Problems with Intimacy Dilemma #1 are best understood as dysfunctional intimacy-distance regulation patterns that stem from unregulated negative emotions associated with negative intimacy schemas. Three dysfunctional patterns are (1) intimacy avoidance, (2) intimacy sabotage, and (3) resentful compliance with partner requests. Table 7.1 presents common examples of these three problematic intimacy-distance regulation patterns, along with possible treatment goals and strategies for each.

Intimacy avoidance is a common strategy for protecting the self from hurt in a close relationship. However, couple partners who overprotect their feelings risk sacrificing the lifeblood of their relationship. In contrast, healthy coping means regulating intimacy and distance in our relationships, so that we achieve a dynamic balance between the two. Table 7.1 lists five common types of intimacy avoidance: (1) concealing the self, (2) failing to initiate intimate contact or passively waiting for the partner, (3) sex avoidance or

Table 7.1 Intimacy schemas associated with problematic intimacy-distance regulation behavior

Intimacy-Distance Regulation Pattern	*Associated Schemas and Automatic Thoughts*
Common Intimacy-Avoidant Behaviors *Conceals self	*Schema: I am unlovable.* Automatic thoughts: *My partner will reject or disapprove of my true self. *If I air these thoughts (feelings, needs), it will lead to the demise of the relationship. *My partner does (will) not like my body. *I can't ask for XX; my needs will overwhelm my partner. *Schema: Intimacy should be easy.* Automatic thoughts: *Talking about things on my mind only makes them worse. *If I can't see a benefit to me, then I don't need to share it with my partner.
*Fail to initiate intimate contact; grow apart	*Schema: Intimacy should be easy.* Automatic thought: *Denial: Relationship is fine (until they realize they're not in love).
*Passive, waits for partner to act	*Schema: Partner is indifferent.* Automatic thoughts: *I want attention/talking/sex with my partner, but I expect to be rejected. *I don't know what to do or say, and he or she will laugh at me. *I have no desire for sex/closeness with my partner because my partner does not care about me. *He or she says/does (or doesn't do) that because he or she doesn't care about me. (I don't want to be hurt, so I'll distance myself.)

(*Continued*)

Table 7.1 (Continued)

Intimacy-Distance Regulation Pattern	*Associated Schemas and Automatic Thoughts*
*Sex avoidance; restricted sexual repertoire	*Schema: I am fragile.* Automatic thoughts: *I look foolish if I am sexually uninhibited. *My partner has hurt me before; I need to avoid getting hurt again. *It is better to play it safe and save face than to risk humiliating rejection or exposure. *Because intimacy opens me up to my own pain, guilt, or anger, I must protect myself from upset by avoiding intimacy. *Talking about that would embarrass me, make me feel weak, or appear weak to my partner. *I must appear cool and in control at all times, or I will be irreparably humiliated.
*Fails to attend to partner's sexual preferences and pleasures	*Schema: Pleasure-seeking is shameful.* Automatic thoughts: *The purpose of marriage is to care for children. Couple intimacy (or sexuality) has to come second. *Sex is the last priority, after duty and responsibility.
*Distance in order to maintain gender roles	*Schema: Men and women must be different.* Automatic thoughts: *I must, at all costs, live up to the standard of strong, independent manhood. *What he or she does won't affect me because I'm independent.
Distance with Negative Behavior: Common Behaviors	*Schema: Intimacy should be easy.* Automatic thought: *I push my spouse to behave in certain ways because I want to feel the way I used to feel. If we don't, we should end the relationship and get a divorce.

*Partners take on roles of criticizer and passive resister	*Schema: Partner has the power.* Automatic thought: *I push my partner to do things because I'm not strong/competent enough to do them myself. *Schema: Things should always go right.* Automatic thought: *He or she must see the error of his or her ways and comply or something terrible will happen. (We'll break up, I'll never be happy or fulfilled.)
*Competitive, combative behavior pervades intimacy-distance regulation	*Schema: I am fragile.* Automatic thought: *If I can make my partner angry with me, I'm off the hook for more intimacy which is difficult or impossible for me to deliver.
*Initiation—clumsy, indirect, ineffective, confusing	*Schema: I am fragile.* Automatic thought: *I can't bear to be rejected. *Schema: Intimacy should be easy.* Automatic thoughts: *If I have to initiate or if my partner doesn't seek me out, it doesn't count or mean anything. *If I ask, he or she will only do it because I asked him or her to.
*Reciprocation—partners fail to reciprocate effectively, rush in to solve each other's problems	*Schema: I am Mr. or Ms. Fix-It.* Automatic thought: *I can't bear the way he or she solves problems; he or she really should do it my way.

(*Continued*)

Table 7.1 (Continued)

Intimacy-Distance Regulation Pattern	*Associated Schemas and Automatic Thoughts*
*Reciprocation—partners respond punitively to initiation, and there's no reinforcement for initiating	*Schema: Intimacy should be easy.* Automatic thought: *I should be able to say what I want (and do anything I want) in my relationship. *Schema: Partner is indifferent.* Automatic thoughts: *He or she doesn't care, so I can't hurt him or her that badly. *He or she doesn't care, so I have to really up the ante (threaten to leave, take the kids, etc.) in order to get his or her attention.
*Declining—partner declines too often or declines as if rejecting *Withdrawing—withdraws quickly or without sensitivity	*Schema: Intimacy should be easy.* Automatic thoughts: *I should be able to say what I want (and do anything I want) in the context of this relationship. *He or she should know I love him or her without my having to say it every other day.
*Resisting withdrawal—coercive, guilt-inducing, or accusatory	*Schema: Partner has the power.* Automatic thoughts: *If he or she loved me/desired me/enjoyed my company, he or she would stay. *My partner withholds from me because he or she doesn't really love or care about me.

	Schema: Mr. or Ms. Fix-It.
*Initiate, invite through guilt induction, blame, and accusations that partner doesn't do enough	*Schema: Things have to go right.* Automatic thoughts: *I must make my partner behave correctly, so that I can feel how I'm supposed to feel. *Otherwise, I will not be happy in this relationship any more. *I can change my partner so that he or she will be better able to meet my needs. *If my partner sees the error of his or her ways, he or she will make more time for me (leave me alone). *Marriage in the movies and on television is an accurate reflection of marriage in real life. *If my partner/relationship can be improved, then improvement must be sought.
*Use partner disclosures to attack self of the partner (no holds barred)	*Schema: I am a victim.* Automatic thoughts: *He or she's taken advantage of me; he or she could do better but refuses. *For hurting me, you deserve to be punished. I want you to hurt like I've hurt, then maybe you won't be tempted to hurt me again like that.
*Fails to fulfill responsibilities; "forgets"	*Schema: I am fragile.* Automatic thoughts: *My partner shouldn't expect too much of me. *My partner should take care of me.
Resentful Compliant Behavior *Comply with partner request or desire but withhold pleasant mood, agreeableness, or affectionate expression	*Schema: I am fragile.* Automatic thoughts: *If I say no, we'll fight or he or she will hold a grudge and punish me later. *He or she will say I'm a bad husband or wife for not doing this for him or her, and he or she will be correct. *I must sacrifice myself to stay married and avoid conflict.

restricted sexual repertoire, (4) failing to attend to partner's sexual preferences, and (5) distancing in order to maintain gender roles.

When viewed from the outside, intimacy avoidance may seem to make little sense. Therapists likely see a loving spouse who wants access to his or her partner's inner life. They see the anguish and loneliness that the complaining partner feels as a result of being left out of the other partner's world. It is easy to side with the partner who is complaining about lack of intimacy.

The therapist should avoid this pitfall if possible. Instead, therapists should learn what is motivating intimacy avoidance from the client's perspective. This means finding out what the client thinks might happen, or what it might mean, if he or she were to be more expressive and forthcoming in the relationship. If the client has no desire for more intimacy, the therapist should discover what it is in the client or the relationship that yields this outcome. These queries can reveal avoidant partners' intimacy schemas or negative behavior in lonely clients that distances their partners, creating the very condition that the lonely individual wants to avoid.

Behavioral Interventions for Low Intimacy Due to Intimacy Avoidance

Behavioral intervention goals for intimacy avoidance include (1) improving the relationship climate by increasing the positive experiences that the couple has together, (2) improving the partners' intimate communication skill in order that their "intimacy initiatives" be reciprocated more frequently, and their "intimacy declines" be less risky for the initiating partner, and (3) increasing partners' skill at recognizing the connection between their own behavior and their relationship outcomes. Interventions to address these goals are (1) increase positive behavior in both partners, through behavioral contracting or giving days, and (2) teach intimate communication skills.

Increase positive behavior through behavioral contracting. Behavioral contracting for enjoyable couple time can increase intimacy in couples whose low levels of relational intimacy stem from one or both partners' consistent avoidance of intimacy. It does so by increasing the amount of time that couples spend in enjoyable, potentially intimate activities. Increases in pleasant companionship can increase goodwill which in turn creates a favorable relationship climate within which intimacy can grow. Hannah brought Jacob into therapy because his intimacy avoidance resulted in her intimacy needs not being met. Here is how their therapist helped them to introduce couple time back into their relationship.

Therapist: A straightforward way to make your relationship more rewarding is to make a conscious effort to increase the positive experiences that the two of you have together. This means planning things to do together that will take you away from your day-to-day work and obligations and allow you to have some time just to enjoy life together.

Hannah: I've tried to get him to do things with me but haven't succeeded.

Therapist: Let's start by talking about what it was like for you before you had children. What did you do for fun?

Hannah: Well, we did a lot of drinking. And dancing. We went clubbing a lot with our friends. We had a lot of friends then.

Jacob: But after the kids came, we stopped the drinking.

Therapist: And that was a good thing.

Hannah: Yes, I have no desire to go back to that.

Therapist: What other common interests did you share? … It sounds like the things you liked to do—dancing, having sex—were pretty romantic things. Real date-night kinds of things… . Now you don't want to drink the night away any more, but what about dancing?

Jacob: I would enjoy going dancing. …

Therapist: How about this Saturday night? Are you free to go dancing?

Hannah: I think so… .

Therapist: Who wants to take responsibility for finding a good place?

Jacob: I can do that.

Therapist: Great, Jacob. You're meeting Hannah more than halfway here.

Jacob: Before we had the kids, I used to make plans for us. And before we had money problems.

Therapist: If you stay away from drinking too much, going dancing can be a reasonably economical night out… .

Therapist: Next session, I want to hear about your night dancing, what it was like to rediscover a shared interest from way back when.

Hannah and Jacob's therapist made a mini-contract with them, that they should go out dancing one night during the upcoming week and that Jacob should find them a place to go. By getting started on the planning in the therapist's office, the couple has already taken a step toward adding positive couple time back into their lives. Even if the couple does not complete the homework assignment, they can address the interfering factors with the therapist in the next session.

Teach intimate communication skills. Currently, Jacob has a tendency to avoid intimacy, and Hannah fights with him over this. Jacob's avoidance and Hannah's tendency to distance him further through her criticisms has resulted in their having conflict over intimacy and an overall level of relational intimacy that fails to meets Hannah's needs. Hannah's unhappiness in turn disturbs Jacob. The therapist's next step is to help the couple find a more constructive intimacy-distance regulating process by teaching them how to respond in a constructive way to their own needs and to their partner's intimacy initiatives or withdrawals. Partners feel empowered when they make conscious choices about how they want to respond.

Therapist: Although you may not agree on how to get there yet, I hear both of you wanting your relationship to be more rewarding, and from you especially, Hannah, I hear you wanting more closeness with Jacob. Do I have it right?

Hannah and Jacob: Yes.

Therapist: Now we can work on how to communicate in such a way that each of you makes it easier to talk and spend time comfortably with the other. Do you have an idea about that already, Jacob? What could Hannah do that would make it easier for you to talk with her?

Jacob: I talk to her if I feel like it, but I guess I don't feel like talking much. I don't want to upset her—I worry about things.

Hannah: You see the problem, though? You don't want to upset me by talking to me, but then you upset me more by shutting me out. When he gets like that, he doesn't want my company. So we're like two silent strangers living in the same house.

Jacob: I always come out of it don't I?

Hannah: Yes you do, but I have to wait forever until you do—at least that's how it seems.

Therapist: So Hannah can you summarize what you think Jacob's concerns are? Try to summarize what he said without criticizing what he said or trying to make him think something different. Just restate it.

Hannah: I know Jacob feels pressured to talk to me just because it's so important to me. He wants relief from that pressure however he can get it. And he thinks it's worse to worry me than to shut me out.

Therapist: Does she have you right there, Jacob?

Jacob: Yes. …

Therapist: What about Hannah's concern? Can you summarize that, Jacob?

Jacob: Hannah, I know you want me to talk to you more. You want to know all my thoughts, my worries, my bad dreams. It's very sweet, and I appreciate your caring, I really do. It's just that it doesn't help me, and I can see the effect on you when I do tell you things. You start getting worried, too, and then we're both worried.

Therapist: OK Jacob, can you just summarize what Hannah said and stop with just that so that she can feel understood by you?

Jacob: Right, Hannah, you want me to tell you my worries, to confide in you more. You'll feel closer to me if I do.

Hannah: You've got it.

Therapist: Hannah, let me check with you. How did this conversation affect you? What are you feeling now?

Hannah: Well, it's good. At least we're talking, Jacob. I do feel like I understand you better even if I don't agree.

Jacob: Maybe it's OK that we don't agree. I feel good about this conversation, too. You're really listening to me now.

Therapist: As soon as you stopped judging each other, you began to have a really intimate conversation. You've each shared something important about yourself and each of you has listened to the other person without criticizing and has shown that you understand by summarizing each other's points. Hannah, what I'm thinking is that it might be worthwhile to experiment with conversations like these, with your only goal being to understand each other better instead of agreeing. Experiment and see if this is enough for you to feel closer to Jacob—maybe this is a better way for you two to get close.

This therapist used the couple's presentation of their problem and their disagreement about it as the scenario within which an intimate communication opportunity could be created. She did this by encouraging each partner to summarize what the other had said and to avoid judging or criticizing it. These two skills are the hallmark of listening to difficult messages, which itself is necessary if a couple wants to turn a difficult conversation into an opportunity for intimacy. The therapist encouraged each partner to share their experience of the conversation, so that each could get direct feedback on the impact of his or her communication.

Cognitive and Affective Interventions for Intimacy Avoidance

Intimacy avoiding behaviors often stem from people's desires to manage uncomfortable emotions and are guided by intimacy-related assumptions, expectations, and standards. Behavioral interventions alone risk leaving couples with short-term gains, unless interventions with the partners' intimacy-related beliefs and emotions are also used. Cognitive intervention goals associated with Dilemma #1 problems include (1) decreasing anxiety and impulsive reactions to Dilemma #1 by helping partners to accept its inevitable presence in their relationship, (2) decreasing frustration and anger stemming from efforts to impose unrealistic relationship standards on themselves and their partners, (3) increasing intimacy by helping partners to effectively soothe their anxieties and hurt feelings, (4) help partners to distinguish the emotional impact of their own thinking processes from that of their partner's behavior, and (5) help partners to find alternative thinking patterns that allow them to enjoy intimacy with their partners more fully. Intervention choices depend on the controlling intimacy schema, as illustrated below.

Intimacy avoidance due to the belief "I am fragile." For many of us, feeling emotionally vulnerable—when we are open to being hurt by another person—is associated with anxiety. In order to avoid the uncomfortable anxiety, some people develop a lifelong habit of ignoring their emotions and are thereby able to avoid acknowledging or even detecting what they feel. They avoid or withhold intimacy because it threatens to refocus their attention on anxiety-arousing aspects of themselves that they have worked hard to avoid. Because avoiding intimacy allows them to avoid their own negative thoughts and feelings about themselves, they are negatively reinforced for their intimacy avoidance, and their pattern becomes self-sustaining. The person who avoids intimacy in order to avoid feeling anxious often endorses the intimacy schema, "I am fragile," which is expressed in their automatic thought that they "can't stand" the anxiety that opening up might reveal.

Intervention: Identify the behavior-outcome connection. Helping the client to identify the consequences of his or her intimacy avoidance can be fruitful. However, in order to help the client have success with this approach, the therapist should first assist the client in identifying the reasons for the avoidance and take a sympathetic attitude toward them. People often avoid for very good reasons. If the therapist mistakenly joins the other partner in pressuring the avoiding spouse to move toward more intimacy, the therapist will not only damage the therapeutic alliance with that partner but also exacerbate the avoidance, because the avoiding spouse will feel misunderstood. Further, although people who habitually avoid intimacy may express a willingness to open up more in order to make their partners happy, it is even more likely that they will do so if they see a clear connection between their own distress in the relationship and their avoidant behavior.

Intervention: Self-empowerment training. Self-empowerment training addresses intimacy avoidance that is motivated by a lack of confidence in the self to take emotional risks and weather the consequences. Kerry's therapeutic goal was to actively experience an alternative, more positive sexual self-schema. Her automatic thoughts included, "I feel/look stupid when I'm having sex," "I feel exposed when we have sex," and "I'm not a sexual person." Kerry's avoidance suggests that she believes she is too fragile to tolerate the anxiety of trying new sexual activities with Rich.

Self-empowerment training for Kerry involved taking ownership of her own sexuality. Kerry treated her sexuality as a commodity that she gave out when she was in the mood. Kerry did not think of her sexuality as for herself, capable of giving her pleasure. "It's fine once we get started, but it's hard for me to get started," was how she described her sexual experience.

When her therapist suggested to her that she begin thinking of her sexuality as her own gift to herself, she was pleased with the idea. They worked together to redefine the word "sexy" in reference to Kerry's self-image. Instead of thinking of "sexy" as wearing too-tight dresses and heavy makeup ("does sexy have to mean floozy?"), she focused on wearing clothing with a flattering fit, soft, sensuous fabrics, and subtle makeup. She began experimenting with her hairstyle. Each day when she walked to work from the parking lot, she made a point of holding her posture erect and enjoying the breeze in her hair. She made appointments for manicures. Kerry experimented with creating an internal image of a strong and sexy woman. She and her therapist discussed cultural icons that fit the description (e.g., Sigourney Weaver in the classic movie, *Alien*). She called up an image of the strong, sexy woman at least once a day to reinforce her new self-schema. The "strong, sexy" image was incompatible with her "I am fragile" schema and helped her become more assertive with Rich about how they could make their sexual relationship more fulfilling for her.

Intimacy Avoidance and Negative Partner Schemas: "My Partner Is Indifferent"

Partner schemas that reflect unrealistically negative views of the partner are as problematic as are unrealistically negative self-schemas. Negative interpretations of the partner's behavior or intentions often provoke more emotional overreactions than ordinary, day-to-day irritating behavior might seem to warrant. Dorothy and Alvin were growing apart because Alvin's inconsiderate behavior (untidiness) activated a negative partner schema for Dorothy, "My partner is indifferent." Alvin forgets where he puts things, forgets the errands she asks him to do, and loses track of hours that have passed while he reads. Via the activation of Dorothy's belief that "My partner is indifferent," Alvin's behavior elicits overblown, lingering anger, and hurt in her. When Dorothy confronts

Alvin, her verbalizations reveal her automatic thoughts: She tells him that he is a selfish person who does not care about nurturing, loving, or supporting her. The impact on their relational intimacy is clear. Dorothy distances herself from Alvin sexually and emotionally because she feels used by him, consistent with her belief that he really doesn't care about her. In their first treatment session, Dorothy told Alvin what she most wanted him to change, and he contracted with her for some specific changes.

Intervention: Self-empowerment training. Dorothy needed to perceive herself as more empowered to manage the intensely negative emotions that Alvin's behavior elicited in her. In Dorothy's case, avoiding the activation of intense negative emotion in response to Alvin's "selfishness" was key to helping her maintain a higher level of relational intimacy with Alvin.

In the example below, Dorothy and Alvin's therapist worked with Dorothy to help her to feel more empowered. For Dorothy, this meant taking some of her focus off of Alvin and the changes that he was making and paying more attention to what she needed to do for herself to maintain contentment in her life with Alvin.

Step 1: Persuade Dorothy that self-empowerment will improve her quality of life. The first step for the therapist is to persuade Dorothy that working on her own self-empowerment does not mean that she is letting Alvin off of the hook for the changes he has promised to make. Dorothy and Alvin's therapist uses persuasion #1 from Chapter 6, which says, "While your partner is making changes, this will help you feel less upset in response to his or her behavior."

Step 2: Work to change unrealistic intimacy schemas that undermine self-empowerment. Because Dorothy was so focused on Alvin and whether he loved her or not, it made sense to focus the self-empowerment training on Dorothy's schema, "My partner is indifferent." The therapist works conjointly in this session with Dorothy and Alvin with the goal of helping Dorothy to think differently about the problem.

Therapist:	Let's start with the incident this week—we've talked about what Alvin did that upset you. Now let's look at why you think he did that.
Dorothy:	It's because he doesn't think about me or my needs—all he thinks about is what he wants to do. So I ask him to do something and four hours later he's completely forgotten.
Therapist:	What has led you to think that he forgets for that reason?

Dorothy: He forgets all the time.

Therapist: Is it primarily what you ask him to do that he forgets? Does he remember everything else? … Let's look at the evidence for your assumption that Alvin forgets what you ask him to do because he doesn't care about you. What about other situations—those that don't involve you—does Alvin forget other things he has to do?

Dorothy: There are those, it's true. Like when he wanted the shelving put up in the garage … when the guy showed up, no Alvin! Because he'd forgotten they were meeting that day.

Therapist: So what if you asked Alvin if he's kind of like the absentminded professor whose head is so full that a few things spill out!

Alvin: I've been accused of that! There's something to that; I can't deny it.

Therapist: Were you forgetful before you met Dorothy?

Alvin: Much worse than now! Being accountable to Dorothy and the kids has cleaned up my act.

Dorothy (laughing): I'd hate to have seen you before.

Alvin: I think you would've, I agree! … *(Dorothy asks Alvin about his forgetfulness).*

Therapist: Dorothy, let's go back to your interpretation about why Alvin forgets what you tell him sometimes. Does checking this out with Alvin offer you a believable explanation for why he's forgetful?

Dorothy: Well maybe you're just forgetful, Al. It's just you!

Therapist: So let me check with you, Dorothy—are you still wondering if Al forgets things because he doesn't care about you?

Dorothy: I'm wondering if I really thought that or just said it because I thought he'd be more diligent if I did … it doesn't make a lot of sense now.

When the opportunity presented itself for Alvin to acknowledge his forgetfulness without having to explain why it didn't indicate any lack of caring on his part, he jumped in and acknowledged it. Once Dorothy was able to see that Al was even forgetful about things that meant a lot to him—such as the garage shelving—she was able to reevaluate her hypothesis that he only forgot things that were important to her because he didn't care about her.

Dorothy also learned from this experience that she had more control over how upset she felt than she had previously believed. By changing her interpretation of Alvin's behavior, she enabled herself to feel secure about Alvin's love even while deploring his forgetful habits. Dorothy discovered that she was happier when her "Partner is indifferent" schema was not being activated so frequently and when she was not so distant with Al as a consequence.

Intervention: Acceptance training. Acceptance training often works by helping partners to blame less and understand their partners as "complete packages" more. It was helpful to Dorothy to realize that Al's forgetfulness did not stem from a lack of caring about her needs, but Dorothy was still left with the reality of living with a forgetful husband. Through acceptance training, Dorothy could learn additional strategies that would help her accept and remain calm when confronted with certain undesirable aspects of Alvin's behavior. Acceptance training could also help Alvin accept that Dorothy's need for a partner who shoulders some of the household burden was part of who she was. Alvin would have more intimacy and less frequent arguments with Dorothy if he accepted that her tolerance for disorder was not ever likely to be the same as his. Acceptance training for Alvin would focus on his accepting that he had some responsibility for maintaining their home at a level with which she could remain content. Alvin's willingness to make a behavior contract with Dorothy is the first step.

In an individual session with Dorothy, which allowed the therapist to focus completely on her thinking processes, the therapist worked with her on identifying and challenging her automatic thoughts about Alvin that kept her from accepting him as he was and wanting to be close to him. The therapist began with a capsule summary that reestablished the connection between the schema modification work she had done in the last session with Alvin and their agenda for this individual session. She then proceeded with acceptance training.

Therapist: We're working under the assumption that a lot of the distance between you and Al is due to how you interpret what Alvin does as well as what he actually does. Because thinking itself can elicit strong negative emotions, this intervention teaches you how to work on your way of thinking about Alvin so that you can be more realistic and more matter-of-fact about what he does or doesn't do. You start this process by "catching" your automatic negative thoughts. …

Dorothy: I still have a problem with getting Al to do his share around the house. There's no way I'm going to happily do it all, so what do I do about that?

Therapist: Once you get past all the automatic negative thinking that makes you feel so awful, you are in a better position to think about solving that problem. What have you tried so far?

Dorothy: I've tried showing him how unhappy he makes me. Sometimes I even stay unhappy just so he'll see how bad he makes me feel.

Therapist: That's when you two start getting distant from each other, right? When you stop talking or having sex?

Dorothy: True. That makes me feel as bad as I make him feel, maybe even worse.

Therapist: OK, it sounds like chilling Alvin out until he shapes up doesn't work. So let's work together to think of some more ways to manage that will work for you. Now that you don't have to worry about how he feels about you whenever he's forgetful, you're freed up to brainstorm about how to respond to his forgetfulness. …

Both Alvin and Dorothy agreed that Alvin could be more prompt and reliable when it came to honoring his commitments to pitch in around the house. Neither liked the times when Dorothy was distant and cold to Alvin. This agreement over the causes of their problems was presented to them as a strength that would help them do well in therapy. Alvin and Dorothy's dual plan of action was therefore: (1) Alvin would work on his contract to change the habits that were most upsetting to Dorothy and (2) Dorothy would work on her interpretations of Alvin's forgetfulness in order that she feel less upset, and, in turn, would be less inclined to put distance between Alvin and her. The second goal was accomplished via the therapist's teaching Dorothy how to generate and use realistic alternative interpretations of Alvin's behavior as a way of helping her to accept Alvin for the person that he was, problem solving to get her needs met with Alvin, and ultimately, helping her to remain open to experiences of intimacy with Alvin while still demanding that he improve his record of unreliability.

Summary

Intimacy avoidance is elicited and sustained via intimacy schemas. Partners can be inhibited because of their belief that their private selves are unlovable and will be rejected. Perhaps they have concluded that their partners don't care about them because at times in the past, their partners' responses have been insensitive. People may also censor themselves if they think of themselves as emotionally fragile and unable to handle their emotional reactions to rejection. Others may protect themselves from guilty feelings associated with seeing their partner upset with the content of their disclosures.

Treatment for couples complaining of intimacy avoidance aims to improve the climate in the relationship by increasing positive behaviors. It especially targets thinking patterns that are connected to intense or prolonged negative emotional states. As avoidance is frequently aimed at preventing or neutralizing negative emotions, the therapist works with the client to identify the emotions being avoided and then helps the client evaluate and change thinking patterns and beliefs that contribute to the avoidance.

Distancing with Negative Behavior

Why would someone who wants more intimacy in his or her relationship seek it out with recriminations and guilt inductions, trying to shame the partner into spending more time with him or her? Why would someone look forward to seeing his or her partner all day only to confront the partner with criticisms as soon as he or she said hello? These behaviors may well represent intimacy ambivalence affecting behavior, working outside the person's awareness but nevertheless motivating a closeness-distance dance. The following section presents interventions for clients who seem to sabotage their own efforts to make intimate contact with their partners. Instead of offering appealing intimacy initiatives, these individuals seem to push their partners away at the very moments that they most desire intimate contact. This section addresses several common aversive behavior patterns that can create distance. These aversive patterns include (1) intimacy sabotage via criticism and combative behavior, (2) negative, distancing intimacy initiation, reciprocation, declining, or withdrawing, (3) sabotaging intimacy through laziness, and (4) distancing via resentful compliance with partner requests.

Although these behavior patterns are not always associated with intimacy avoidance via negative behavior, they frequently have this effect. In the context of intimacy-related problems, such as lack of intimacy, conflict over intimacy, or lost love, the therapist should explore the intimacy-regulating function of negative, relationship-sabotaging behavior.

Clients who go on the attack when their needs are not met are usually averse to appearing vulnerable. They may resemble some of their avoidant counterparts described above in the convictions that they hold about the shamefulness of emotional vulnerability and the importance of avoiding it and appearing tough at all costs. The therapist is advised, as before, to identify the thinking patterns that lead to the avoidance of up-front, honest, and vulnerable communication about wants and needs and its replacement with attacks on the partner.

Intimacy Sabotage through Criticism and Combative Behavior: Example 1

Couples who present to their therapist with complaints of repetitive, irresolvable conflict may be sabotaging intimacy with that conflict. Conversely, the negative behavior that perpetuates the irresolvable nature of the conflict may be serving to maintain intimacy homeostasis at a safe (i.e., nonanxiety provoking) level for one or both partners. The common wisdom has been that escalating cycles of negative communication poison the climate in the relationship for intimate contact. Therapists should also check on the possibility that the conflict, instead of sabotaging a desired state of relational intimacy, serves one or both partners as a maladaptive, intimacy-distance regulation process.

Partners can sabotage opportunities for intimacy by being critical, demanding, or argumentative. This behavior can be defensive, protecting an individual with a vulnerable self-image from exposing that vulnerability. By keeping the partner at more than arm's length, these behaviors insure that the partner will not get close enough to see the whole self.

Intervention: Evaluate automatic thoughts. It is sometimes the case that a client who learns how to avoid applying a dysfunctional intimacy schema in one situation finds it being activated in another. This was the case for Dorothy from the example above. In the following incident, Dorothy concluded that she became unreasonably angry with Alvin over a different issue—Alvin had called to say he would be late getting home when the two of them had planned an outing to an art fair. Although this was not a case of Alvin being inconsiderate or forgetful, Dorothy's "Alvin is indifferent" schema generated a familiar string of automatic thoughts.

Dorothy withdrew from Alvin as she had in the past but, before doing so, accused him of not being eager to see her and not making an effort for the sake of their relationship (i.e., she engaged in intimacy-sabotaging behavior right before they went on an outing). Needless to say, they did not have much fun at the fair.

Dorothy's therapist first helped her to evaluate her automatic thoughts as she had learned to do with Alvin's forgetfulness. She was able to come up with believable alternative interpretations of Alvin's being late that reduced the intensity of her negative emotions. It was also important to help Dorothy and Alvin recover from this backsliding by assuring them that backsliding is a normal part of change, and that eventually, the old "partner is indifferent" schema would be aroused less and less frequently.

Intimacy Sabotage via Criticism and Combative Behavior: Example 2

Often, behavioral changes begun early in therapy come readily because people are motivated to reduce the painful fighting scenes and please the partner. The partners may even have two or three weeks of honeymoon following their first two or three sessions of therapy while they enjoy the relief and feel hopeful again. However, when one or both partners are stuck in their efforts to cope with Intimacy Dilemma #1, the intimacy ambivalence is likely to express itself in some other way. The advantage of dealing with some of the negative behavior first is that Dilemma #1 then often emerges in more recognizable form and can be addressed directly.

One wife (Michelle) said, after a few sessions of couple therapy, "You know, now we're not fighting as much, and yet we're still not connected. We play with the kids, we visit our families, we have fun, but we're not connected. It's like we're friendly roommates who occasionally have sex. I don't feel close to him."

Intervention: Normalize intimacy ambivalence. Repetitive conflict and criticism of the partner usually function as an intimacy-distance regulating process that serves its function outside of the awareness of the partner who engages in it. Michelle and Josh had been engaging in fruitless arguments when they came into therapy, which had distracted Michelle from the lack of intimacy in their relationship. Now that they were fighting less, Josh and Michelle wanted to address their lack of intimacy. Their therapist thought that a good first step would be to help them explore and thereby understand more deeply their intimacy ambivalence.

Josh and Michelle's therapist suspected that the couple fought in order to maintain a connection that was difficult for them to attain with positive behavior. In order to get more comfortable with moving in and out of intimate contact, the couple needed to perceive the intimacy-distance regulation process as a normal part of couple relationships. Often, couples who fight do so because they cannot tolerate constant intimacy and do not have the skills for a friendly moving apart.

To help couples explore their feelings about intimate contact, the therapist can ask questions such as, "what encourages intimacy between the two of you? What discourages it? (Are these things in the external environment or between the two of you?) What kinds of feelings do you notice as you spend leisure time together? Do you relax and have fun? Do you get bored, restless, anxious? Do you think about other things, such as work or children? When your partner initiates, when you sit down to talk, when you approach having sex, what is your reaction? Can you identify the thoughts connected to that feeling? As you think about the situation, what is your desired outcome? What would be the best way for these kinds of interactions to end? These questions increase a couple's awareness of the intimacy-distance regulation process and the various ways that discomfort with intimacy might express itself (i.e., distracting oneself, feeling bored, and so forth).

Michelle recognized that her tendency to find fault with Josh was self-protective; it created the safe distance with him that she had maintained in previous relationships by not fully loving the men in her life. Michelle's therapist helped her to see the connection between her ambivalence about being intimate with Josh, her critical behavior, and her feelings of irritation. Once Michelle was aware of her intimacy ambivalence, she was open to finding more constructive ways of dealing with her ambivalence than being irritable and critical with Josh.

Negative Behavior in Intimacy-Distance Regulation

Some couples cannot comfortably move in and out of intimate contact. For a myriad of reasons, they either fail to initiate intimacy effectively or have problems when one or the other declines or withdraws from contact. Some relationship partners feel hurt every time they ask and the other says "no," even when "no" is said nicely and even when they know they ask for a lot. People who are in relationships with overly sensitive partners, who predictably get upset about hearing "no" or "not now," may give up on direct, straightforward communication and instead find a hundred reasons to fight. The fighting creates distance and allows them to push apart periodically, albeit in a most painful and destructive manner. Their fighting has become a way of distancing with negative behavior. These couples benefit from learning alternative intimacy-distance regulation strategies and from interventions that help them feel more comfortable with inevitable, periodic rejections.

Problems with intimacy initiation. Frustrated partners are at risk for introducing aversive behavior into their intimate overtures. Early in intimate relationships, we seek intimate contact with appealing, attractive behavior and have high hopes of reciprocation (Jacobson & Christensen, 1996). Eventually, however, we receive a negative response from our partners; we are rejected. Depending upon how hurt and sensitive we are, we may react to the other's rejection with unpleasant behavior. Further, each partner's less agreeable side becomes apparent under stress, fatigue, or emotional neediness. Thus we confront the first choice point of the dilemma: to maintain the attractive, appealing behavior in order to persuade the other to take a moment for "couple time," to express anger or disappointment, or to withdraw in the face of rejection.

Sometimes partners lack skills for inviting their partner in a pleasing way. Many partners have defensive responses embedded within their initiations (e.g., "how's that headache tonight?" or "how much work do you have to do this evening?" or even, "will you once again spend all your time with your photography and act as though I'm not even here?"). Defensive, self-protective behavior sometimes results in a self-fulfilling prophecy and decreases the likelihood that partners will reciprocate. Further, if initiations are too oblique, partners increase the risk that the other will fail to read their minds. Indirect, self-protective initiatives can become self-fulfilling prophecies when the rejection they were supposed to prevent becomes a reality and, eventually, an expectation. Rejections from the partner can appear to affirm our worst fears (e.g., "I knew he or she wouldn't want to") and invite reactive, impulsive responses, such as, "I knew you would say 'no' before I even asked, so why do I bother?" It is not difficult to imagine couples confronting the irony that their behavior invites rejection just at the moment that they feel most vulnerable.

One form of distancing through negative behavior begins when anger about frustrated intimacy needs is outside of awareness, and intimacy initiation reveals both the desire for intimacy and the anger toward the partner. In this case, combative behavior expresses frustration and the desire for intimacy in the same breath. If clients use aversive behavior in conjunction with intimacy initiation often enough, they condition their partners to associate intimacy initiation and negative interaction. Here are some examples of combative intimacy initiation that ironically arise from unmet needs for intimacy:

> "Have you noticed we haven't had sex in a month?"
> "There you are again, doing your couch potato number in front of the TV."
> "Why don't you lose some weight? Then maybe I'd feel attracted to you again."

At other times, negative behavior seems to come out of a lack of awareness on an individual's part as to the impact of her negativity on her partner, as in this example:

> "Surprise! I brought you something!"
> "I wish you wouldn't buy me things, dear. Remember last time you bought that purple scarf, and I had to take it back? You know purple is my worst color. It's better if you just give me the money, and I buy something myself."

The longer intimacy needs go unmet and the more frustrated and angry people become, the more tempted they are to escalate their efforts to persuade the other with negative, coercive, or critical communication. In more severely distressed relationships, combative intimacy initiatives often alternate with hopeless withdrawal (or partners alternate taking one or the other of these roles).

Other problems with intimacy engagement can occur when one or both partners attempt to initiate without seeming to do so. Sometimes, the belief guiding this behavior is that engagement is not worth anything unless the partner initiates it ("how else do I know that he really wants to be with me?"). With especially sensitive partners who can pick up quickly on one another's nonverbal signals, this may work well most of the time. It can backfire, however, when partners do not read each other's intentions accurately and (frequently) end up arguing about something either related or unrelated to intimacy. The result in both of these cases is that efforts to engage one another intimately backfire and relational intimacy decreases.

Intervention: Behavioral guidance and communication training. To increase effective intimacy initiating, therapists can structure "perception check" sessions in which couples check with each other to find out how best to express their needs, wants, and preferences to one another (e.g., they can ask, "How could I say this without putting you on the defensive?"). The therapist can help by suggesting that they communicate their needs and wants with modulated *more-than* or *less-than* statements rather than *always* and *never* statements (Baucom & Epstein, 1990). Also helpful is when the therapist teaches couples to verbalize the problem in relational instead of "right-wrong" terms. This strategy can be compared with what Jacobson and Christensen (1996) call joining around the problem. Joining around the problem occurs when partners cooperate to solve a couple problem instead of competing to assign blame to one or the other. Joining around a problem creates a team spirit in the partners and increases the likelihood that they will want to work together.

Problems with reciprocation. Partners may not know how to reciprocate the other's initiatives in a way that facilitates intimacy. During verbally intimate interactions, partners may give advice or rush in to solve a partner's problem. They blame themselves if they can't offer concrete assistance, or they blame the partner for not following through on their advice. They may think that they must take away their partner's pain.

Some problems with reciprocating reflect the partners' bewilderment about what to do or say in response to the other's confidences. To avoid feeling incompetent or clumsy, partners may distance themselves. Both partners' intimacy needs are thereby frustrated, and many will blame the other, further reducing relational intimacy. People who endorse the "I am Mr. or Ms. Fix-It" schema may find it especially difficult to provide support to their partners when the other self-discloses problems or worries. Instead of listening sympathetically and offering encouragement, Mr. or Ms. Fix-It feels inadequate because he or she fails to see anything constructive that can be done if he or she cannot fix the problem. Feelings of inadequacy can result in the individual withdrawing from intimate interaction quickly or being angry and impatient with the partner for bringing problems that cannot be solved.

Therapists can address these issues by demonstrating to partners the gift that listening is to someone who is talking. Intimate communication training emphasizes sharing and listening to the inner life of one's partner when the partner shares. The therapist can encourage couples to see talking about problems as a form of intimacy.

It is also true that some of a partner's most intimate disclosures may be things the other does not want to hear. Partners sometimes have to work up their courage to sit down with the other in order to raise and discuss a problem in the relationship itself. If the discussion leads up to an implied or explicit request that the other partner change his or her behavior, partner support may not be forthcoming.

Intervention: Teach intimate communication skills. The therapist can use the Behavioral Checklist: Intimacy in Couple Interaction in the Intimacy Signature Dilemma #1 packet to systematically observe the couple's interaction and note the presence or absence of the skills on the checklist. Following that, it is worthwhile to check on whether partners are able to perform any behaviors that are missing, if asked. If not, therapists can provide intimate communication training.

It has been my experience that it is rare to find couples who cannot learn intimate communication skills quickly. Rather, their difficulties more often arise from negative emotion that overwhelms their best communication ability. Couple partners may fail to demonstrate their communication skills because they have not learned to calm themselves when they are upset. It may be best to teach self-soothing skills along with communication skills for individuals who cannot communicate effectively when upset.

The most useful communication skills for reciprocating intimate talk are active listening skills and the communication of respectful acceptance. These intimate communication skills can be taught in tandem with cognitive modification exercises that aim at changing emotion-intensifying thinking processes. Also useful are negotiating and problem-solving skills when couples need to find solutions that meet their different needs and wants.

Problem solving with the partner requires that each has some clarity about what he or she wants. Couple sessions in which each identifies behaviors they want from the other can be useful. Resulting lists can be incorporated into the Giving Days exercise discussed in Chapter 4. Sometimes, it is helpful to work with a partner to find out what is behind their focus on "being right" if they frequently default to this nonproductive process.

Problems with declining. Clients may also have problems declining their partners' initiatives gracefully. They can decline intimacy too frequently in response to their partners' initiation, or they can decline disrespectfully or flatly, conveying a message of personal rejection to the initiator. They can also attack the other when he or she declines. It is no surprise that experience shows that the latter two sets of behavior tend to go together.

Declining a partner's intimate overture creates problems when it communicates rejection of the partner (e.g., "Oh come on, leave me in peace!"

or "Why do you always need to talk, talk, talk"). The initiator's response to being declined is also important. Graceful acceptance of a partner's decline, such as leaving the scene with no comment and absorbing oneself in something else, allows this initiate-decline sequence to end without negative emotional consequences. An unremitting pattern of initiate and decline—whether overtly rejecting or simply not reciprocating—will nevertheless create problems no matter how tactfully the decline is communicated or how gracefully it is received. Lack of reinforcement for initiating will result in a decrease in initiation and ultimately will lead either to conflict about intimacy or a low intimacy relationship.

Conversely, the initiator can respond to hurt feelings caused by the partner's declining by attacking, blaming, or criticizing the partner for declining. In the latter case, the response to being declined is punitive, and itself creates intimacy problems by conditioning an association between intimacy initiating and negative emotions.

It is also true that the resistant partner may believe that the partner who is pressing wants something other than mutual intimacy. People seek intimate time for a variety of reasons, some of which have little to do with wanting to share themselves and to better understand their partners. Sexual intimacy, in particular, can be used like a drug to relieve stress and lift spirits. Partners pick up on this motivation, and it may not sit well with them. It is also true that partners may initiate intimate self-disclosure for the purpose of catharsis. In some cases, the information shared can overwhelm a listener.

Intervention: Teach a relational perspective. A relational perspective can help couple partners understand why a carefully phrased decline response to intimacy initiation is important for the future of intimacy in the relationship. A relational perspective, seen in Figure 7.4, communicates to couples the reciprocal nature of their behavior with one another. The bottom half shows how the rejecting response reduces the likelihood of initiation from the rejected partner. Rejecting, annoyed responses to a partner's initiative often emerge out of guilt: The declining partner feels guilty for saying "no" to his partner and feels angry at the partner for "making him" feel guilty by initiating. As the person in the declining role begins to understand the long-term consequences of rejecting instead of just declining, the therapist can use behavior guidance to help that partner find ways to prevent (as much as possible) the negative consequences.

Problems with withdrawing. Intimacy withdrawal creates problems if one but not both believe that the interaction should continue. In this case, one attempts to keep the other engaged. Sometimes, resistance is positive and

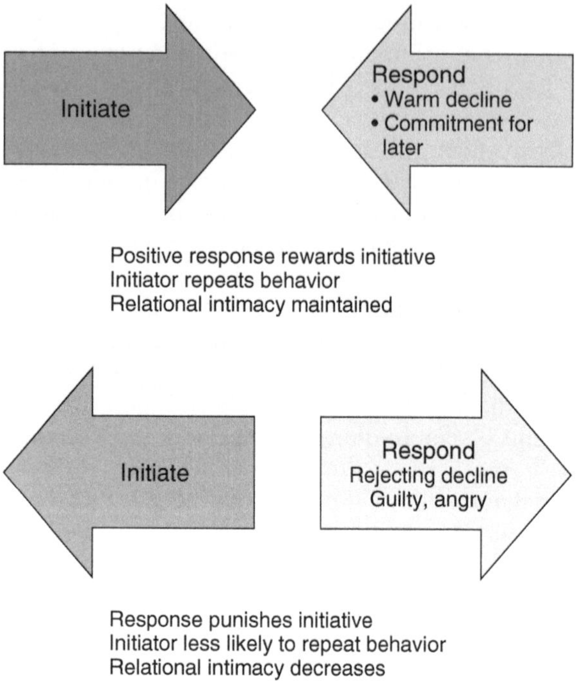

Figure 7.4 A relational perspective on declining without damaging intimacy

playful; however, it can also be coercive, guilt-inducing, or accusatory. It is not uncommon for therapists to hear that one partner is following the other around, demanding a response while the other refuses it. One wife complained that her husband "always wanted sex, was always ready," where she in contrast did not enjoy sex much and was eager to get up and resume other activities. Another husband complained that he needed "down time" and that his wife's needs to "tell him all the bad things that happened" was too much for him, and that she wouldn't let him go when he had heard enough. Steven and Stephanie exemplify couples who have problems withdrawing and with resistance to withdrawal. Steven uses premature withdrawal punitively in this example.

As they went in to have sex, Stephanie said, "Do you really love me?" Steven responded with irritation in his voice and turned away from her, saying, "Don't you know I do?" She said, "The only way you show it is by having sex. Otherwise, you shut yourself off from me." He said, "I'm just tired a lot; why do you have to interpret that as a sign that I don't love you?" He then sighed in frustration and said, "I've lost the urge to have sex" and started changing into his exercise clothes as if preparing to go to the gym. Stephanie followed, him, saying, "You see what I mean? As soon as I want anything from you, when I don't just smile and get right into bed, no questions asked, you withdraw from me." He replied coolly while continuing to make his way to the car, "I'm just not in the mood for sex anymore, Stephanie. It's no big deal; don't make it into one. If we keep talking, it's just going to get worse, so I'm going to the gym now. Let's see how we feel when I get back." With that, he left the house, and Stephanie felt furious, rejected, and sad.

Problems with withdrawal may be minimized if the one initiating withdrawal responds warmly and sensitively to the resistance (without necessarily capitulating). The example of Stephanie and Steven shows how problems escalate if an angry, withdrawing partner "ups the ante" by turning withdrawal into rejection. Insistent, negatively toned resistance increases the likelihood of outright rejection; similarly, an escalated response to resistance could increase the likelihood of demanding, negative behavior from the resistor.

As with other problems with intimacy-distance regulation, couples who have sabotaged their intimate interactions with hostile and rejecting withdrawals and angry, coercive resistance can benefit from learning to see more clearly that their undesirable outcomes are in part a consequence of their own behavior. Behavioral guidance and intimate communication training can help partners identify and practice alternative, less damaging intimacy-distance regulation behaviors.

Intimacy-Sabotaging Laziness

Intimacy-sabotaging laziness grows out of the schema that "intimacy should be easy" and assumes that a partner will always be there and always fulfill one's needs without requiring one to put out much effort. Donald and Ronnie had a habit of sustaining their relationship on minimum effort. Here is an example of how they distanced one another from indifference and laziness more than from combativeness:

Donald: Want to get a babysitter for Saturday? I guess we really don't have the money do we! The electric bill was really high this month. ...
Ronnie: So here it is 10:00 on Saturday night and we still haven't gone out. What happened to us?
Donald: I guess I just got involved in watching this movie, and the time slipped away.
Ronnie: I guess I wasn't that motivated anyway. I'm going to bed early.
Donald: I'm watching another movie—I'll come later.

These partners do not put effort into finding couple time and enjoying intimacy. It is easy for them to drift apart without knowing what happened because they do not accept that maintaining a deep, intimate connection requires some effort.

Intervention: Schema modification. Donald and Ronnie's therapist helped them to articulate their shared "intimacy should be easy" schema and explore the way that it operated in their relationship. Donald had expressed some distress at the lack of fun in their relationship. Donald and Ronnie's therapist began by helping the partners articulate the "intimacy should be easy" schema they shared. The next steps served to increase the partners' awareness of the advantages and disadvantages of continuing in the same vein. The final step would allow them to test out their experience of their chosen course of action, and to evaluate the advantages and disadvantages of that course of action. They could then discuss it with the therapist and make a conscious choice about how to proceed from then on. Whichever choice they made, they would be making it with awareness of the consequences.

Intimacy Sabotage via Resentful Compliance

Resentful compliance is a mutually punishing cycle that begins with coercive behavior in response to unsuccessful bids for intimacy. According to Jacobson and Christensen, coercion is a way to "up the ante" associated with partner demands. However, coercion has especially destructive long-term effects when it follows a partner's declining an intimacy initiation. If coercive responses are repeated too often by the disappointed initiator, this pairing of appeals and coercion can classically condition the partner on the receiving end to associate appeals for intimacy with negative, aversive follow-up. Once that association has been conditioned, partners may comply unwillingly, saying "yes" to avoid the subsequent coercion, but then feel resentful, thus poisoning intimate interactions. Successfully avoiding the other's coercion negatively reinforces compliance with demands, and the compliance positively reinforces the coercive behavior, resulting in a cycle of avoidance and punishment that sabotages intimacy.

Intervention: Identify the behavior and the consequences. As with other repeating, self-sustaining cycles of negative behavior, it is helpful here to teach partners that their own behavior is part of the mechanism that keeps the negative behavior cycle going. Explaining the principles to them is a useful first step. Following the explanation, it is helpful for the partners to examine the automatic thoughts that occurred immediately prior to the interaction as a way to help them see how they respond to both their partner's behavior and their own thoughts.

Intervention: Evaluate the schema. Intervening with resentful compliance is most effective when aimed at thinking patterns that elicit and sustain the behavior. It is common to find that the self-schemas "I am a victim" or "I am fragile" are activated by a partner's coercive behavior. The automatic thoughts that link the activating event with the schema include, "If I say no, we'll fight or he or she will hold a grudge and punish me later" or "he'll say I'm a bad wife for not doing this for him and he'll be correct." Self-empowerment training, particularly with the inclusion of assertiveness training, can be effective with the partner who is unassertive and complies resentfully.

Conclusion

Because intimate relating is associated with strong emotions and because efforts to relate intimately can go awry, leaving emotionally vulnerable partners hurt, people experience ambivalence about intimacy and develop habitual patterns of thinking and behaving that protect them from being hurt while allowing for joy and intimacy. Couple interactions vary systematically in order to maintain intimacy homeostasis, or that level of relational intimacy that allows each partner to maximize positive feelings and minimize risk of negative ones. Three types of behavioral sequences are associated with intimacy-distance regulation—initiating intimacy followed by either reciprocation or declining intimacy, and withdrawing from intimacy. Together, these efforts control the way intimate partners enter into, withdraw from, and avoid intimate interactions. How these interaction sequences are enacted determine the couple's level of relational intimacy—the more often initiations are offered and reciprocated, the more relational intimacy; the more quickly partners withdraw from intimate interactions, the less relational intimacy. To further complicate their efforts to maintain a satisfying intimacy homeostasis, each partner brings with him or her intimacy schemas that not only reflect generalizations about their interactions with each other but also reflect experiences in previous relationships and in their families of origin.

The most common presenting patterns in couples seeking therapy are intimacy avoidance with low intimacy, lost love, conflict over intimacy, negative behavior that sabotages intimacy, and excessive coercion and compliance that sabotage intimacy and love. By helping couples to increase their positive experiences with one another, therapists can help them create a safer relationship climate for intimacy. With schema modification work, therapists can help partners to develop more realistic expectations of their partners, themselves, and their intimate experiences, and thereby have less anxiety and hurt and more intimacy with one another.

8

INTIMACY DILEMMA #2: HOW MUCH I VERSUS HOW MUCH WE?

If I am not for myself, who will be for me?
And if I'm only for myself, what am I?
Hillel, 1st century Jewish sage

When we form a new intimate relationship, we often hope that "two can become one." We detect in ourselves a not-quite conscious yearning to merge with our partners, to share their dreams and hope that they will share ours, to enjoy another's sympathy and understanding, and to have a companion who will enjoy what we enjoy, vote for the candidates we support, and worship where we worship. The first flush of infatuation seems to promise that each has found a "soul mate," someone who looks at the world much as they do themselves and who will validate their outlook on life (Hatfield & Rapson, 1992).

The romantic hope of finding one's soul mate has some basis in reality. Intimate interactions with our relationship partners can create experiences of oneness and transcendence of individuality (Monsour, 1992). The most memorable intimate moments with partners offer experiences of being part of something larger than oneself. Erik Erikson (1953) argued that sexual intimacy was especially likely to elicit such experiences. Sexuality invites two bodies to function as one with each being the instrument of the other's gratification. It also requires each to maintain a heightened sensitivity to the other's needs and wants, needs that are often different from those of self.

In return for the opportunity to feel mystically connected to another person and to perceive the other as sharing in our joys and burdens, our intimate relationships oblige us to be thoughtful of the other's needs and to care deeply about the other's welfare. The picture becomes complicated when the benefits of intimacy create psychological challenges that we must negotiate successfully in order to maintain a deep intimate connection with our partner.

Why I versus We?

Intimate relationships intensify inner conflict between our opposing motivations to become one with another and to remain separate, unique individuals. Ideally, when in love, we want to celebrate and accommodate our partners. We want to be attuned to our partner's needs in order that our partners enjoy life with us. As intimacy increases and a committed, interdependent union takes shape, we increase our familiarity with our partner's ways of understanding the world and with his or her dreams of the future. With our partners, we also share our own thoughts, dreams, and ideals. For intimacy's sake, we risk the open exposure of self in order to be loved just as we are.

Nevertheless, intimate relationships create two simultaneous and sometimes contradictory internal pressures: We want to invite our partners to share our own dreams, and we want to celebrate and support our partner's dreams. These two internal pressures guarantee that the dream of two becoming one is never realized, and indeed, an intimate relationship often teaches us that we don't want this particular dream to come true. Dilemma #2 arises because too much accommodating causes us to lose touch with ourselves, whereas too little appears selfish and damages our connection with our partner. If we try to withdraw from or avoid the conflict, we lose our intimate connection with our partners or may risk losing the relationship altogether. Relationship partners often try to resolve these internal pressures by remaking themselves to be more similar to their partners or to more closely fit into their partner's dreams for the future and the relationship. Conversely, they may attempt to remake their partners to more closely match their own ideals and dreams for future happiness. Both behavior patterns are expressions of the same motivation, to make the dream of two becoming one come true, but one privileges the merging of souls over one's own individuality whereas the other seeks two to become one while keeping one's own individuality besides.

Dilemma #2, I versus we, emerges logically from risks associated with intimacy's rewards (listed in Chapter 1). Intimate relationships lend meaning to life and affirm the self, yet there is also a risk. We can enjoy the self-expansion that identification with our partners provides yet rely too heavily on our partners and lose something of ourselves. We can appreciate our partners for sharing our dreams and lifestyle habits while simultaneously pressuring our partners to alter their ways of being to more closely resemble our own. Partners try to implement one or more problematic responses to Dilemma #2 by: (1) failing to maintain the self, (2) failing to accommodate the other partner, or (3) failing to maintain a deep intimate connection with the partner. Each of these unbalanced reactions to the risks of Dilemma #2 stem from problems with psychological differentiation.

Psychological Differentiation versus Enmeshment and Detachment

Individuals who fail to honor their true selves, fail to accommodate their partners, or fail entirely to establish or maintain intimate relationships, are often those who have problems with *psychological differentiation.* Differentiation, a concept introduced by family systems theorist Murray Bowen (1960), is defined here as the ability to sustain a deep intimate connection without losing sight of one's own or one's partner's unique self. An individual who is psychologically differentiated can share him- or herself intimately with a partner, accept intimate disclosures from the partner, and negotiate for solutions to conflicts without demanding an excess of self-sacrifice from him- or herself or the partner. Psychological differentiation refers to each partner's capacity to perceive the other as unique and different from the self and to maintain a deep intimate connection despite or even because of this reality.

From a cognitive-behavioral perspective, psychological differentiation is a group of theoretically related emotion-regulation and interpersonal skills that permit reasoned, respectful responding within the potentially volatile interactions of an intimate relationship. Psychological differentiation is associated with three groups of behaviors and emotion management skills that together allow partners to minimize the risks of Dilemma #2.

Challenges and Skills of Psychological Differentiation

The skills and behaviors that constitute psychological differentiation serve three functions in the intimate relationship: (1) maintain the self within the intimate relationship; (2) maintain accommodating, respectful, and accepting behavior toward the partner; and (3) maintain the intimate relationship in the face of I versus we challenges. Psychological differentiation and its component skills are shown in Figure 8.1.

Maintain the self within the intimate relationship. "Maintaining the self" in the context of the intimate relationship involves two overlapping skills. For the first, *independent functioning,* the person maintains an intimate connection with the partner while simultaneously functioning independently. The individual sustains a level of self-care and fulfills his or her various responsibilities (i.e., finding a purpose in life, managing own work habits, monitoring own spending and saving, diet, health care, addictions, relationships with children, friendships, extended family relationships, exercise, or sleeping habits) without requiring an excess of vigilance, support, or guidance from the partner. The individual does not acquiesce to a partner's efforts to monitor or take over these functions nor does the individual engage in reactive displays of independence.

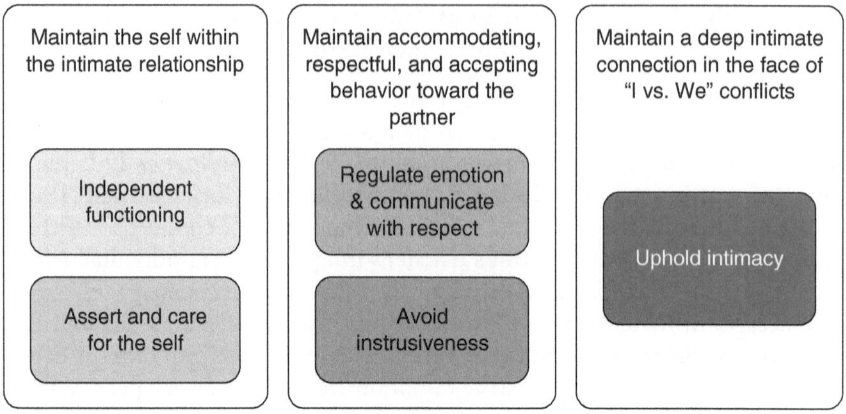

Figure 8.1 Psychological differentiation and its component skills

For the second, *assert and care for the self,* the person is able to express and pursue aspects of the self—needs, wants, opinions, beliefs, interests, goals, values, and tastes—even when these interests, opinions, and so forth are not shared by the partner. In case of conflict, the individual does not go overboard to sacrifice him- or herself in the interest of unity, approval, conflict avoidance, or validation. Further, the individual does not tolerate abusive behavior from the partner or otherwise allow the partner's behavior to severely compromise quality of life (e.g., through excessive drinking, affairs, irresponsible spending habits, and so forth).

Maintain accommodating, respectful, and accepting behavior toward the partner. Respecting the partner involves the following two overlapping skills. For the first, *regulate emotion and communicate with respect,* the individual demonstrates empathy for the partner's aims, needs, wants, opinions, beliefs, values, and tastes even when those are different from the individual's own. Each can listen to and accurately understand the other's perspective. Each can validate the other by communicating that the other's viewpoint is understandable even if different. In case of conflict, the person does not demand an excess of self-sacrifice from the partner, nor does he or she attempt to change the other's needs, wants, opinions, etc. to be more similar to his or her own. The individual can comply with the partner's wishes or desires without feeling that he or she is losing self-respect, identity, or a battle of wills. Each partner can accept the other's influence (see Gottman, 1999, on the importance of the latter).

These skills are combined with the skill of *regulating emotion* because we have recently discovered in our research at the University of Texas at Dallas that these load together on the same factor. In order to maintain accepting, respectful communication, the individual keeps his or her emotional reactions proportional to the events in the relationship (for the most part). He or she neither overreacts nor does he or she artificially suppress emotions in an effort to appear indifferent. The individual can pause, weigh different aims, and reflect on what to say or do without excessive impulsivity. For a detailed discussion of the importance of emotion regulation as a means of decreasing conflict and its negative aftermath, I recommend *The High Conflict Couple,* by Alan Fruzzetti (2006).

Finally, the respectful individual can also *avoid intrusiveness* with regard to his or her partner's activities. He or she does not attempt to regulate or take over tasks for the partner that adults ordinarily manage for themselves (e.g., finding a purpose in life, managing work or health habits, and so on).

Maintain the intimate relationship in the face of I versus we challenges. The individual who *upholds intimacy* can maintain relational intimacy despite partner differences and disagreements. Upholding intimacy means that one does not have to sabotage the relationship with bad behavior (as described in Chapter 7), distance from the other, or abandon the relationship as one's only means of coping with Dilemma #2 challenges. Instead, the individual attempts problem solving with the partner and can tolerate negative emotions within the intimate relationship.

In sum, a psychologically differentiated individual can listen to, accommodate, and respect the partner without losing sight of his or her own needs and without sabotaging, distancing from, or abandoning the relationship. No one is perfectly psychologically differentiated all the time; I versus we is a dilemma experienced by all couples. Acquiring psychological differentiation skills, however, minimizes the negative impact of Dilemma #2 on the relationship and on each individual's mental health. It also enriches the potential for intimacy for the couple.

Differentiation, Enmeshment, and Detachment

Psychological differentiation has been contrasted with *enmeshment* and *detachment.* The term enmeshment, originally coined by Minuchin (1978), refers to over-involvement and over-identification of partners with one another. Enmeshed partners "weave their lives and identities around one another so tightly that it is difficult for . . . them to function independently . . . the boundaries that define individual autonomy are so weak that functioning in individually differentiated ways is radically handicapped."[1] Enmeshed individuals believe that their partners exert irresistible power over them. They experience their partner's preferences, interests, inclinations, and reactions as nearly irresistible forces, in the face of which they must either capitulate or resist. Because of this perception that the partner has all the power, the enmeshed individual often reacts with disproportionate anxiety or anger to

1 www.mentalhealth.net (2006)

things that the partner says and does. In a flurry of intense emotion, the enmeshed partner must decide whether to fight it out with the other or withdraw to a "safe" distance. Enmeshed partners may attempt to control their partner's behavior as a way of regulating their own volatile emotions.

In contrast, detached partners are "so independent in their functioning that it is difficult to figure out how they are related to one another" (Minuchin, 1978, p. 30). Detached partners function independently of one another and may appear to be healthier than their enmeshed counterparts. However, they too have failed to address Dilemma #2 effectively; they are unable to maintain relational intimacy without capitulating to their partner's demands or fighting desperately to avoid capitulating. According to Minuchin (1978), "healthy relationships [with differentiated partners] are thought to be described by the space between enmeshment and detachment" (p. 30). Enmeshment and detachment are opposite reactions to the same Dilemma #2, I versus we struggle.

Some partners are in the process of developing differentiation skills. A defensive and even aggressive assertion of personal empowerment and independence can accompany someone's effort to avoid enmeshment. The enmeshed person will not self-consciously assert his or her independence because it hasn't occurred to him or her, and the differentiated individual knows he or she is independent and personally empowered so he or she doesn't need to assert it. It is the person moving out of dependency and guilt that must assert it in order to believe it him- or herself and in hopes of persuading the partner.

Individual partners in enmeshed or detached relationships may each respond in the same unbalanced way to Dilemma #2 (i.e., both are enmeshed or unrelated), or they may take complementary or opposing positions, as in the pursuer-distancer pattern (Boszormenyi-Nagy & Spark, 1973). In the latter case, one partner pushes for more intimacy whereas the other grows more distant.[2] Pursuer-distancer couples are polarized in the sense that one argues for togetherness and intimacy whereas the other argues for autonomy and privacy. In reality, every couple partner has a need for intimacy and a need for autonomy (Ryan & Deci, 2010). The polarized partners fail to see the reasonableness of "both-and" and instead fight with each other, each devaluing the other's wants and needs. What two polarized partners have in common, regardless of the polarity about which they argue, is a tendency to get stuck in their respective positions and to fail to hear or acknowledge their partner's perspective and the subsequent lack of intimacy in their relationship. A process for helping couples to become less polarized, and thereby address Dilemma #2 more constructively, can be found below in the treatment of Doug and Carla.

Examples of less versus more differentiated behavior are displayed in Table 8.1, organized by the differentiation skill involved. The table also shows how

2 For another way of understanding polarized couples, see Bartholomew and Horowitz (1991) for a description of the avoidant-anxious couple pairing.

Table 8.1 Behavioral differentiation process

Differentiation Skill	*Enmeshment versus Detachment (Less Differentiated)*			*More Differentiated*
	Enmeshed		*Detached*	
	Active	*Passive*		
Independent functioning	Demands that the partner let him or her be in charge and make choices and decisions. Inflexible, demeans partner's aims.	Demands that the partner support his or her dependency.	Independence without intimacy. Goes about his or her business without coordinating with the partner.	Can articulate and pursue dreams and goals and make and implement decisions with the partner, but does not require undue support. No extreme displays of independence or dependence.
Assert and care for self	Sacrifices own aims or distorts or hides true needs, feelings, beliefs, and thoughts to avoid partner disapproval or conflict.	Partner's needs, wants, and demands perceived as irresistibly powerful, demanding acquiescence.	Withdraws into a stance of indifference.	Maintains, pursues, and expresses own needs, wants, opinions, beliefs, interests, goals, values, and tastes that are different from partner's and still maintains intimacy. Tolerates partner differences without distancing.

(*Continued*)

Table 8.1 (Continued)

Differentiation Skill	*Enmeshment versus Detachment (Less Differentiated)*			*More Differentiated*
	Enmeshed		*Detached*	
	Active	*Passive*		
Regulate emotions and communicate respect	Demands that partner think, feel, and behave as self would; overblown anger, sadness, or anxiety in response to partner's communication or actions.	Disproportionate negative emotion in response to partner; cannot understand or refuses to understand partner's thoughts, emotions, or perceptions if they are different from self.	When partner selves are at crossed purposes, distances or withholds intimacy, or abandons the relationship in order to hold onto own aims. Displays little affect in response to partner.	Emotionally responsive without overreactivity; listens to partner's perspective; demonstrates understanding and empathy; accommodates partner's needs and wants; accepts partner as the expert on partner's preferences.
Avoid intrusiveness	Monitors activities that are reasonably within the other partner's responsibility.	Permits partner to monitor activities that should reasonably be within his or her own responsibility.	Mostly ignores or fails to participate in partner's daily life.	Monitors him- or herself and lets the partner do his or her own self-monitoring.
Uphold intimacy	Stays in the relationship although difficult to uphold intimacy; escalates demands for support, concessions, and sacrifices from partner in light of conflict; punishes with anger.	Stays in the relationship; withdraws, stops communicating, and withholds self when confronted with conflicts.	Hides self, even develops secret life when overwhelmed by partner's needs and wants.Leaves the relationship.	Keeps conversation open even when partners must discuss difficult issues. Maintains positive view of partner and allows acknowledgment of differences.

enmeshed behavior can be active or passive. Enmeshed individuals who want to be active will attempt to control their partners. Enmeshed individuals who are inclined to be passive will use guilt induction or threats to insist that the partner take care of them.

Fostering Psychological Differentiation

Fostering psychological differentiation skills is an important strategy for helping couples to more effectively cope with Dilemma #2, I versus we. Differentiation can be fostered within an intimate relationship through changes in behavior, cognition, and affect management. Changes in behavior foster differentiation when they encourage partners to develop well-defined, autonomous selves that can collaborate and compromise without causing either to feel smothered or overpowered. Enmeshed partners can also be encouraged to cultivate separate friends, activities, and interests as a way of enhancing their perceptions of themselves as unique and separate individuals within the intimate relationship. Changes in behavior encourage more togetherness in unrelated couples. For these couples, learning to share previously separate interests and friends counters a growing distance that has served the purpose of maintaining their separate identities.

Couples can foster differentiation in one another through their communication. Communication fosters differentiation when it expresses acceptance for, or even lauds, partner differences. Therapists can teach partners to demonstrate an active interest in the other's perspective through communication and listening skills and through changing negative interpretations of the other's communication. Partners can be encouraged to develop and practice self-statements in which they remind themselves that the other's unique perspective is interesting and different rather than dangerous. When each partner is responsible for expressing his or her own point of view and takes responsibility for communicating it clearly, this also fosters differentiation.

When partners are comfortable balancing time alone with time together, they foster differentiation. When each has time to hear his or her own thoughts and enjoy his or her own interests, the partners are fostering each other's differentiation. When the partners come back together, they have experiences to share with one another, each as a separate and unique individual. Sometimes partners are ready to change habitual behaviors because they are more differentiated than when they met and simply need guidance as to how they can best do that.

In addition to being fostered by changes in behavior, differentiation can be encouraged through intimacy schema evaluation. Once clients have begun identifying their automatic thoughts, the therapist can work with the client to identify themes that underlie the thoughts. These themes are the self-, partner-, and relationship-schemas that, once explicit, are subject to evaluation. Evaluating schemas frees clients from simply reacting to the emotions that they generate. Ultimately, the client can entertain alternative beliefs that may more accurately capture the current situation and the self that he or she is at present.

Finally, affective interventions, particularly those targeting clients' self-soothing skills, can be useful in fostering psychological differentiation and reducing conflict associated with Dilemma #2. As clients improve their own self-soothing skills, they depend less on their partners for soothing and are likely to do better at managing their emotions during couple conflict. Self-soothing is especially helpful for partners who feel overwhelmed when the other makes demands; pausing to think is helpful for those who have difficulty managing their emotions while negotiating with their partners. Self-empowerment training also fosters psychological differentiation skills, as upcoming examples will demonstrate.

Treating Problems with Maintaining the Self

This chapter addresses I versus we dilemmas that require couple partners to maintain and assert the self. These dilemmas push partners toward developing a strong sense of self within the context of their intimate relationship. The next chapter will address the remaining two I versus we challenges—dilemmas that require partners to attend to and respect the partner, and those that require partners to maintain a deep intimate connection in the face of Dilemma #2 issues.

Problems with maintaining the self take two general forms: (1) Partners try to micromanage or take over adult, executive functions of the other that are best left to the individual (e.g., as mentioned above, health care, family of origin issues, and so forth) and (2) partners fail to assert and care for their interests in the face of the other's attempts to persuade, manipulate, or even bully to get what they want and, as a result, lose touch with who they are and become resentful. Although problems with the first are important to resolve for couples to function well, they are not likely to be tangled up in intimacy issues and so will not receive detailed treatment in this book. Problems with maintaining an autonomous self are often tightly interwoven with intimacy issues, however, either as a consequence or a precursor of intimacy problems.

Problems with asserting and caring for the self tend to be driven by self-schemas that devalue the individual's own power, entitlement, or competence and that overrate the partner's power or underrate his or her devotion. Table 8.2 lists some schemas that are likely to lead to problems maintaining the self. The left-hand column shows the different variations on the basic intimacy schemas listed in Chapter 6.

For couples presenting with Dilemma #2 complaints, these schemas promote hiding of the self. They also promote a pattern of excessive compliance that sometimes alternates with explosions of anger or "vacations" (i.e., escapes from the oppressive responsibility of excessive compliance). Either pattern inhibits intimacy.

Table 8.2 Schemas associated with Dilemma #2, I versus we

Description	*Schema*
Dilemma #2 Problematic Beliefs	*Self-Schemas*
*I fear, or am convinced, that no one could love me if they knew my true self. *My needs will overwhelm my partner, and I must keep them to myself. *I must only show the self that my partner wants to see, or my partner will stop loving me.	I am unlovable.
*I fear that my partner will reject or humiliate me if I speak up, and I "cannot stand" it if that happens.	I am fragile (I can't stand it, etc.).
*I have no power to get what I want from my intimate relationship. *I must sacrifice myself for my partner (and—often added—my partner must notice, reward, and appreciate my self-sacrifices). *My partner could avoid causing me hurt but doesn't and therefore causes hurt on purpose.	I am a victim (of my partner, of this marriage, etc.).
	Partner-Schemas
*I have no choice but to capitulate to or aggressively protest my partner's demands.	Partner has the power (it's not worth it to fight, etc.).
*My partner has negative intentions toward, lack of interest in, or lack of empathy or concern toward me.	Partner is indifferent.
*My partner can't know about or can't handle certain responsibilities, and I must handle them.	Partner is fragile.
	Relationship-Schemas
*I have a high standard of conduct for myself, my partner, and for intimacy. If I demand enough from my partner, I can make my standards a reality.	Things should always go right.
*In order to be a real woman, I must be soft and compliant, and my behavior must conform to cultural or religious ideals and requirements. My partner must also fulfill the requirements of being a real man (or vice versa).	Women and men must be different (real men don't . . . , etc.).
	Fear Scenario
*If either I or my partner or our relationship does not proceed as we planned, the outcome will be terrible (i.e., a breakup, a failure of mental or physical health, delinquent or mentally ill children, etc.).	My future is predetermined.

What follows are couple problems that can be usefully assessed and treated as Dilemma #2 issues. Each emerges because of risks associated with intimacy. For each example, I will show how the presenting problem is a manifestation of an 'I versus we' dilemma and how problems with psychological differentiation prevent the couple (or individual) from addressing the problem constructively. I will also show how assessing and working with schemas can help partners to increase psychological differentiation skills and to implement resolutions to 'I versus we' dilemmas.

It's hard to accept that partners have different needs and wants. Relational intimacy depends upon interactional intimacy (e.g., self-disclosing communication) and upon a willingness to reveal the self even when it means disagreement with (or disapproval from) the partner. This sharing of the unique self requires sufficient self-awareness to permit the individual to ascertain and then communicate what he or she thinks, feels, and wants. It also requires the ability to assert and care for the self when one's partner tries to persuade one to change something that one cannot or will not change. It is a willingness to disappoint the partner in the interest of honest self-presentation.

One risk of Dilemma #2 is that a partner will give up on sharing his or her needs and wants because of an unacknowledged belief that (1) the partner is inordinately powerful and (2) there is no way to get one's own needs met when the two are at crossed purposes. In this case, the person either risks losing touch with the self (i.e., stops being able to access or express his or her needs and wants) or knowingly submerges the self, building up resentment that interferes with intimacy. When a partner increases his or her level of differentiation and begins asserting and caring for him- or herself openly in the relationship, he or she also confronts the beliefs that forced him or her into hiding in the first place.

Carla and Doug sought treatment after Carla stopped a 15-year habit of submerging her own wants and needs to comply with what Doug wanted. As a result of Carla's increased differentiation, the two found themselves stuck repeatedly in irresolvable conflict, as neither knew how to resolve their conflicts now that Carla no longer capitulated to Doug's wants and needs. In this incident, Doug wants Carla to join him and his family for their annual family reunion. He asks, why she can't give up just one weekend to go with him? Carla exercises her new-found assertiveness skills by expressing what she wants, which is to bow out and enjoy a quiet weekend at home alone. She asks, why he can't go on his own just this once? He argues that his family, for all their quirks, would be hurt if she didn't attend as would he. Carla and Doug are ill-prepared to deal with this I versus we incident after solving their problems in Doug's favor for so long.

How Carla and Doug perceive the conflict, what they feel in the face of the conflict, and the flexibility with which they can approach the conflict's resolution are each dependent upon Doug's and Carla's respective differentiation skills. Each must accept that they will have different wants and needs that at times cause conflict. If Carla perceives Doug and his wants as presenting her with an irresistible mandate, then she is more likely to capitulate with resentment (a sign of intimacy schema, "my partner has the power"). If she fights his request with all her strength, it is to avoid having her will overwhelmed by the power she perceives in Doug's request. For his part, Doug must learn to address his fear scenario in which he pictures himself with a lifetime of attending family events without Carla.

The couple's therapist developed a strategy of (1) intimate communication training, to help the partners to openly express their wants while also listening to and demonstrating their understanding of each other's points of view, (2) dual monitoring training, to help the partners monitor and communicate their own feelings while still listening to and demonstrating understanding for the other's wants, (3) acceptance training, to help Carla and Doug accept (perhaps with sadness) that each of them wants something different and that there is no obvious collaborative solution, and (4) problem-solving training, to help them find as mutually beneficial a solution as possible.

The following dialogue illustrates how a therapist can combine the intimate communication training, the teaching of dual monitoring, the acceptance training, and problem solving together with traditional cognitive therapy skills of collaboration, normalizing, and schema work to help couples solve irreconcilable conflict by increasing differentiation skills.

Therapist: Your fights occur partly because neither of you feels understood (i.e., *a lack of intimacy*) and partly from the emotions that overtake you when you have these disagreements (i.e., *a sign of enmeshment*). Let's begin with each of you saying what you believe—and why if you want to—and the other person listening carefully to be sure that he or she understands the message (*intimate communication training*). . . .

Carla: Yes I get furious; he always seems to want things his way.

Therapist: *[Normalizing.]* Well, that just makes Doug a pretty ordinary guy, you know? Because most of us want things to go our way. In a marriage, though, we learn pretty much the hard way that we will not get our way every time. Most of the time, we can handle not getting our way. But sometimes, we get really upset; all of us do at one time or another. That's because the argument means more than what appears on the surface. Follow me? . . . The way to figure out what that meaning is and to resolve the problem it's creating begins with monitoring your emotions. *[Teach dual monitoring.]* So while you are speaking and while you are listening to the other person, notice carefully what you are feeling. This means this conversation will go more slowly than what you're accustomed to, because instead of reacting to your emotions, you will notice them. To begin, Carla I'd like you to say what you want and why, and I'd like you, Doug, to listen carefully and get her point. Notice what you are feeling as you do that, Doug. Ready? . . .

[Carla states her case.]

Therapist: What are you feeling, Doug?

Doug: I feel really angry. She thinks it's OK to skip out on my family's reunion. This is a big deal to my family. She's a part of it, and they'll be hurt if she doesn't show up.

Therapist: *[Working on identifying schemas.]* OK, great, you've identified what you're feeling *and* you've heard what Carla wants (along with your own objections to it). This is just how dual monitoring is supposed to work. Let's see if we can get to the belief behind your anger. . .

Doug: I believe that married couples owe it to each other to participate in family gatherings. She owes it to me, but she's trying to weasel out of it. . . .

Therapist: OK! For you, attending each other's family gatherings is part of being married. Would you like Carla to show you that she understands your perspective? . . . *[Therapist reassures Carla that understanding does not equal agreement or capitulation, after which Carla restates to Doug's satisfaction.]*

Therapist: *[Moves back to identifying the schema.]* Now, may I play devil's advocate for a moment? What does it mean to you if Carla misses one of your family gatherings? Are you afraid of setting a trend?

Doug: Well this family reunion itself is a big deal. But yes, I also don't want Carla to think she can skip out of my family get-togethers any time she wants to.

Therapist: So this is something you want Carla to understand: That you believe in this sharing of family time.

Carla: Believe it or not, Doug, I agree with you.

Therapist: For the sake of exploring your feelings, Doug, may I ask, why not make an exception this time?

Doug: I don't know. The reunion's a big deal. The family will be hurt. It sets a bad precedent.

Therapist: It sounds like you have a fear scenario about this. An expectation that if you give in this time, then she'll run off with this and avoid all your family gatherings or most of them.

Doug: Yes, I think she might do that.

Carla: That's not fair, Doug. I've never asked to skip one of these in all the years we've been married. Even though, I don't really enjoy them that much.

Therapist: *[Returns to dual monitoring training.]* Carla, are you noticing feelings as you discuss this with Doug?

Carla: I'm actually not angry. Slowing down (*as a part of dual monitoring*) has helped me to notice that I'm actually sad. Sad that Doug doesn't want me to have this time to myself and sad that I just can't find it in myself to do what Doug wants. Because I know it would make you happy, Doug.

Therapist: *[Acceptance training.]* When you have accepted differences, you feel sad because you realize that you won't get exactly what you want. It's often a quiet sadness, though, instead of the emotional agitation before acceptance.

Carla: I think that's why I feel sad—that by getting what I want I play into your fear [scenario], Doug, that I'll take advantage of you and stay away from your family. I'm sad that you could think that about me, but I'm more sad realizing that I can't get what I want without hurting you. So, I'm thinking that now is not the time for me to get my time to myself.

Doug: I appreciate that, Carla—although this doesn't seem like something I should be grateful for, your doing what any wife would do.

Therapist: *[Acceptance training.]* Can you accept that Carla feels differently about the reunion than you do? That she has some needs of her own, for some alone time, some peace and quiet? And that she's postponing the fulfillment of her needs in order to give you what you want?

Doug: OK, I can accept that. Does it always have to be this way? That somebody has to give in?

Therapist: *[Problem-solving.]* You're in a good position, now that you know exactly what Carla wants, to find another way for her to get her quiet time besides skipping your family reunion.

Carla: I know just what you could do, Doug, that would give me some peace of mind. Take the rental house repairs off my to-do list. . . .

This dialogue from Doug and Carla's therapy illustrates the use of collaboration, cognitive interventions (normalizing, schema work, and problem solving), and intimacy-enhancing strategies (dual monitoring training, acceptance training) with the aim of increasing partners' psychological differentiation and in turn increasing mutual understanding and preventing irreconcilable conflict. When they each focused on their own feelings and tried to understand them, Carla and Doug stopped arguing about their respective positions; the therapist was therefore able to proceed directly into acceptance training.

My partner made me do it. One form of the I versus we dilemma that couples face is a certain instability of self-concept that accompanies the taking on of new roles as a result of the relationship (i.e., husband, wife, parent, daughter-in-law). These roles expand the self-concept beyond its previously defined boundaries. Partners' self-concepts are also expanded when they incorporate the informal roles that they play as a result of their unique combination of personalities. One will become the responsible one whereas the other is the dreamer; one is the financially conservative one whereas the other lives for today; one is the neatnik and the other is a total slob. These informal roles result from the partners' personality differences. Human beings engage in a variety of psychologically defensive maneuvers to avoid having to make changes to self-concept (e.g., Epstein, 2003). Because of this built-in conservatism, the self-concept effectively limits each individual's possible responses in an intimate context to those that are consistent with existing self-schemas.[3]

Problems with Dilemma #2 can arise when the new relationship roles challenge long-held beliefs about the self. The I versus we dilemma for each partner is to maintain continuity with the self-concept as it existed before the relationship while still being flexible enough to incorporate into the self-concept the new roles that the relationship brings.

Ken's conflict between who he is with his new wife and his more well-established self-schemas exemplifies this dilemma. Ken came to his marriage believing that he was generous and giving to a fault. He had grown up in a family in which he was the "do for others" sibling. For Ken, being a giver was an important aspect of his self-concept. After he married Linda, however, his identity as a giver was challenged. Linda tended to ask for more until he said no. However, Ken could not

3 For example, research on relational self-construal has shown that people who define themselves primarily according to the roles they play in their relationships are more likely to go out of their way for relationship partners than will those whose self-construals come primarily from individual characteristics and accomplishments (Gore, Cross, & Morris, 2006).

reconcile his saying no with his identity as a giver. He blamed Linda for "bringing out the worst" in him and for "never being satisfied no matter what I give."

When they started therapy, Ken and Linda initially complained of irreconcilable conflict and a growing distance between them. Linda and Ken's therapist used four strategies to help them resolve their disagreements more effectively: (1) *teach realistic expectations* of what each could do for the other, given the other constraints with which each also had to cope, (2) *self-empowerment training* for Ken, to put him more fully in charge of what he agreed to do for Linda and in what time frame, (3) *acceptance training* for both, as part of developing realistic expectations of the other, and (4) *behavioral guidance,* aimed at improving their communication to encourage Linda to give Ken more strokes for the efforts he made to please her and to encourage Ken to speak more clearly about his needs and to negotiate more effectively with Linda.

The therapist first helped Ken to apply more realistic expectations about Linda and about himself. Ken's self-concept as a tireless helper exceeded his normal human limitations. His expectation that Linda would anticipate his needs and help him to do what he couldn't do himself was also unrealistic. Second, self-empowerment training helped Ken take charge of his own breaks even when Linda wasn't so supportive. The therapist used three of the mini-interventions of self-empowerment training—persuasion, schema evaluation, and schema modification—to help Ken normalize and accept his need to take breaks without giving up his concept of himself as a "Mr. Fix-It." The strategy also helped him to stop blaming Linda for his inability to give himself breaks. The therapist has set the stage for Ken to begin asserting himself via realistic modifications in his heretofore rather rigid and unyielding self-concept. Ken's concept of a "giving person" was childlike and had likely crystallized while he was growing up in his family of origin. Now, Ken could refine his old self-concept into one that was more adult and allowed for normal human frailty.

It is often useful to begin self-empowerment training in an individual session. In part, this is because partners who are not self-empowered are distracted by the blame they place on their partners. Indeed, it is easy for a sympathetic therapist to get caught up in the complaining spouse's "I am a victim" schema, because the description of the spouse's behavior is consistent with that schema. The individual session reinforces the message that self-empowerment is something one must do for oneself and does not depend on any particular behavior from the partner. Partners can be enlisted to provide support and encouragement for self-empowerment, but because asserting the self may put one at odds with the partner, the support cannot be a precondition for self-empowered behavior.

Self-expansion versus remaking ourselves to our partner's specifications. The search for an intimate partner stems in part from yearnings for self-expansion (Aron & Aron, 1996; see Chapter 1). When our partner's desirable characteristics become extensions of ourselves in which we take pride, we may brag about them as though they were our own. Our partners can also help us expand ourselves by serving as role models and sources of inspiration. Through our partners, we can learn the virtues that we have neglected in ourselves: if we are orderly and conscientious, we can learn to relax; if we are happy-go-lucky, we get more organized.

The urge to expand ourselves via a relationship with a partner can go awry if we find ourselves working too hard to live up to our partner's standards for what he or she wants us to be. If we admire our partners and fail to also appreciate ourselves, we can get caught in an enmeshed pattern, in which we try to change our personalities to be what our partners want us to be. Theorists Carl Rogers (1959) and Abraham Maslow (1968) have argued that submerging the self in order to accommodate the self-concept to someone else's ideals sabotages one's own personal growth and well-being and is a recipe for negative self-regard and depression. Submerging the self can cause a buildup of resentment toward the partner and is not a workable long-term strategy for resolving Dilemma #2 challenges.

Victoria is currently struggling with Dilemma #2 in her relationship with Preston, in that she has internalized Preston's ideals for her as her own. Preston thinks that Victoria is too insecure, and she agrees with him. Both Victoria and Preston believe that their mutual resentment and resulting lack of intimacy stem in part from Victoria's "insecurities." Victoria sought therapy because she accepted her husband's view that if she could resolve her insecurities, she and Preston would be more intimate. Here is Victoria's individual assessment session with her therapist.

Therapist:	So you find it difficult to trust him when he stays out so late at night, but you wish you could trust him. You know, I think a lot of wives would wonder about where their husbands were if they were out until 1 A.M. so often and didn't call.
Victoria:	Part of his work is taking clients out for dinner and drinks and getting to know them. I still resent it even though he's a great breadwinner. I don't blame him for being upset with me, but I still worry. He works so hard, is so devoted, he deserves to have a wife who trusts him. So I'm here to try to be more secure.

Victoria is at risk for losing her "I" in the "we." Her initial goal for therapy was to remake herself according to Preston's wishes. This is not a realistic goal nor will the effort to achieve it, at least on those terms, be helpful for Victoria's mental health. Her unsuccessful effort to suppress her emotions is already causing Victoria distress and causing conflict in the marriage. Empowering Victoria, via cognitive change, to perceive a request that Preston change his behavior to help her to feel less anxious could be beneficial to Victoria and to the marriage if Preston is flexible enough to accommodate her.

Victoria's therapist recommends self-empowerment training because, once empowered, Victoria will be better able to assert and care for herself without distancing Preston.

Therapist: *[Self-empowerment training—Persuasion.]* So you and Preston both have been trying to change you, so that you won't feel anxious about his late nights. But you've been trying to do it in a way that doesn't usually work—and that is, by trying to remake *you,* so that you stop feeling what you're feeling. That hasn't worked very well has it?

Victoria: That's because of my history, I think.

Therapist: *[Normalizes to validate Victoria's feelings as understandable.]* Your history may make it more difficult for you to trust Preston under these circumstances, but I'm not willing to blame your history entirely. I think that a lot of wives—a lot of spouses—would feel uncomfortable with the late hours Preston keeps. *[Persuasion to try self-empowerment training.]* So my first choice would be to help you validate yourself, accept your own feelings as understandable and reasonable. Then, as you feel more self-confident, I can work with you to develop a strategy for addressing Preston about this.

Victoria: Hmm, so you think most wives would feel insecure about this?

Therapist: Yes, I think most wives would not like it much.

Victoria: You know, though, when I'm being reasonable, I really don't think Preston is fooling around. But his behavior is secretive—like when he doesn't answer his phone or he's not honest about how late he's going to be. That gets me going—if he would just call and act like he's sorry he's going to be so late. Like he understands my feelings.

Therapist: *[Therapist provides a benign alternative framework.]* Yes, a mature, pulled together Preston would do all those things. But Preston has his own struggle with this issue, doesn't he. He feels guilty about the impact on you, and because guilt and anger are closely linked emotions, he avoids dealing with the guilt directly by not dealing with you.

The therapist's framework validates Victoria's feelings of anxiety under the circumstances and helps her to see that the problem does not stem solely from her insecurities. Armed with the alternative framework and the validation, Victoria is freer to reevaluate the circumstances surrounding her problem and to modify her expectations of self to accommodate an understanding

Table 8.3 Steps in Victoria's self-empowerment training

Model empowered, differentiated response.
Teach cognitive self-soothing methods.
Help Victoria identify and modify her self- and partner-schemas.
Change less realistic to more realistic expectations of Preston.
Role-play/rehearse self-expression skills with Victoria.

of Preston's contribution to the problem. This new understanding reduces Victoria's tendency to mold her ideal self to fit with Preston's expectations.

The next steps in the therapist's strategy for helping Victoria are aimed at increasing her level of differentiation. For Victoria, this means (1) maintaining a vision of her ideal self that is her own, not borrowed from Preston, (2) soothing her own anxiety, and (3) communicating soft rather than harsh messages in order to uphold intimacy with Preston in the face of their conflict. Self-empowerment training provides the therapeutic strategy for accomplishing these goals. The therapist's selection from the self-empowerment intervention menu is reproduced in Table 8.3.

When clients are unable to picture or reproduce differentiated communication, the therapist can show the client what it looks like by modeling it and then explaining how each part of that communication contributed to the whole. Here, Victoria's therapist models soothing self-talk and empowered communication.

Therapist: First, we'll work on some things that you can say to yourself that will make you feel less insecure about your own reactions. For example, "It's midnight and Preston isn't home and hasn't called. Now I'm feeling anxious! That doesn't mean there's something wrong with me, though. I think most wives would feel the way I feel. Although I don't have any reason to mistrust Preston, I think it is reasonable for me to expect him to make this easier for me to accept. If I write down what I want to say to him now, it will help me go to sleep. I'll leave him the note and get his reaction tomorrow. OK, now the letter: "Dear Preston, You are out past midnight again, and I'm feeling anxious and having trouble sleeping. It still doesn't feel right to me that you are out so late when you have me and our children here at home. So here is what I would like you to do to help me feel less anxious. I'd like you to call me when you are out late—while you are at dinner or after dinner, before you go to the nightclub. I'd like you to tell me what you're doing, and why you will be out late if that's your plan. I'd like you to

> give me an approximate time when you will get home. And sometimes, I'd like you to apologize for your late nights and the way these nights leave me alone at home taking care of the kids. Sometimes, too, I'd like you to thank me for taking up the slack when you are working late. That will help me to feel more positively about what you do, and I promise to thank you too for how hard you work to provide us with a comfortable lifestyle. I will also continue my therapy and work on reducing my anxiety. I'm ready to talk about it as soon as you are. . . . In the meantime, I love you and appreciate all that you do." OK, you might not include all of that in any given note or any given self-talk session. But I wanted to lay out some of the issues that I think you're dealing with and suggest some of the things you would be asking Preston to do if you were asserting yourself more fully. So what did you think of that process, Victoria?

In this case, the therapist demonstrated what a psychologically differentiated response to Preston's behavior would sound like. A differentiated effort to assert and care for the self does not require distancing but rather is done in the context of intimate communication. The therapist can now refer back to this demonstration to help Victoria stay on track as she works toward becoming self-empowered. If Victoria is similar to other clients who struggle with I versus we issues, then she will revert back to her efforts to remake herself in Preston's image before she fully internalizes the notion that she can assert and care for herself and still be loving and intimate with Preston.

In the next session, Victoria and her therapist work on cognitive self-soothing skills. These help Victoria to ease her own anxiety with realistic alternative thoughts about Preston's behavior. As her anxiety eases, Victoria's problem solving and communication with Preston will come closer to fulfilling her aims.

In the first phase of cognitive self-soothing, Victoria's therapist helps Victoria to see that she is using a thought pattern that worked for her in the past but not in the present. The therapist does not invalidate the thought process, which might cause Victoria to further doubt herself, but rather helps her to remember a time when she used the thought process effectively. Next, the therapist works with Victoria on creating soothing thought processes for coping with Preston's behavior in the marriage. Traditional cognitive therapy technique—evaluating automatic negative thoughts—can work as a part of a self-empowerment strategy for clients who lose their "I" in the "we." Focusing on thoughts about the partner is especially important for increasing differentiation because it helps the client to see the partner as a person in his or her own right.

The last step in Victoria's self-empowerment training involved clarifying for herself what she wanted from Preston and then asking him for it in a direct, nonblaming manner. The therapeutic challenge here is to help the client set a goal that is within his or her power to achieve rather than framing the goal as a change in the partner's behavior, over which the client has little or no control. Victoria, with the help of her therapist, set as her goal to tell Preston in a calm manner that the unpredictability of his late nights, along with the late hours that he kept, was difficult for Victoria and that she wanted him to sit down with her and work out a way to handle the problem so that she could feel more comfortable. Her goal, then, was to communicate effectively with Preston rather than "making" him do what she wanted him to do. She and her therapist then role-played (with the therapist taking the part of Preston), so that Victoria could practice communicating clearly and calmly before she had to face Preston with her concerns. In the end, she was satisfied with the compromise that the two of them worked out (although the solution was not her first choice, she realized that she could compromise without rancor now that she had stopped taking his behavior so personally).

In sum, the steps Victoria and her therapist took to increase Victoria's feeling of self-empowerment with her husband and to decrease her tendency to blame herself for their arguments comprised a subset of the microinterventions listed in Chapter 6 for self-empowerment training. Self-empowerment works best when it is tailor-made for the individual seeking it, and not every client will need to work through every step. The therapist can determine which of the steps to take for a particular client on the basis of the particular self-empowerment issues with which the individual struggles.

Conclusion

In this first chapter on Dilemma #2, I versus we, I have presented a model of self and intimacy that elucidates several ways that intimate relationships challenge the self. Partners risk depending too much on the other to boost their own self-esteem, hiding parts of themselves that are risky to expose, and excessively complying with the other's wants in order to please. Dilemma #2 problems also emerge because two partners are bound to have differences that sometimes express themselves in opposing intentions. These conflicts are often complicated, because the individual is of two minds: The individual wants to please the partner and make the partner happy, and the individual wants to pursue his or her own aims without obstacles. Unresolved inner struggles become outer struggles when guilt and resentment build and are directed at the partner. Psychological differentiation refers to a set of skills that helps individuals maintain a deep intimate connection with their partners while taking responsibility for their own struggles. In this chapter, I have addressed presenting problems and treatment plans for individuals who have difficulty asserting and expressing themselves in intimate relationships. In the next chapter, I address the problems associated with the other two aspects of psychological differentiation: accommodating the partner and maintaining the intimate relationship.

9

THE URGE TO MERGE, DILEMMA #2, AND THE CHALLENGES OF DIFFERENTIATION

[There is always a part of the self that is] "not included in the self-affirmation of the collective."
(Paul Tillich, 1952, p. 99).

In this chapter, I address the two remaining challenges associated with Dilemma #2, I versus we, (1) managing emotions in order to listen to and demonstrate understanding of one's partner, and (2) maintaining relational intimacy in the face of relationship difficulties. Here I address couple partners who try to change one another (enmeshed) or who withdraw entirely from intimate connection with the other (unrelated).

In Chapter 8, I identified psychological differentiation as a set of skills and thinking processes that allows partners to maintain a high level of intimacy in their relationship while simultaneously acknowledging the self and other as unique individuals. Psychological differentiation can be distinguished, on the one hand, from enmeshment, putting pressure on the self or other to change in order to increase sameness, or, on the other, from unrelatedness, withdrawal and distancing in the face of pressure to accommodate. The ability to maintain intimacy while appreciating each partner's uniqueness sets the stage for effective and even intimate communication in the face of conflict.

Yearning for a Soul Mate

One reason why it is difficult for partners to increase differentiation is their belief that their attraction to one another is based on their similarities. People want soul mates and are attracted to others who seem to be similar to themselves. As they communicate their views and their dreams, people are thrilled to find someone else who shares them. These early intimate interactions are validating, offering each the reassurance that he or she is not alone (or crazy) in viewing the world as he or she does. Further, the new partners are eager to give the validation that each knows the loved one craves. They may even validate the other at the expense of their own self-expression and withhold a different, contradictory, or incompatible personal view because it would disrupt their partner's experience of validation (and the couple's new-found intimacy). Partners believe that their similarities have drawn them together and assure that theirs will be a match of soul mates.

Intimacy initially reveals similarities, but in the long run, it also reveals differences. Partners who are convinced that they've found their soul mate may be dismayed to learn that the other person is not only similar but also significantly different from them. They may be more alarmed when their differences cause conflicts of interest, thereby challenging their altruistic motives toward each other. Because they believe partners have to be similar, enmeshed partners are anxious about the relationship's viability in the face of differences.

Getting Stuck in Power Struggles

Once their differences are revealed, partners are liable to engage in power struggles. Each time their differences create a conflict of interests, partners face questions. "Which of us will get our way this time?" "What would it mean to me to let my partner do this his or her way?" "When must I assert my own way of doing things?" "How do we resolve it if neither wants to give in?" Two partners confronting each other, each trying to get his or her own way, appear on the surface to be struggling for power and influence over the other. Intractable power struggles are more complicated than they appear, however. These struggles often reflect partners' attempts to improve their relationships without the benefit of differentiation skills. Each believes he or she has identified the best route to their mutual well-being. Further, each expects the two to become one. When the other refuses to give up on his or her point of view, a power struggle ensues.

Power struggles are often the result of less differentiated partners' attempts to resolve Dilemma #2 by changing the partner to become more like self. Less differentiated partners attempt to remake their relationships in their own respective individual images, both for their own good and for the good of their relationships as they perceive them. These efforts make things worse instead of better because partners lack the skills to work with their differences constructively. Partners may also experience assertiveness on the part of the other as disloyalty.

Although partners' initial attraction may stem from perceived similarities, ongoing relational intimacy depends as much upon the partners' ability to accept their differences. Interventions aimed at increasing psychological differentiation are, at least in part, efforts to increase partners' acceptance of one another. Partners are more likely to self-disclose if they trust that the other will accept what they say without trying to change them (e.g., Laurenceau, Barrett, & Pietromonaco, 1998).

Helping partners to increase their levels of psychological differentiation therefore requires that therapists target communication and problem-solving skills in conjunction with beliefs about good relationships. Partners' ability to accept one another's differences and to maintain a deep intimate connection in the face of those differences is achieved via the attitudes and skills associated with differentiation.

Increasing Mutual Respect and Acceptance via Changes in Partners' Psychological Differentiation

Being able to listen to and express understanding for a partner's viewpoint when it conflicts with one's own is an important aspect of relational intimacy. Therapists can help couple partners improve this ability by helping them to increase their psychological differentiation. Although increases in differentiation can be accomplished with cognitive, affective, or behavioral interventions, it is often most effective to target dysfunctional thinking patterns and beliefs about relationships first and then proceed to help partners change their behavior. Changes in emotional reactivity and in behavior can result from interventions aimed at the cognitive aspects of enmeshment or unrelatedness. Some highly reactive individuals may also need to learn skills specifically for managing their emotions. I first take a closer look at enmeshment and how to help enmeshed partners change.

Attitudes and Expectations Associated with Enmeshment

Psychologically differentiated individuals expect their partners to have different ways of thinking and doing things than they do. In contrast, enmeshed partners have expectations of sameness (usually unacknowledged): They expect to have the same goals, the same paths toward achieving their goals, the same emotions, the same sense of fairness, and the same wants and needs. They often experience difference as disloyalty.

Expectations of sameness handicap enmeshed partners' efforts to resolve Dilemma #2 conflicts in several ways. To begin with, enmeshed partners' expectations of sameness lead them to perceive their partners as extensions of themselves. Because of this perception, it is easy for them to recognize ways that their partners could help them achieve their own goals but more difficult to perceive how they could be helpful to their partners.

Further, enmeshed individuals believe that their partners can learn to "do better," which often means think, feel, and behave the way that they themselves do. They often adhere to the psychologically naïve belief that their partners are infinitely malleable and can change because they hear a logical argument in favor of their behaving differently. When couples report that they have been fighting about the same issues with the same arguments repeatedly with no change in their approach, it is often because they adhere to the belief that "next time" they will come up with the perfect argument that will change their partner's thinking or behavior to more closely resemble their own.

A related belief that is often held by enmeshed individuals is that their partners are willfully withholding a change that would make themselves happier. Enmeshed partners persist in their efforts to persuade the other to give them what they want because they perceive willful withholding. The belief that motivates the repetitive conflict is, "It would be so easy for him to do this for me. If he doesn't, it is because he's a jerk."

In sum, enmeshed partners believe that they and their partners must be the same, that their partners are malleable and can change if they hear the right argument, and that partners who do not change are willfully and maliciously withholding themselves. As a result of these beliefs, arguments of enmeshed partners are often coercive. Through seemingly impeccable logic, pleas, angry recriminations, withdrawal and sulking, or a multitude of other coercive strategies, enmeshed partners attempt to influence one another to change their ways. These change efforts are intensely frustrating, partly because partners confront their helplessness when attempting to change each other and partly because each is mystified by the other's recalcitrance. The mystification stems from the less differentiated individual's unrealistic expectation that two can be like one.

Addressing the Cognitive Distortions Associated with Enmeshment

When working with enmeshed couples, it is useful to begin treatment by focusing on cognitions that are shared in common by enmeshed partners, as it is difficult for partners to stay calm or to change their behavior until their attitudes and expectations are modified. Two cognitive interventions that can be used very early in treatment are normalization and development of realistic expectations. Therapists can help to normalize a couple's struggles with Dilemma #2 by teaching partners that people typically come into their relationships with their own separate viewpoints and their own aims on numerous issues. The therapist can teach them to expect that working through and resolving differences are a normal part of a couple relationship. Therapists might even suggest that partners can learn to be intrigued by one another's differences and thereby enhance their relational intimacy through their discussions of their differences. The development of realistic expectations helps couple partners rethink their goals and desired outcomes for their interactions. Couple partners are more likely to listen to one another and to communicate understanding and respect when they do not expect to unify or become one.

In the individual session laid out below, the therapist combines realistic expectations and normalization to help Charlie, who was in the habit of trying to change his wife Brittany's way of handling money. Charlie's efforts to change Brittany had not resulted in her changing her behavior but did succeed in frustrating Charlie and had damaged their intimate connection.

Therapist: As part of asking her to live within a budget with you, you can acknowledge the good things about her that motivate her to spend too much. Like, when you argue about budget, you could be praising her generosity.

Charlie: But I don't want her to think that she can just spend whatever she wants.

Therapist: Let me give you an example of what I mean—you don't just appreciate you also say what's important to you. "You know, Brittany, I'm really touched by how much you love the kids and grandkids, and how you've taken them under your wing. And I know we've argued a lot about how much you spend on them every Christmas, and I think because of all that arguing, I haven't let you know how much I appreciate the love you show them. And I know they appreciate it, too. So would you be willing to talk with me about how we can stay within our budget while still being generous to the family?" . . . You wouldn't find yourself in the odd position of trying to change something that you actually like about Brittany—her generosity . . . that gets us to the next piece of this. Tell me about how you expect her to change.

Charlie: Well, I expect her as an adult to be able to stay within a budget. When I met her, she had no savings at all. She spends every penny she makes and more. Her daughter had to put herself through college. . . .

Therapist: OK, so you expect her to change her way of handling money.

Charlie: I don't think that's unreasonable.

Therapist: What's unreasonable is expecting her to see the handling of money the way you do. You see money as a cushion against hard times. She sees it as a way to express her love. I think you're walking against a steep incline when you try to change that basic value. What you can more likely do is ask her to respect your views on money while you simultaneously agree to respect hers.

Charlie: In other words, have a gift budget.

Therapist: Good idea—and a savings budget for you. Decide how much you want to put into savings. Decide how much you can afford to spend on gifts. Honor her desire to be generous with your family. Then work on ways to afford it. . . . The advantage of these solutions is that they acknowledge the value of being generous at Christmastime. And you are out of the business of changing the way Brittany thinks about money. Of trying to make her more like you. People don't usually marry someone who is just like themselves. And you and Brittany are no exception.

This therapist worked with Charlie to help him to see his marital dilemma as normal (by validating what he wants from Brittany). The therapist also helped Charlie to see that the reason he was so frustrated was that he was trying to achieve a goal that wasn't in his power to achieve, which was to make Brittany value money in the same way that he did. Instead, the therapist suggested that there are ways to encourage Brittany to be more cooperative with him that don't require him to invalidate her needs.

Intervening with emotion and behavior. Partly because they expect "oneness," less differentiated partners are at risk for becoming overwhelmed with anxiety when they confront a different viewpoint or desire in the other. They may fear being "swallowed up" in their partner's game plan. Expending energy to change one another, they are too anxious or angry to devote their efforts to perceiving the internal logic of their partner's perspective.

Teaching partners how to calm themselves before they speak is a useful intervention for couples struggling with Dilemma #2. The first time, the therapist can soothe partners' emotions, which permits them to evaluate the impact of emotional soothing on their conversations before they learn to do it themselves. Later, the therapist can teach partners rapid self-soothing and pause before speaking in order to calm themselves down and communicate constructively during an intense interaction.

Bob and Amanda used to get so upset with each other during their sessions that their therapist had to shout at them to stop talking. Here is how their therapist introduced ujjayi breathing as a rapid self-soothing intervention.

Therapist: Hold it! You two sound pretty upset . . . before we continue, let's all get calm together with a technique called ujjayi breathing. You breathe deeply through your nose while keeping a space in the back of your throat open so that you can hear your breath going in and out. Watch me do it and then we'll all do it together. . . . How would you feel about our making a deal that each time the discussion gets too heated, we pause for ujjayi breathing? The more we practice in here, the more likely you'll be able to use this to calm yourself down outside of our sessions.

Amanda and Bob's therapist should also assign it for homework and encourage them to practice it when they are not upset, so that when they do need to calm down, they can use it on the spot for self-soothing.

Dual monitoring is another useful technique for encouraging partners to listen to and attempt to understand one another. Respectful listening, a requirement for intimacy, may seem to the less differentiated individual as the path to capitulation. It is difficult for less differentiated individuals to fully absorb the partner's message while simultaneously maintaining self-understanding. The less differentiated partner erroneously experiences him- or herself as facing an impossible choice between self and other. Intimacy is reduced or compromised when acknowledgment and understanding are confused with capitulating.

The therapist who seeks to teach dual monitoring to enhance a couple's coping with Dilemma #2 selects a conflict that the couple has brought into therapy, then communicates the goals of the exercise. This therapist validates the new level of psychological differentiation that Carla has already demonstrated in the relationship: maintaining the self.

Therapist: Carla, I hear that you don't want to just capitulate on this issue—you believe you've done that too much in the past. So now you are erring in the opposite direction—you're communicating aggressively and not getting Doug's return message. This process you're on—being assertive and speaking your mind—is healthy and a good direction for you. [*Therapist validates.*] So now the challenge is combining it with listening and getting Doug's message without losing your own.

Carla: It's true, I always ignored myself. I did whatever he said—I was little submissive wife, Miss Be Quiet. . . .

Therapist: Well, it's important that Miss Be Quiet not return; this will not improve your relationship. What will improve it, though, is you continuing to feel more confident that you will speak up, say what you mean, and not back down just to avoid a fight. As you feel more confident, you'll be able to combine your assertiveness with careful listening and understanding of Doug's messages to you.

Doug: That would be nice.

Therapist: Carla, would you be willing to work on this combining of assertiveness and listening today? [*Set goals.*]

Carla: Well, I think I listen to him, you know, but sure I'm game.

Therapist: You do listen, until you get emotional. Most of us have the same problem. [*Normalization.*] This is a strategy to help you with that, so that the two of you can communicate more effectively. It's called dual monitoring. I'll explain it as we go along. Doug, your role here is to respond to the work that Carla is doing. She'll be working hard to improve your communication, so we'll have to put any issues that arise for you aside temporarily. Can you live with that for now? [*Identify one partner as working and one as assisting.*]

Doug: Yes, this sounds like it will be a good thing.

Therapist:	Doug, if you would, please repeat what you said a minute ago. Then, I'd like you to sit quietly, if you're comfortable with doing so now and let Carla work through this dual monitoring process.
Doug:	OK I said, it seems like she's criticizing me all the time, always finding fault. I can do no right, even though I have so much respect and love for her, and she's always on my case. [*Assisting partner communicates message.*]
Carla:	You know that's not true. We've been getting along so much better; it's only in here that I bring things up.
Therapist:	OK, hold it; this is the point, Carla, where dual monitoring is really helpful. It will help you to focus on what you are feeling, on what you want, and what is the best way to get there. So let's put this on the whiteboard—six columns. Take a minute to check in with yourself, breathe in slowly, and tell me what you're feeling. [*Present the six-column chart—see* Table 9.1.]
Carla:	I know what I'm feeling. I'm angry, he's saying that we're fighting all the time. . . .
Therapist:	OK, I'm writing "angry" on the whiteboard in column 1. Any other feelings that should be up here? . . . OK, how angry are you, 1 to 10?
Carla:	I'm pretty close to a 10, I'd say a 9.2. [*The working partner identifies the emotion aroused by the assisting partner's message and rates the strength of the emotion.*]
Therapist (laughter):	Fair enough; a 9.2. OK, the next part is to notice what's making you angry; you said Doug's saying he thinks you criticize him a lot. Right?
Carla:	That's right. . . .
Therapist:	Now does this also capture it? Doug is sharing a perception of his that doesn't fit with your perception, right?
Carla:	It's not fair; I'm making an effort to let things go, to laugh things off.
Therapist:	Take a minute and focus inside yourself, Carla. Take a deep breath or two to help you focus inside. What are you reacting to?
Carla:	The unfairness of what he said, it's wrong.
Therapist:	Would you accept my description? That his perception of how it's been is different from yours?
Carla:	Yes that's true.
Therapist:	And his perception is more negative than yours.
Carla:	Yeah no kidding!
Therapist:	OK, I'm writing this in the second column here. "Different and more negative perception." Is that

Table 9.1 Six-column worksheet for dual monitoring intervention

Internal Monitoring: (What do I feel? Rate emotion 1–10.)	External Monitoring: (What I see and what I hear from my partner.)	Automatic Thought Monitoring: (My interpretation of my partner's message/ behavior, automatic thoughts.)	My Immediate Goal/My Long-Term Goal:	Alternative Interpretation: (Is my interpretation helping me to achieve my goal?)	Internal State: (Rate emotion1–10.)

acceptable? . . . OK? Now—next step—how do you interpret his more negative perception?

Carla: Well, I don't know where he gets it! Last weekend, we went out and had a great time, we saw our friends. . . . Sunday we went out for breakfast and had fun; it wasn't until last night that I was telling him. . . .

Therapist: What does it mean that he is thinking more negatively than you? What's the implication if he doesn't see how things have improved between you?

Carla: Well if he can't see that, I don't know how we're ever going to make it.

Therapist: OK, do I have your interpretation correct? If he doesn't see the improvement that you see, you will never make it as a couple. Is that right? [*Identify the thought that accompanies the emotion.*]

Carla: Yes, he has to see what I've been trying to do.

Therapist: OK, so what does it look like here? Could some or most of your anger come from your seeing a lot riding on his perceptions?

Carla: Well, I don't know; I guess if I was that negative, I'd be wondering if it would ever work. [*Here Carla identifies a fear scenario of hers.*]

Therapist: OK, let me put that up here in the fourth column, that is, your interpretation of what it means that he is perceiving this. Now what was your reaction to this interpretation—your strategy when you were communicating with Doug?

Carla: He just sees things so negatively. . . .

Therapist: What was your strategy? What did you hope to convey to Doug?

Carla: Well, I had to defend myself. To defend our marriage.

Therapist: OK, to defend the relationship, to show him that it is viable and healthy. Would you agree, Carla, that this is what you were doing just now?

Carla (laughter): I'm trying to clear up his muddled thinking!

Therapist: And when I see this, it makes total sense to me; given this interpretation, I can see why you'd have so much anger, and I would think maybe some fear, too? That you won't make it together?

Carla: Yes, I want it to work.

Therapist: You know, my experience has taught me that people who argue hard on a point, like you were doing earlier in the session, are mad, but they're also fearing something, like the anger is saying, "How dare you scare

	me like that." I'm thinking of your arguments about Doug's driving, they're kind of like that.
Carla:	OK.
Therapist:	So would it be fair to say that the goal here is that you want Doug to relieve the fear? Even though the emotion that you're expressing is anger? [*Identify the communication goals associated with the emotion, the thought, and/or the message.*]
Carla:	I think you're right. We've worked so hard, who wants it to fall apart now.
Therapist:	So, as you think about your purpose, to get that reassurance, that relief from the fear, can you think of another way to accomplish that, besides expressing anger?
Carla:	Well, I could ask him for reassurance, couldn't I?
Therapist:	That would be more direct, wouldn't it.
Carla:	Yes, it would. And I'm getting more direct, so it fits with how I want to be with Doug.
Therapist:	Was it difficult to get to the fear? To identify it?
Carla:	At the time, I just knew I was angry.
Therapist:	That's what this process is for. To get at emotions—and goals—that are below the surface. That requires some thought, some introspection to get to them. It's easy for all of us to just react; this is harder. It is worth doing when we actually get the outcome we desire.
Carla:	Yes, I can see that.
Therapist:	I'll give you some of these sheets to take home. While you're learning, you may have to do the exercise after you've had an argument, or after you've had an interaction with Doug that didn't go the way you wanted it to. Then when you've done the exercise, you can get back to Doug and start again more directly, asking for what you're wanting.
Carla:	Well you know, I'm not so good with homework.
Therapist:	Homework gets you where you want to go faster—but we can also keep practicing here in our sessions. What do you think Doug? You were complaining about how Carla argues with you; does her arguing make more sense now?
Doug:	Yeah, she thinks I'm going to give up on her or something. But how could she possibly think that after I've said so many times how much I love her and how much I want us to be together.
Therapist:	OK great, Doug, you've just helped Carla with the last step here. You've given Carla a reminder that you are

not considering leaving her! And your worries that you voice here should not be taken that way. Would that be accurate?

Doug: Absolutely.

Therapist: So tell me, Carla, having walked through this step-by-step process and hearing what Doug has to say about his intentions, how do you feel now?

Carla: Well I'm laughing, so I guess I'm not angry now!

As this dialogue suggests, Carla still needs more practice with simultaneously listening to Doug and determining what it is that she's feeling and wanting. Dual monitoring provided her with a route by which to reach her goals. It helped her to identify her goals and her fears and helped her to distinguish between what she imagined was going on with Doug and his actual message.

In sum, addressing a couple's difficulties with listening and showing understanding usually requires interventions that also target thinking processes and emotion. Oftentimes, cognitive interventions set the stage for the emotion-focused and behavioral interventions to work. Cognitive interventions help couples to see their different needs, wants, goals, and perceptions as normal and to replace coercive efforts to change each other with listening, understanding, and constructive problem solving. Some differences are especially challenging to live with, however, and with this in mind, I turn next to differences in intimacy needs.

Understanding Differences in Intimacy Needs

Couple partners who have long-standing differences in their intimacy needs and wants are especially aware of the importance of intimacy and can find themselves chronically unfulfilled in their relationships. Further, it is difficult for partners to demonstrate understanding for one another when their needs go unmet. These next sections discuss the problem of different needs and some interventions for addressing them.

Needs for intimacy are universal even if people vary widely in the strength of their intimacy needs. For my understanding of individual differences in need strengths, I am indebted to Henry Murray's (1938) personality theory, which was built on the premise that there are dispositional differences in need strengths that will cause people to perceive different potential benefits in interpersonal situations and, in turn, to behave differently. Murray assumed that we are motivated to selectively attend to those aspects of a situation that correspond to our most strongly felt needs. According to Murray, needs are evident in the "figure" that the individual selectively perceives and responds to in the "ground" of social interaction. The extent to which specific needs organize perceptions and behavior in a given situation will vary depending upon the felt strength of the need at the time.

I understand problems with acknowledging and respecting partner needs in intimate relationships to occur because each partner's behavior is organized by the needs that are most salient to him or her at that moment, and that partners can simultaneously pursue the fulfillment of opposing needs. When goals are at cross-purposes, as when one partner wants to interact with the other and the other wants to pursue other goals, the need fulfillment strategies of two partners will be mutually incompatible. If partners have stable differences in need strengths, then their incompatible aims will repeat themselves across many interactions.

There are many reasons why some incompatibility of needs is inevitable. First, partners can hail from different cultures with different norms. Cultures (including specifically American subcultures) "groom" people for different levels and forms of intimacy. Cultures vary in their norms for public displays of affection, hugging and kissing, the amount of time for interaction that partners expect to have with one another, and the amount of sharing of one's inner life that is expected in close relationships. Second, families have their own idiosyncratic norms for intimacy. Normal variations among families result in offspring who are better prepared for some levels and forms of intimacy than others. Some families touch but don't express emotions; some families are comfortable with nudity and talk openly about sexuality but have little tolerance for members' emotional needs; some families encourage self-exploration and disclosure whereas others believe in taking life as it comes, and so forth. In brief, healthy functioning families may demonstrate a variety of patterns of intimacy tolerance based, in part, on what kinds of intimacy are deemed acceptable or comfortable in the culture of the family of origin and what kinds are discouraged.

Third, intimacy needs vary across the life cycle. For example, men's needs for sexual intimacy appear to be strongest when they are young adults and decline in intensity as they grow older (McCarthy & McCarthy, 2003). Husbands and wives alike forgo the fulfillment of many intimacy needs during their middle adult years when careers and growing children are so demanding but want to strengthen their intimate connection once children are launched (Whitbourne & Weinstock, 1986). Finally, partners' intimacy preferences may be just one of a myriad of partially inherited personality differences that affect close relationships (e.g., O'Rourke, Neufeld, Claxton, & Smith, 2010).

Given that partners are more likely than not to have different intimacy needs and preferences, even the most satisfied and harmonious partners will eventually confront those differences and attempt to resolve them. These variations in people's needs for intimate contact can be a source of intense frustration and distress because the more disparate the partners' needs are coming into the relationship, the more difficult it is for either of them to get their needs fulfilled. If partners fail to identify ways to meet their respective intimacy needs, they are likely to find themselves dissatisfied with their relationship. Partner compatibility issues are best approached with the assumption that the strength of people's needs for intimacy are rooted in long-established dispositions that can change in degree but are unlikely to be completely altered by therapeutic intervention.

Frank and Barbara's struggle with Dilemma #2 illustrates the way that differences in intimacy needs can create problems. Barbara is the more frustrated partner because she has unmet intimacy needs and because she interprets as rejection Frank's seeming to need less intimate contact than she does. Whereas unmet needs can cause pain, negative interpretations of partner differences exacerbate the pain of the unmet needs that result from those differences (Christensen & Jacobson, 1996), and this is what is transpiring with Barbara. Frank and Barbara's problems are further complicated by the fact that both partners display the enmeshed pattern of coping with Dilemma #2, which means that each attempts to coax the other into seeing the world as he or she sees it. This conversation between Frank and Barbara illustrates the dilemmas faced by enmeshed couples struggling with differences in intimacy needs.

Barbara: What's the point of being together if I spend most of my weekends alone or with girlfriends?

Frank: [*Defending himself, attempting to change Barbara's perception that they don't spend enough time together and to persuade her to think more like he does.*] C'mon, Barbara, we go out together every Friday and Saturday night, and we do fun things. We stay together and get up and have breakfast together. Then I want to go do my own thing. What is so important about having me with you every minute?

Barbara: When you put it that way, I feel so unloved. Besides, we don't go out every Friday and Saturday night. Last Friday night you had that dinner. . . .

Frank: I invited you to come with me. We could have been together.

Barbara: You know I don't get along with those people. Why do you keep planning things with them when you know they don't like me, and I feel so uncomfortable around them.

Frank: They're my friends, Barbara. Besides, you're wrong that they don't like you. Maybe they think you're shy or something, but I don't see any evidence that they don't like you.

Barbara: You've seen Joan—I think she has a crush on you. She barely greets me. . . .

Frank: You're being ridiculous, Barbara! Joan is happily married. Besides, how often do I make plans with them?

	Maybe three times a year? I would think you could put up with them that often for my sake.
Barbara:	[*Brings the conversation back.*] My point is, we don't get together every Friday night. And when we miss a Friday, you don't make it up to me. We just spend less time together, and it doesn't seem to bother you. I would love it if just once, we could go for a drive or go to the park on a Sunday afternoon.
Frank:	Tell you what. Let's plan on going this Sunday. I don't mind at all our making plans for a Sunday afternoon. You just think I don't want to.
Barbara:	You mean that?
Frank:	I do. This Sunday we'll go for a drive into the country and go walking.

Frank and Barbara's conversation illustrates a good faith effort to cope with differences in intimacy needs. Barbara's unmet intimacy needs are evident when Barbara has to ask Frank for more time over and over. Barbara finds herself in this role because her "intimacy bank account" gets depleted sooner than Frank's does. She notices first when the two have not had much time together. Frank does not realize yet that he cannot solve their problem by offering additional together time to Barbara on a one-time basis. Frank's thoughtful solution will make Barbara happy for a weekend, and Frank will be happy that she's happy. However, when Barbara complains again, as she inevitably will, Frank will be especially aware of his 'I versus we' dilemma where intimate time with Barbara is concerned. He may be more motivated to please himself because he pleased her the time before. He may also judge that his previous efforts to make her happy are going unappreciated.

Like other 'I versus we' dilemmas, problems with differences in intimacy needs are resolved most effectively when partners have good psychological differentiation skills. Barbara's and Frank's communication reveals each of their problems with differentiation and, by so doing, reveals how improbable it is that they have resolved this issue. Frank begins their discussion by refusing to acknowledge Barbara's complaint or the feelings that go with it. Instead, he wants to persuade her that her perception of their time together is flawed. He hopes that she will change her mind and decide that in fact they have plenty of time together, which is his perception. For her part, Barbara interprets Frank's effort to change her mind as an indication that he does not miss their time together as much as she does. Further, she interprets that apparent truth as a sign that he does not love her as much as she loves him. She assumes that the only way to experience and express love is the way that she does (i.e., by wanting lots of time together), and that Frank's being different from her indicates inadequate love on his part. Both of them lose the focus of the argument for a time when they argue about Frank's friends and Barbara's perception of them (Frank again invalidates Barbara's perception of his friends by refusing to acknowledge it and trying to convince her to perceive them as he does). Frank, to his credit, ultimately comes up with a solution, one that involves his devoting a Sunday to a joint activity that he knows Barbara will enjoy. However, the couple has not yet addressed their primary I versus we difficulty, which is that they are different and are currently unable to accept and demonstrate respect for one another's differences. Instead, they will find themselves replaying this argument many times again.

Frank and Barbara have different intimacy needs, but in fact they are struggling with more than that. Frank enjoys intimacy with Barbara as much as she enjoys it with him. Rather, Frank has a need for quiet, alone time that overrides his needs for intimacy and compels him to postpone fulfilling the latter. For many of us, strong needs for autonomy, separateness, and alone time can compete with needs for intimacy in the context of an intimate relationship. To resolve apparent differences in intimacy needs, many couples will also have to address their different needs for autonomy and alone time. It is to the challenges that these needs pose for couples that I turn next.

The Flip Side of Intimacy Needs: Needs for Autonomy and Separateness

It is usually easy for a therapist to understand and validate a lonely partner's unmet needs for intimacy. Yet it is wrong to see the less lonely partner as someone who simply has a weaker, less salient need for intimacy. Although this may indeed be the case, it is also likely that their efforts to fulfill autonomy and separateness needs create problems with relational intimacy.

Autonomy refers to a person's ability to endorse and organize his or her own activities (Ryan & Deci, 2010). Autonomy allows people to select the domains within which they will operate, with those domains, in turn, creating the self-schemas with which people will organize (and expand) their self-concepts. The need for *separateness* includes the need for time alone and for time to pursue interests and friends that one's partner does not share. It includes the need to be physically apart from other people, a need to be free from the observing public eye, from interruptions and distractions, from noise, and from demands on one's attention.

Needs for intimacy exist in "dialectical tension" with needs for autonomy and separateness (Baxter & Simon, 1993). This means that intimacy and autonomy needs are fulfilled through different behaviors and activities (e.g., Larson, 1990). Dialectical tension exists because the intimate interactions that meet needs for intimacy do not meet needs for autonomy whereas the pursuit of interests, activities, and goals that fulfill autonomy needs do not necessarily meet intimacy needs. Dialectical tension also refers to the way that autonomy and separateness can foster intimacy. As people's needs for separateness are fulfilled, their needs for intimacy become more salient, and the fulfillment of those intimacy needs becomes more rewarding. Healthy adult functioning requires both intimacy and autonomy (e.g., Bakan, 1966; Blatt & Blass, 1996; Erikson, 1950; Guisinger & Blatt, 1994, Ryan & Deci, 2000), with the fulfillment of each creating the optimum conditions for the other. Indeed, trait autonomy has been associated with less defensive and more understanding responses to disagreements (Knee, Lonsbury, Canevello, & Patrick, 2005). Intimacy and autonomy are, therefore, each essential but dialectically opposed needs.

Needs for autonomy and separateness are similar to needs for intimacy in that they are unlikely to change dramatically. Further, the consequences of ignoring individual psychological needs can be disruptive to a couple's relationship or can lead to behaviors that sabotage developing intimate relationships. On the one hand, when the partners sacrifice too much of their separate interests, goals, and friendships because they think this is necessary to preserve their level of intimacy, then one or both partners is likely to have feelings of being smothered. On the other hand, if partners put all of their time and energy into separate pursuits, then they will find themselves experiencing less intimacy and fewer relationship rewards as a result.

We can now revisit Frank and Barbara's dilemma and get a new perspective on their struggles. First, the notion that couple partners can have stable differences in intimacy needs and in autonomy and separateness needs helps the therapist understand why the couple repeats this conflict over and over. Frank and Barbara struggle with their difference in intimacy needs, while they must also address Frank's efforts to fulfill his strong needs for separateness and alone time, needs that are greater than Barbara's. In fact, taking Frank's needs for alone time into account can help the therapist avoid overestimating the difference between Frank and Barbara's intimacy needs. Frank's needs for intimacy are closer to Barbara's than is apparent from their interactions, but Frank is willing to give up some intimate time with Barbara to satisfy his needs for alone time. Barbara enjoys some alone time, but her desire for intimate contact overrides that need, and she is willing to give up some of her alone time to be with Frank.

Second, the notion that irresolvable conflict often stems from a lack of psychological differentiation on the part of one or both partners helps the therapist make educated guesses about the way that Frank and Barbara understand their conflict and why they fail to resolve it. Frank and Barbara each believe the other should *and could* be more similar to him- or herself. Barbara believes that people who love each other miss each other when they are not in frequent contact. She uses her own window of time—a few hours or a day—as the standard and concludes that anyone who can wait longer does not love very much. Further, she believes that if Frank does spend more time with her, he will see how enjoyable that time is and become more willing to spend the time.

For his part, Frank misses Barbara when they are apart, but he doesn't think about missing her before a couple of days go by. Frank's appreciation for quiet, alone time is stronger than are his feelings of missing Barbara during the two or three days after he has spent time with her. Once those days have passed, missing Barbara begins to take precedence for Frank and he is eager to see her. Because Barbara has already missed him for days once he is ready and has pressured him to get together with her, she rarely gets the opportunity to see how happy he is to see her after two or three days. So it seems to her that he never misses her although she is missing him very much.

Because of his belief that Barbara's needs are malleable, Frank's solution to their dilemma is to attempt to manipulate Barbara's perception of the amount of time they spend together. He does this by failing to acknowledge Barbara's complaint and by arguing with her about her perception. Further, he is betting that if he spends this Sunday with her, she'll be happy enough to give him more space the next time he wants it. He has not shared this hoped-for trade-off with Barbara, however. Further, Frank will have neglected his own needs for a time and will likely feel the lack of separate time as the week goes on. Missed alone time affects his mood, and the following weekend, he may find himself determined to guard his alone time more jealously. Barbara will then again feel bereft, not understanding why they don't spend their whole weekend together. At that point, they will start the argument again. Because Frank and Barbara have not accepted that they are different, they cannot work together to decide how to have a good relationship despite their differences.

Finally, the notion that Dilemma #2, I versus we, is an ordinary dilemma faced by all couples allows the therapist working with Barbara and Frank to give them hope that their problems can be resolved and their relationship preserved. By teaching the couple the dual monitoring technique, for example, therapists provide couple partners with a process for simultaneously evaluating their own feelings and listening to their partners' messages. The technique also helps each partner determine the thoughts that elicit those feelings and how to translate feelings into wants and needs that can be communicated. Further, they learn how to do so while maintaining a respectful, open stance toward their partner's needs. In sum, understanding that differences in partners' needs can cause Dilemma #2 challenges offers multiple pathways for intervention with troubled couples.

Special Challenges Associated with High Needs for Autonomy

Although high autonomy needs do not necessarily signify a lack of love or aversion to intimacy, people with strong autonomy and separateness needs can have special problems with intimate relationships. They may seek to fulfill their autonomy needs by going about their business as though they did not have obligations to the other partner. They create distance when they make plans and decisions without consulting the partner.

Individuals who have strong needs for autonomy can have intimate relationships, but they must pay attention to their behavior in order to reconcile their obligations to intimate partners with their needs for autonomy. Their expectations for how much time and attention they must devote to a relationship to sustain it may be unrealistically low. Once the strong autonomy needs are acknowledged by both partners, accommodations can be made to allow the high-autonomy individual to meet some of his or her needs without sabotaging the couple relationship. A partner who seeks to fulfill strong needs for achievement may create the same behavioral pattern in the relationship as the high-autonomy individual does in his or hers.

Normally, seeking opportunities to fulfill autonomy and separateness needs should not reflect upon the partners' desires for intimacy with one another. Most frequently, it represents the normal rhythms with which partners regulate the fulfillment of intimacy and separateness needs. Possibly, the worst problems associated with differences in autonomy needs may stem from partners' misinterpreting the significance of those differences, confusing them for lack of love, commitment, and caring.

Nevertheless, two interrelated problems arise in the interpretation of bids for separate activity. First, they can be misinterpreted as bids for distance, causing distress to the partner who is misinterpreting them. Second, the communication around their misinterpretation can itself cause problems. When partners wrongly confuse bids for separate activity with bids for distance, they may perceive a lack of love or the possibility of infidelity in such activities. Their accusations and bids for reassurance strain the relationship. Even if not communicated, their interpretations of the partner's needs for autonomy and separateness cause them internal distress and may ironically sabotage relational intimacy.

To further complicate this dilemma, sometimes bids for more autonomy are in fact used to disguise efforts to increase distance and may be mistakenly taken at face value. Partners will claim that they need time alone when they really mean they want distance from the other but don't want to confront the other with the reasons. They can then play head games with the other partner, who intuits the distancing but wonders if he or she is wrongly interpreting normal desires for separateness. Couple therapists should avoid dismissing the concerns of partners who claim to perceive the partner distancing them and interview them carefully to determine on what basis they make their claims.

The therapist has the same dilemma as the confused partner when a client in couple therapy claims that he wants more time for separate activities or quiet, alone time. The therapist must determine if these requests can be taken at face value or whether the client is using them to disguise relationship troubles, including an affair. The individual interview gives the therapist the best opportunity for learning as much as possible about the client's needs for separateness. The best assessment method is for the therapist to ask directly, such as in the following examples:

"Is there anyone else in your life besides Maria, another woman?"

"What have you done to try to work this out with Maria? Are there any compromises that you've tried before that haven't worked out?"

"All these activities that take you away from home, is it possible that these provide you with a good opportunity to get away from an unhappy situation at home?"

"It's normal for couple partners to want to push each other away sometimes. Do you ever feel that you want to do that with Maria? How often? What do you do when you feel the urge to get away?"

It is important that the therapist support partners' efforts to fulfill needs for autonomy and separateness while simultaneously offering them realistic expectations with regard to their fulfillment. Intimate relationships may not retain their level of intimacy if partners place too high a priority on fulfilling separateness and autonomy needs and neglect their intimate connection with their partner.

Helping Couples Cope with Differences in Intimacy and Autonomy Needs

Because differences in intimacy, autonomy, and separateness needs cause intense emotional reactions in the partners, they are especially likely to challenge the psychological differentiation skills of the partners. It is difficult to accept something about the partner that will result in one's own needs not being fulfilled. It is therefore common, at least in my own practice, to see differences in need strengths and problems with accepting and respecting the partner's perspective going hand-in-hand to create irreconcilable conflict over intimacy.

Helping couple partners to demonstrate acceptance and respect for one another's perceptions and needs requires a multipronged approach. Joan and Gayle's therapy shows how one therapist combined five of the therapy techniques discussed in this book to treat a couple who had trouble acknowledging their differences and addressing them. The five strategies used in this example are: (1) soothe partners' anxiety and frustration; (2) teach realistic expectations; (3) increase emotion tolerance; (4) teach identification of problematic intimacy schemas and fear scenarios; and (5) teach them effective communication strategies such as pause before speaking.

Joan initiated the contact with the therapist because her intimacy needs were not being met. One complaint was that her partner Gayle did not make herself available for conversation after Joan came home from a hard day at work. Joan was angry because she was convinced that if only Gayle would try harder, Gayle could be as emotionally available as she, Joan, needed her to be. She was convinced that Gayle would try harder if she loved Joan enough. Joan did not think of herself as especially demanding and considered herself a strong, independent person who only wanted what was reasonable: some time and attention from her partner. In general, she got annoyed with Gayle for wanting so much time for herself and her work. The ensuing arguments would create distance between Joan and Gayle. Gayle gets angry and defensive in response to Joan's pushing Gayle to give her the intimate contact she needs. Gayle works hard to get Joan to acknowledge her experience but without much success. Further, Gayle attacks Joan, accusing her of having no interests and depending too much on Gayle for company.

Joan in this example is experiencing a high level of anxiety because her relationship problems are activating a fear scenario she has about intimate relationships. Her fear is that she and Gayle will stop trying to make each other happy and will experience deterioration in their relationship quality as a result. Joan had experienced this kind of deterioration in a previous relationship. She swore she would not go through that again and believes that she can avoid this outcome by remaining vigilant and refusing to settle for less than perfect.

Gayle and Joan's therapist used the multistep process described above to help them accept and cope effectively with the differences in their needs, as illustrated in the following dialogue.

Therapist: [*Soothes Joan's and Gayle's intense emotions by acknowledging their messages and demonstrating understanding.*] I can hear how frustrating this whole disagreement is for both of you. Neither of you wants to reject the other, but somehow you find yourselves doing just that. Gayle, I can hear that you are hurt that Joan doesn't understand your needs for quiet, separate time and that it's frustrating to you that she interprets them as a sign that you don't enjoy her company. Joan, I hear you being overextended at work and looking forward to spending time with Gayle, whose life is less stressful, and enjoying letting her take care of you. It seems like a small thing to you, and yet it also seems that Gayle withholds from you.

Joan: I think I do understand Gayle's need for solitude and quiet. I just don't understand why she gets overloaded with my company so quickly. And it's true, when I come home from work, I'm not very good at showing understanding when Gayle seems to just be thinking about herself.

Therapist: And the stronger your needs are, the more stressed you've been and the more time and attention you need from Gayle, the less able you are to take a step back and try to understand her needs at that moment, especially when those needs are different from yours.

Joan: I guess I have been feeling tired, washed out, and like I don't have much to give. And I get angry because Gayle seems stingy to me, stingy about her time and attention. . . .

Therapist: OK, let me ask you a couple of questions to see if I can understand better how all of this plays out with you two. [*Therapist begins laying out realistic expectations by normalizing their dilemma.*] Every couple has times when they don't see enough of each other, don't get enough time to be together as a couple, and want more intimacy. Between the two of you, who is the first to notice when this happens with you?

Joan and Gayle: I do/Joan does. . . .

Therapist: And which of you is the first to notice when you haven't had enough quiet time, separate time, alone time?

Joan and Gayle: I do/Gayle does.

Therapist: And this difference—that Joan notices lack of together time and Gayle notices lack of personal time—could this be at the heart of a lot of your arguments?

Joan: It's that—but it's also that I want that time right after I get home. I'd like that to be "us time."

Therapist: So, you are OK with being the one who usually notices when it's time for you two to be together, when you haven't had enough time?

Joan: Hmmm. I guess I've been angrier about that lately. That's been part of this overall angry feeling I have. Why doesn't Gayle ever say that she misses spending time with me?

Gayle: I do!

Joan: OK, maybe now and then, but it's usually me.

Therapist: I think you all are dealing with a basic difference between the two of you. [*Therapist normalizes their dilemma and suggests realistic expectations.*] Although everyone needs intimacy and everyone needs solitude sometimes, you two do not have exactly the same needs. Joan, you seem to need more intimacy than Gayle whereas Gayle needs more solitude than you do. As a result, Gayle mostly notices first when she hasn't had alone time in awhile. And Joan, you end up being the one who notices when the two of you need to reconnect and have intimate time. I think this is about a personality difference that may have little to do with love.

Joan: Well I didn't ever really think that Gayle didn't love me, just that she was selfish with her time.

Therapist: So this is a different, and I think a more realistic way to understand what Gayle wants. She is different from you and needs more alone time. I'll be honest with you and tell you that this is probably a stable difference. Gayle is more introverted than you are, Joan. Introverts get overloaded with external stimulation more quickly than extroverts. Loud music, parties, city life, conversation—put two people in those situations and the more introverted person will be ready to stop before the more extroverted person most of the time. Introversion is a continuum though—if you all were too different, you might never have been attracted to each other enough to form a relationship. Does my description fit your experience, Gayle?

Gayle: Yes, that sounds like me. I start feeling overwhelmed and want some quiet. But that's only temporary until I can come and visit again. Joan's always taken that so personally, I haven't known how to handle it.

Joan: I'm afraid if I leave it all up to you, we'd get together once a month or something. I'm afraid it would mean the end of our relationship.

Therapist: [*By encouraging them to perceive and accept their differences, the couple's therapist is mapping out a path toward more psychological differentiation.*] Fortunately, Joan, Gayle has you, and she can count on you, simply because of who you are, that you will not let the two of you drift apart.

Gayle: That's right, I do value Joan's opinion on this. I just want Joan—you—to accept me for who I am too.

Therapist: What I'd like to work on with the two of you is to find some kind of process for working with your differences. [*Normalizing.*] This is something every couple must do because people rarely hook up with their identical twin. The way you two have been dealing with this has made you both unhappy, but differences by themselves don't have to do that. I'm going to suggest a two-pronged approach, one that requires each of you to make changes. Sound good?

Gayle and Joan: Yes.

Therapist: First I want to work on the expectations that you have for each other. Why don't we start with each of you articulating what it is that you expect or hope for from the other as far as this issue goes?

Gayle: I would like you to be more understanding about my alone time. Don't take it so personally; I do love you. I just need alone time.

Joan: The problem with your alone time is you don't always act like you're happy to see me. So, I don't feel loved or appreciated.

Therapist: OK great, you're communicating with each other about what you want. Gayle, do you feel like you know what Joan wants from you?

Gayle: I think I do, but maybe I don't because I think I'm giving her what she wants and then she's disappointed.

Therapist: And some of the anxiety and uncertainty you both feel is because you don't actually know what it will take to make the other person happy. [*Therapist offers behavioral guidance.*] One way to get around that is to communicate very specifically about what you expect. For example, Joan, I think it would be useful if you could let Gayle know just how much time you want for talking after work. Do you want 15 minutes or more like an hour? Once Gayle knows that, you're both on the same page and can talk about the problem more constructively. . . . [*The couple practices providing more specific information to one another with the therapist's assistance.*]

Joan: You know, I feel like we have a better understanding of each other than before. But, it seems like I end up just having to give up on getting my needs met. Is that really a good thing to do?

Therapist: [*Therapist offers realistic expectations. This is also a step toward acceptance training.*] You know, I think every relationship involves partners giving up on getting some of their needs met. If you trust in your partner's good intentions toward you, that makes it easier to accept the limitations of what each of you can give the other. I think it is realistic to expect some change, especially now that you've identified exactly what would make you happy. But I don't think you two are likely to reverse roles—that is, suddenly Gayle will be the one who wants more intimacy, and Joan will want more alone time. So, one way to stop fighting about this is

> to make peace with yourself about this rhythm that emerges from each of your personalities and work on how to accept that rhythm that is the logical outgrowth of your two personalities coming together.

In these first interventions, the therapist provides understanding and soothing to Joan and Gayle, perhaps the first they've received on this issue. The therapist then formulates the treatment plan as one in which they must problem-solve together around how they handle their different needs.

Relationship architects and their fear scenarios. Realistic expectations of intimate relationships can help couples like Joan and Gayle feel less frustrated and less anxious when their relationships fail to live up to their ideals. Because love relationships and marriage are idealized in popular culture, we often get the message that anything is possible. As a result, it is easy to believe that if we make the effort, we can make our relationships live up to highly idealistic standards, particularly as regards to the fulfillment of our own needs.

Further progress for Gayle and Joan likely depends on Joan's willingness to tackle a fear scenario and the impact that it has on intimacy with Gayle. Joan's response to the anxiety generated by her fear scenario is to become a *relationship architect*. Relationship architects try to fashion their relationships according to their own mental blueprints. As with Joan, their efforts often come out of anxiety about what could happen if their fear scenarios come to pass. Joan's determination to shape Gayle's behavior is a clue that she is operating out of a fear scenario that she has not yet articulated in therapy.

Problems for relationship architects begin when their partners fail to buy into their "relationship blueprint." At first, the architect's efforts to change the partner are made with patience, but as it becomes clear that the partner will not be easily changed, the architect becomes increasingly frustrated. Eventually, the frustration is channeled into attacks on the partner in an escalation of effort to make the partner change his or her ways. The relationship architect is discovering that nothing makes one feel more powerless than putting all of one's effort into trying to make someone else change his or her behavior.

The therapist can help the relationship architect regain a sense of power and control by helping him or her to redirect these efforts toward obtainable goals. Therapists can teach their clients to self-soothe by teaching them realistic attitudes about their own and their partner's imperfect capacities to meet all of their needs. The role of the therapist in this case is to function as the expert on relationships and to normalize the couple's different intimacy and autonomy needs.

As Joan becomes increasingly aware of the content of her fear scenario, she can learn to reduce the anxiety associated with it by modifying it. Joan believed that "things must always go right." Joan's "things must go right" schema coexisted with a fear scenario that carried doomsday prophesies regarding what would occur if aspects of the relationship were not perfect. In the dialogue below, the couple therapist works with Joan to identify her automatic thoughts and to help her identify the fear scenario that elicits her anxiety and, in turn, her anger.

Joan: This week was better. We hung out together Wednesday and Thursday. But then Friday, she went off by herself again. It was OK after we were together the other two nights. But then, Saturday again she wanted to do her own thing.

Gayle: We went out together Saturday night!

Joan: Yes, that night, but Saturday afternoon is special time, and you spent it on the computer.

Gayle: You don't seem to get that I need my quiet time.

Joan: I give you your quiet time! I do it; I make the effort and then you don't give me credit for it. I didn't say a word on Friday. I worked in the garden and then read until I went to bed. You had the whole evening to yourself. Admit it, I was quiet and gave you your quiet time on Friday.

Gayle: Yes, you're right. But I still felt guilty. I just don't know if you'll ever be able to give it to me for real. It seems like you're always hovering, waiting for me to entertain you.

Joan: That is so unfair! Look at Friday—you came home about what time? 7:00 P.M.? I wasn't even there! I was at Walmart. So, you had that time. Then when I got home, I just visited with you for what, about 15 minutes? I know it was 15 minutes because the CNN special had just been on a few minutes . . . so why do you say I can't give you your quiet time? I give it to you all the time.

Therapist: Stop for a moment. Joan, what are you experiencing right now?

Joan: It's just so unfair—how can she think that about me when I try so hard?

Therapist: So you're angry?

Joan: Well, I'm concerned. It's like Gayle doesn't even see me, see the effort I make for her.

Therapist: So, you want her to acknowledge your effort?

Joan: I don't even care if she acknowledges it so long as she knows it's there. I put up with a lot. She wants to spend all this time alone, fine. I can entertain myself. I can get by on two or three days a week of couple time. Fine.

But to try to adjust to that and still have her say that I need her to entertain me!

Therapist: Am I reading you right, then, that what Gayle just said got you pretty upset?

Joan: I can't let her say things like that about me.

Therapist: [*Therapist is working with Joan to identify a fear scenario.*] What does it mean to you, that she did say what she said? Take a deep breath . . . think this through with me. What did that mean to you, what she said?

Joan: Ummm—well I can't let her think those things, about me.

Therapist: What does it mean to you when it seems that she's thinking those things?

Joan: Hmmmm—well, what would happen to us, to our relationship, if she thinks those things?

Therapist: May I follow that thought with you? What would happen? What do you imagine would happen?

Joan: Well if she thinks that, then where would we be? There would be no us.

Therapist: So if she says that, if she thinks that, it's the end of your relationship?

Joan: Well maybe not right away, but eventually.

Therapist: So what Gayle said—it activated a fear scenario. Perhaps you fear that a thought like that in Gayle's head is the beginning of the end?

Joan (pausing): Yes. Gayle is usually so optimistic. When she gets hopeless or thinks bad things about me, I get really upset because I think it's the end of us.

Therapist: You deserve a minute to sit quietly and collect your thoughts! Because that fear scenario is pretty scary. Take some deep breaths—see what you can do to calm yourself. . . . [*Therapist is encouraging Joan to increase her emotion tolerance.*] (After a few minutes), were you able to find a way to calm yourself?

Joan: Sort of—I got a clear idea about some things I want to say to Gayle, to explain how I feel. I felt better as I put those things into words.

Therapist: [*Therapist encourages Joan's self-soothing.*] Excellent—so now you know a way to calm yourself. You formulate an explanation for yourself and eventually communicate to Gayle about why you see her perception on this as deadly to your relationship? Am I getting that right?

Joan: Yes, something like that.

Therapist: Yes?

Joan: I don't know about "deadly"—I want her to see that I am making an effort.

Therapist: Or else?

Joan: I guess, like you said, we may not be an "us" anymore.

Therapist: OK, great! You've got a handle on what your fear scenario is. Now, as a next step, a good way to deal with a fear scenario like this is to check out your concerns with Gayle. Instead of assuming that your worst fears are true as far as how she perceives you, you can check with her directly to learn what her perceptions are. You ask her directly what her perception is.

Joan: OK—so what are you feeling, Gayle?

Gayle: You know, I'm just trying to give to you and do what I need to do both. I don't feel hopeless at all. I'm sorry if I sounded that way.

Joan (exhaling): That was a good thing for me to do, to check with you. I'm realizing that my fear was more about the breakup with Tina than about our relationship. Tina and I did have a similar problem, but we were incredibly cruel to each other whenever we tried to resolve it. It's like I'm holding my breath waiting for you to do that, too.

Gayle: But I haven't done anything like what she did, have I?

Joan: No, you haven't. And if the truth be known, if I think about it, I can't imagine you saying the kinds of things she said to me. You're a much calmer person but also so much kinder and more thoughtful.

In this session, Joan's therapist queried her closely about her automatic thoughts because she suspected that Joan's fear scenario—that Gayle's perceptions would cause their relationship to deteriorate—was affecting her reaction to Gayle. Because Joan and Gayle are relatively new to therapy, the therapist suggested the fear scenario to which she suspected Joan was reacting. Had they been farther along in therapy, Joan might have identified the schema on her own and adjusted her reaction accordingly.

For homework, Joan practiced checking for her fear scenario when she got especially anxious in her interactions with Gayle. With the therapist's help, she was able to identify alternative and more realistic expectations for Gayle and catch herself operating out of her fear scenario. She learned to use alternative explanations to counter the fear scenario (e.g., "Gayle is not deliberately withholding from me. She is human with her own troubles"). The better able she was to counter her fear scenario with this more realistic thought, the more acceptance she was able to convey to Gayle.

Working with differences that have become polarized. In addition to arguing about their differences, *polarized* couples have lost sight of their commonalities. When partners are polarized, each one claims to have a need that the other denies having. Polarized partners have staked out opposite positions on an issue and fail to see any legitimacy in the other partner's position. A more realistic stance for polarized partners would be to recognize that they both have the same needs at different intensities. When partners are not aware of their own needs, it is much more difficult for them to listen to and understand one another, and more likely that they will personalize the partner's needs, seeing those needs as a statement about themselves rather than about the partner.

The first step toward decreasing polarization around intimacy and autonomy is for partners to be able to articulate the advantages of both togetherness and separateness, with neither feeling that he or she is the only one who cares about that aspect of the relationship. Second, partners should be able to identify a combination of joint and separate activities that they pursue that is satisfactory to both. In order to do so, partners may need to confront their standards and expectations about exclusiveness and the possibility that one relationship can fulfill all of a person's needs (or, vice versa, that a relationship can endure if one or both partners fails to tend to it). Third, partners should be able to tolerate each other's separate interests and pursuits without undue jealousy and possessiveness. If partners have behaved in a trustworthy fashion in the past, then one individual's jealousy or possessiveness may need to be addressed with automatic thought monitoring and self-empowerment training. As a converse, the pursuit of individual interests and friendships may have to be delayed if the partner desiring such freedom has abused it in the past by betraying the other.

One therapeutic strategy that can decrease polarization involves calming one or both partners' anxieties about the opposite pole. Anxious partners fear one end of the polarity and ignore their own, similar needs. For example, Joan ignored her own needs for separateness and autonomy because she believed that Gayle's insistence on fulfilling those needs left her deprived and lonely. It is helpful for the therapist to remain conscious of the fact that both partners need both intimacy and autonomy to grow and feel whole, but their anxieties may prevent them from pursuing one or the other.

Contracting for specific time together, and scheduling it, may be necessary before the intimacy-seeking partner can be reassured that the couple will have sufficient time together once he or she has accepted the other partner's wish for more separate time. If one partner is always wondering when he or she will have time with the other, then it will be difficult for that partner to be generous about the other partner's individual activities.

Partners may also need to develop a more equitable division of labor before they will feel free to grant one another more freedom to pursue outside activities. If one partner is out having fun while the other is saddled with the bulk of the child care or household chores, then the burdened partner may not want to be generous. Sometimes, partners must address their different standards for household maintenance before they can resolve this intimacy dilemma, as one issue is often tied in with the other in complicated ways. Partners can polarize around issues of neatness and household orderliness just as they can polarize around intimacy issues.

Differences in needs for intimacy and autonomy are some of the thorniest that couples will face. It is easy to personalize a partner's lesser need for intimacy as a rejection of self. As a converse, a partner's greater need for togetherness and intimacy may feel to the autonomy-seeking partner like an effort to control how he or she spends his or her time and an effort to limit his or her autonomy. Once partners learn to perceive these as personality differences and nothing more, their anxiety about the partner's needs tends to dissipate, leaving them open to listening to and accepting one another and better able to solve the problems associated with their different needs.

Anxiety about the Partner's Behavior Reflecting on Self

Differences in intimacy and autonomy needs are scarcely the only differences that couple partners find difficult to accept. Differences that cause embarrassment or shame by association also cause difficulty, especially for partners who are less psychologically differentiated. The boundary between self and other is more blurry for less versus more differentiated partners. This blurry boundary causes less differentiated partners to over-identify with one another and to thereby take one another's strengths and weaknesses into themselves, to a larger extent than do more differentiated partners. In Chapter 8, I mentioned research that indicates that intimate partners incorporate characteristics of their partners into their own self-concepts, to the point that even normally differentiated partners confuse their own and their partners' resources, strengths, and perspectives (Aron, Mashek, & Aron, 2004). In couples who present for therapy, this incorporation of the other into the self can cause anxiety and lead to a feeling of losing self.

Rita and Nick exemplify the problems that less differentiated partners encounter when they over-identify with one another. Rita found Nick's lack of attention to table manners, his insistence on wearing old, unfashionable clothing, and his rude dinner table conversation uncomfortably embarrassing (Nick enjoys loud jokes and loud laughter). Nick insists that she spoils many of their social outings by enumerating his bad behaviors later and complaining about them. Rita counters that the events are marred for her by the embarrassment and shame that she feels about Nick's uncouth, unrefined behavior.

Rita's feelings of shame would not be possible, had she not extended her self-boundaries to include aspects of Nick's self. By imparting extensive knowledge of the other, intimate interaction opens the door to the expansion of our self-boundaries to include aspects of the other. This self-expansion allows us to feel pride in our partner's accomplishments as if they were our own

(Aron, Mashek, & Aron, 2004; Beach et al., 1996). However, if this expansion of self includes the other's foibles as well as his or her strengths, then we may find ourselves feeling embarrassment and shame over characteristics of our partners, just as though these were our own flaws. In response to these self-conscious emotions, partners may pressure one another to conform to standards. Alternatively, they can increase their level of psychological differentiation and accept the other as he or she is.

Any potential embarrassment we might feel over our partner's social behavior, lack of career success, or appearance is muted when our identities are well differentiated. Differentiation allows us to own our own successes and social graces and similarly allow our partners to own theirs. In contrast, embarrassment is exacerbated when one or both partners' are insufficiently differentiated. To the extent that the self boundary is blurred or (subjectively) nonexistent, partners may be tempted to attack one another for faults that prevent themselves from "looking good" through their association with the other (e.g., in the eyes of a purportedly judging public, extended family, etc.).

One way to begin treatment with partners who over-identify with each other in this manner is with positive reinforcement and validation to each of them in support of their respective positions. The therapist can validate one partner's sensitivity to the social deportments that lubricate interaction. The therapist can then normalize the strong identification that they feel with each other, acknowledging that others perceive them as a couple unit and that identification with one another is a sign of closeness.

The therapist can then suggest that the couple formulate goals that will bring them closer to the midpoint of their polarized positions. With Rita and Nick above, the therapist is suggesting a standard behavior-change goal. Nick has gone overboard in brushing off Rita's concerns and could afford to select behaviors that he could change to accommodate her preferences. The therapist could explain that attraction comes partly from admiring one's spouse in public and that Nick may be jeopardizing their attraction by being too dismissive of Rita's feelings about his behavior.

Nick's therapist may also have to work with Nick cognitively if Nick perceives the behavioral changes as unilateral capitulations to Rita with accompanying loss of self. Nick's behavior in response to Rita's requests suggested that he alternated between a passive enmeshment with Rita (he would not empathize with Rita, nor would he validate her concerns about his social behavior) and an intermediate level of differentiation (his reactions to her requests that he modify his behavior were sometimes more aggressive than seemed to be warranted by the situation).

In Rita's case, a more complicated cognitive behavioral change process is involved. The first goal for Rita is to encourage her to work on herself, with the idea that she will be happier if Nick's behavior does not generate so much negative emotion for her. Her multistage assignment then would involve the following: (1) select one or two behaviors that she wants him to change and ask that he change those (i.e., demanding more is likely to backfire); (2) work on accepting Nick for who he is by identifying alternatives to her negative automatic thoughts about Nick (e.g., his social personality is part of him and he can only change so much to please her; she loves him even though he does not share her value emphasis on proper social deportment); and (3) work on reducing the intensity of her embarrassment by increasing her psychological differentiation. In this case, Rita will work on reducing the extent to which her self-concept as a wife includes Nick's social behavior.

This formulation of Rita and Nick's dilemma suggests that it might be useful to present the idea of differentiation to them. Clients who can think abstractly (i.e., have attained formal operations when it comes to thinking about psychological concepts) can use the concept of differentiation to understand what is going on between them; it can help them to see the wisdom in changing their behavior. It is best if the therapist chooses to present the differentiation concept to clients in whichever way is consistent with the way that they think about themselves and their goals for therapy.

Regardless of how the therapy goal is presented to Rita and Nick, Rita will use schema modification and acceptance training in order to acknowledge Nick's separateness, individuality, and uniqueness as a good thing rather than a burden. Rita will work individually on this change, either in the conjoint session or in separate individual sessions. Either way, Nick will be actively discouraged from interfering in any way with this personal, individual growth.

Thus far in this chapter, I have discussed individual and couple processes that make it difficult for partners to listen to and demonstrate understanding and acceptance of one another. In the last section that addresses intimacy Dilemma #2, I versus we, I turn to couple problems that make it difficult for partners to sustain high-quality intimacy between them.

Sustaining the Intimate Relationship

The third set of skills associated with psychological differentiation, and necessary for couples to make progress coping with their Dilemma #2, 'I versus we' challenges, is sustaining the intimate connection between the partners in the face of Dilemma #2 conflicts. Certainly, asserting and protecting the self and listening to and demonstrating respect for the partner are both crucial differentiation skills. However, without the ability to simultaneously sustain the intimate connection, these skills would not be sufficient for building a deep intimate connection with another. The ability to maintain this intimate connection without either partner losing part of the self is the hallmark of differentiation (Schnarch, 1997).

Erik Erikson may have been the first psychologist to note that experiences of intense intimacy can threaten to dissolve the perceived boundaries of the self in an individual who has not yet established a firm identity. According to

Erikson, an individual who lacks a firm identity will feel smothered by shared experiences of intimate connection, and this perception of being smothered will generate anxiety and an urge to pull away.

Intimate relating can cause boundaries between selves to blur; to some extent, the blurring of boundaries is an indication of love and commitment (Aron et al., 2004). Paradoxically, intimacy also creates the opportunity for partners to engage in self-clarification with each other (Prager, Fuller, & Gonzalez, 1989).

Intimate talk encourages individuals to talk about themselves and to identify and communicate about important aspects of self that are elicited via relational processes. Self-clarification not only reveals the self to the other, it also reveals the self to the self (Derlega & Grzelak, 1979). For example, a mother may not be explicitly conscious of her desire to raise her children in a permissive environment until she confronts her husband's desire to provide a stricter upbringing. A husband may not have thought to communicate to his wife about his desire to start their retirement fund while they were still in their twenties until he confronted his wife's hope that they would travel extensively before they had children. Through the intimate opening up of the self, partners not only learn about each other, but they may also become more self-aware as they hear their own views contrasting with those of their partner.

Both the boundary-blurring and self-clarifying characteristics of intimacy can create discomfort in individuals who do not have sufficient differentiation skill to manage them. We have already discussed two responses to these challenges to the self that can create problems for intimacy in a relationship: hiding or burying the self to avoid conflict or pressuring the partner to change him- or herself in order to fulfill one's own needs. A third problematic response is to create enough distance to neutralize the Dilemma #2 challenge. This distancing may involve a reduction of intimate relating between the partners, or, for more vulnerable individuals, this neutralization may require that they end the intimate relationship altogether. In the last few sections of this chapter, I discuss several psychological factors that can contribute to an individual's distancing or ending an intimate relationship in order to avoid confronting a Dilemma #2, 'I versus we,' challenge. This chapter concludes with suggestions for treating such avoidant individuals.

Upholding Intimacy in the Face of Dilemma #2 Challenges

Dilemma #2, 'I versus we,' makes the dream of two-becoming-one a paradox, something that is longed for and resisted simultaneously. This conflict between longing for and dreading for two to become one is often difficult for intimate partners to identify and label (Silverman, Lachman, & Milich, 1982). The threat of losing their identity or individuality can cause minimally differentiated individuals to sabotage relationships just as they are becoming intimate. A problem integrating intimacy and individuality may lie behind many instances of serial broken relationships. People who break off their relationships only to miss their partners and regret the breakup later may be victims of a "we overwhelms I" version of Dilemma #2.

Minimally differentiated, unrelated partners have the same Dilemma #2 conflicts as those discussed above for enmeshed partners, but they respond to them differently. Unrelated partners often loathe the kind of coercive, cruel quarreling that enmeshed partners engage in. As a result, when they are frustrated because their partners will not do things their way, they withdraw and distance from their partner rather than engage in conflict.

Compared with enmeshed partners, unrelated partners are often more overtly, consciously afraid of losing themselves in their relationships. For example, when individuals become part of a couple, they feel some pressure to change habits from their single days. Unrelated partners may fight this pressure to change, because they believe that letting go of those habits will cause them to lose themselves. As a result, an unrelated partner may hold onto a monthly trip to the singles bar with his or her single friends or hold onto a separate bank account because the individual believes (subliminally or overtly) that he or she will lose something of him- or herself if he or she does otherwise. The individual may keep secrets from the partner and engender mistrust, just because he or she feels compelled to hold something of him- or herself back in order to avoid feeling that he or she is losing him- or herself.

Other unrelated partners may expect "two to become one" as enmeshed partners do. These partners distance in order to avoid acknowledging their partner's divergent needs. For these partners, empathy and acceptance mean giving up their "two can become one" fantasy. Because they will not behave coercively, however, they instead create distance, perhaps disguised as a pretense of communal harmony that allows them to avoid acknowledging Dilemma #2 issues, but that makes real intimacy impossible. When they get weary of the pretense, they may start looking around for a new partner. Because they have not confronted their "two can become one" fantasy for what it is, they continue to dream of the ideal soul mate that is waiting to be discovered.

Helping unrelated clients to avoid flight when confronted with Dilemma #2. Eddie exemplifies someone who had not heretofore been able to cope successfully with his simultaneous longing for and resistance to intimacy. He had come to therapy to work on his habit of becoming intimate with a woman only to break up with her afterward. He had been feeling depressed over breaking up with a woman who had refused to reunite with him afterward despite his entreaties. Once he started feeling better, however, Eddie dropped out of therapy; he had met a new woman and believed his problems were over. When Eddie repeated his old pattern with the new woman, however, he became depressed and sought therapy again. This time, his therapist was on the lookout for the "we overwhelms I" pattern. The therapist asked Eddie about each of the women he had broken up with. Here is what he said about the most recent one.

Therapist: So tell me, what happened with Sheila.

Eddie: She was a wonderful woman. She was fun to be with, a great hostess—always inviting people to the house, cooking up a great meal. . . . [*Eddie tells a couple of stories about how wonderful Sheila was.*]

Therapist: So it's clear why you were attracted to her, right? Why did you end up leaving her?

Eddie: Well in Sheila's case, I didn't leave. She called it off and won't even talk to me.

Therapist: I gathered from what you told me earlier, though, that before she called it off, you had been drifting away, feeling disenchanted with her.

Eddie: Yeah, I guess so. It's hard to remember what I was thinking.

Therapist: The best way to figure out what goes wrong, though, is to try to reconstruct what you were thinking and feeling that led you to drift away. Were there things about her, about the two of you together? Or was it something inside of you? Once we understand what your experience of being with her was, we'll understand better how to prevent it from happening in the next relationship.

Eddie: I remember I didn't like her demands. She was upset because I didn't spend enough time with her and I didn't make a big deal of her, you know, buy her flowers, tell her I love her, that sort of thing.

Therapist: Do you think she was unreasonable in how much of that she wanted?

Eddie: No, well, I don't know. She was always buying me things—a shirt, something for my workshop, videos. She was always doing something. I was a fool; I didn't appreciate her.

Therapist: Maybe she was too much? She was so expressive with all that, was she closer than you wanted?

Eddie: I guess I felt a little crowded. . . . [*Eddie explores his recollections and ties some things together.*]

Therapist: I notice that it's hard for you to remember how you felt now that you're far away from her. Yet, while you were with her, something wasn't right; otherwise, why not do all the things that keep her happy and keep the relationship going well, right?

Eddie: Mmhmmm.

Therapist: What I wonder is: was there a feeling you had when you were together with her, in the relationship, that you don't have now that you're out of it? That at the time, you wanted to escape but that once you're out, it's gone? [*The therapist is testing the hypothesis that it was not so much Sheila that Eddie wanted to escape, but a feeling state that he could not regulate while in the relationship.*]

Eddie: I just remember I didn't want to bother with telling her I loved her or planning things for us to do together. That was the feeling, like it was a bother.

Therapist: Like once you're in the relationship, it starts feeling like a burden?

Eddie: Something like that, although I can't imagine why I would have felt burdened.

Therapist: [*The therapist tests the hypothesis that Eddie was running from an I versus we challenge.*] Sometimes, when people feel like that, it's because they start to lose something important if they let themselves get totally involved—maybe their independence, their ability to go and do as they want when they want—was it something like that?

Eddie: If I had done things the way she wanted, that would have been a problem. But I didn't do things her way, and I lost her.

Therapist: OK, so you made a choice: You did your own thing hoping she'd stick around; she'd be available when you wanted to be with her, but that wasn't enough for her, right?

Eddie: If only I could have given her what she wanted. She just wanted me. I think she loved me for myself. All I did was rebel against her.

What Eddie's therapist noticed was that, with one exception (her demands), Eddie spoke of his ex-girlfriend in glowing, even idealized terms. He described her as smart, well-spoken, kind-hearted, and sexy. In retrospect, he couldn't remember why it hadn't worked out. Only through detailed questioning did the therapist begin to get a picture of what Eddie actually felt and did during the relationship. Eddie felt crowded—the "we" of the couple seemed to overwhelm his "I" of individuality. To preserve the "I" that he unconsciously believed he was losing, Eddie tried to keep his girlfriend at a distance, coming and going as he pleased without checking in with her. It seemed that Eddie only appreciated her once he was far away from her.

The challenge in working with Eddie (like other unrelated clients) is that he escapes from intimacy just as he is close to becoming aware of the anxiety it generates for him. His only conscious emotion is annoyance, and he notices that he isn't enjoying being with the woman as much. He starts wanting to spend time alone. But a little time alone isn't enough for him to feel comfortable; he needs more distance to feel that he is back to himself. So he creates more distance than alone time can create; sometimes he starts fights, usually indirectly by behaving inconsiderately or irresponsibly. Eventually, the relationship is no fun for either of them, so someone initiates a breakup.

The therapist's challenge was to help Eddie get another perspective on his intimacy-avoidance, one that would allow his own behavior to make sense to him. Once it made sense, he would be in a better place to address it head on. The first step was to find a place where Eddie and the therapist agreed on what was going on. In this case, it was that Sheila (and the women before her) were great and that it wasn't their fault that Eddie couldn't make a relationship work with them. So the therapist was able to say the following:

> "So there are two possibilities here: Either you're attracted to people who end up not being good for you to be involved with, or there's something about being involved that's troubling to you. You've resisted any suggestion I've made that maybe Sheila [and the others] were a pain in the neck one way or another, so I wonder if there isn't a wise part of you that knows you're not ready for a relationship and that makes sure these breakups happen even though you're sad afterward. Perhaps that's the wise part of you that brought you here, that knows you have some work to do on yourself before you settle down with someone."

This goal-setting intervention opens the door for an exploration with Eddie of why he might not be as ready for a relationship as he believes himself to be. It communicates to Eddie that he is wise to avoid involvement before he is fully ready for it and promises that he can hope for more from a relationship than what he has been able to create thus far. This labeling of his intimacy-avoidant side as wise is an alternative perspective for Eddie, also known as a *cognitive reframing*. The purpose of the reframing is to help Eddie to address his intimacy-avoidance in therapy without the loss of self-esteem that comes with the condemning of a part of oneself. In fact, at this point in his therapy, Eddie's level of differentiation was not sufficient to permit him to sustain an intimate relationship over the long term.

A second step is to explore with Eddie how he feels when he's not with the woman, whether they have broken-up or are still together. There are several attractions that might be drawing Eddie out of intimate contact with his partners. Possibly, he cannot simultaneously chart his own path while also dealing with the intimacy demands of another person. Because he believes he cannot do both at once, he sacrifices what he needs to do for himself in order to make the woman happy until he starts getting uncomfortable, at which point he distances her. Distancing her is the only way he knows how to get to do what he wants and needs for himself.

The minimally differentiated person who is unable to sustain an intimate relationship is often running toward the "freedom" to chart his or her own path in life. For this individual, being a part of a couple leads to a panicky feeling of being jailed. Sometimes, the intimate relationship replicates the experience of living under parental control. When this is the case, exiting the relationship gives the person the same feeling of freedom that he or she felt when moving out from under his or her parent's supervision. Leave-taking feels exhilarating, if only for a while. Unrelatedness is even more likely when the person's self-concept is wholly tied up with the plans for his or her future. In this case, if the individual compromises any of those plans (i.e., "but I always pictured myself living in the Texas ranch country"), the individual feels that he or she is giving up his or her whole self. Breaking off the relationship, then, allows the individual to resurrect a plan for the future that would bear no compromises to include another person. In Eddie's case, the attraction was to the feeling of being "footloose" he got as soon as he broke off his relationship. The feeling was fleeting, however, because Eddie wants an intimate partner.

The third step, once Eddie has thoroughly explored the meaning that singleness and relationship have for him, is to work with Eddie individually on either being happy single until he has his own self-direction more thoroughly charted, or, if he still wants a relationship, teaching Eddie (in the abstract for the moment) about differentiation and intimacy. If he decides he still wants a relationship, the therapist may help Eddie through *anticipatory socialization,* a process by which a person is prepared for the contingencies of a situation that lies ahead. The preparation will change his expectations of intimate relationships, so that he will perceive the 'I versus we' dilemma as normal and will develop sufficient tolerance for it to stick with a relationship once he has it. Eddie's therapist can work to help Eddie change his concept of where he is in his own growth and development versus what he needs to bring into a relationship.

Choosing passion and sacrificing intimacy. Some people are like butterflies, lighting on one flower after another, only to fly away as soon as the first petals of new love have come down to earth. They are like Lori, who loves the beginning of relationships and the fusion of selves that characterizes passion. Like a butterfly, however, Lori loses interest when the relationship deepens, and a more differentiated intimacy replaces passion and fusion. It is almost as if they fall out of love as fast as they fall in love.

For Lori, passion is great but mature intimacy is uncomfortable. As intimacy progresses, and inevitably requires more differentiation, Lori becomes uncomfortable. She only wants the two-become-one experience and finds differentiated intimacy either uninteresting or intolerable. In her mind, intimacy that is differentiated does not feel like real love. It is in a word boring.

Lori does not understand that it is intimacy that she is running from, because she thinks of herself as someone who loves intimacy. Lori interprets her love of passion and newness and mutual discovery as a love of intimacy. She avoids confronting Dilemma #2 by never moving beyond the stage of finding similarities with the new love.

Because clients like Lori often have limited awareness of their own emotional life, affective interventions can be useful strategies to help them experience their emotions more fully and thereby come to understand them better. Quite possibly, Lori never experiences anxiety about intimacy because she backs out before it deepens because she feels boredom or a lack of love. Lori's therapist used guided imagery to increase her awareness of what went on as she got closer to her relationship partners.

Therapist: [*During the guided imagery, the therapist pauses frequently to give Lori a chance to access an image and her emotions.*] Let's see if you can recreate the experience that you had when you knew it was over with Jon. This will give us something concrete to work with. Close your eyes and take some deep slow breaths. . . . Let your mind drift back to the last time you were with him. . . . Can you picture it? Where were you? . . . Can you see what he's wearing? . . . What are you doing? . . . [And finally,] how do you feel? About yourself? . . . About him?

Lori: [*Describing the imagery.*] Well, he's mad at me actually. I was upset that he wanted to go to a family picnic without me. He had said before he thought his mother would really like me. But now he was saying he wanted us to get to know each other better before he introduced me to his family, to make sure we really had a relationship. Well what did he think was going on with us all month? We were having sex twice a day! We were spending all our time together. I was really upset, feeling like he was giving me the brush off. And he was mad, looking really disenchanted with me. Although he denied it was true, I could see that those wonderful things he'd said to me had evaporated. I just wanted to get away from him as fast as I could. I cried and cried, like when I came to see you last week; I felt like my life was over. But now, I don't feel so bad. I got out just in time.

Therapist: OK, let me make sure I understand what happened. . . . You interpreted his going without you and his lack of attentiveness that morning, as a sign that perhaps his feelings for you were already waning or that he never meant them. Right? . . . Could there be another explanation for why his mood seemed different that morning?

The therapist uses guided imagery to get as vivid a report of what went on with Jon as she can from Lori. She also wants as vivid a description of Lori's emotions as she can, to determine when Lori was likely to believe that love was over. She discovered that in this case, it was the point at which Jon was no longer obsessed with her, ecstatic about her. It was also the point at which Jon's and Lori's agendas diverged, a confrontation with Dilemma #2 that would require them to differentiate if their relationship was to continue to thrive. What Lori demonstrates here is that her tolerance for differentiation in the context of a love relationship is low indeed. At the close of the guided imagery work, Lori's therapist asks her for alternative interpretations of Jon's behavior in order to begin a process of identifying and evaluating Lori's intimacy schemas. By helping Lori to make the connection between her schemas and her emotions as her relationships deepen, the therapist helps Lori to understand fully why she leaves relationships so soon after they've begun.

A preference for passion over intimacy does not always lead to a person abandoning relationships. Rather, some people may fight with their partners in order to keep the emotions intense, as Vera does. Vera feels small and unimportant when her spouse fails to be attentive toward her. Now that Vera and her husband have been married for a year or so, he is less attentive as he has other distractions. Vera feels bereft but doesn't completely understand why. What she does know is that she is mad at her husband for withholding from her. Without exactly intending to, Vera creates intensity with conflict; she fights with him about wanting more attention. The fights win her that intense attention, however negative, but at least she knows he's still involved with her emotionally. Vera does not feel love or loved without the intensity.

Vera and Lori both intuitively grasp that the calming down of two lovers, the return of their focus to the everyday concerns that follows the period of infatuation, happens when the partners break apart the happy fusion of early love and revert back to their separate selves. Both of them associate love so strongly with the romantic obsessions of early love that each is convinced that normal psychological differentiation in the context of a love relationship is a sign of love waning, and may even be a betrayal of what they had come to expect.

As with the others issues raised by Dilemma #2, I versus we, difficulties accepting the necessity of self-differentiation usually require cognitive interventions, often with intimacy schemas. In order to have relationships that last, these individuals should be helped to develop more realistic expectations of intimate relationships and to modify their fantasies about love to include mature, differentiated intimacy.

Summary

In conclusion, the third competency associated with psychological differentiation is the ability to uphold intimacy, to maintain a relationship characterized by relational intimacy, in the face of I versus we dilemmas. Individuals who have difficulty maintaining an "I" when confronted with the demands of an intimate relationship may flee their relationships, only to wish to have them back or to seek out another relationship. Each time, they hope that this time it will work out. Others create independent lives within their relationships but find that their independent lives have left no room for an intimate connection with their partners. Cognitive-behavioral treatment for intimacy problems offers therapists a conceptualization along with a variety of intervention strategies for helping enmeshed and unrelated individuals find and embrace the self that can be happy in an intimate relationship and who can keep their partners happy as well.

Emotion Regulation

Throughout the last two chapters, I have referred to the challenges that individuals face in managing overly intense negative emotions when they confront Dilemma #2. Increasing psychological differentiation skills goes along with less emotional reactivity, because the person's expectations are more realistic and because losing the self is not at stake.

Emotion regulation training, described in detail in Chapter 5, is useful for helping partners manage intense, negative emotions that arise when less differentiated partners encounter I versus we issues. Emotion regulation training is a five-step process in which clients identify and practice techniques for calming themselves in the face of negatively arousing interactions with their partners. In the next example, Carla's therapist uses emotion regulation training to help Carla calm herself when she is feeling anxious about the implications of Doug's communication with her. The steps for emotion regulation training are: (1) empower the client—frame the training as a way to reach the client's self-stated goals; (2) identify the emotion that is most troubling as a focus of the training; (3) identify and validate healthy goals associated with current functioning; (4) identify alternative, more adaptive strategies for managing emotions; and (5) experiment with new strategies and evaluate them.

This example demonstrates the use of emotional regulation training for Carla who will identify and de-catastrophize a fear scenario with rational alternative thoughts. By "defanging" a fear scenario, she helps herself remain calm enough to avoid negative behavior and thereby decreases the need for distancing. The couple came in complaining that they spent a whole evening being distant from one another instead of having fun.

Doug:	See I remember more or less—Carla at this party [on Friday] was very assertive about when she wanted to leave; she'd had enough.
Therapist:	She used to stew.

Carla:	I went to that party.
Therapist:	Yeah.
Doug:	Well, I said angry, assertive.
Therapist:	What a minute, stop there. What was angry?
Doug:	. . . To go back to Friday night, she made a decision, let's leave . . . . I was having a good time; I could have stayed a little longer.
Therapist:	So were you mad?
Carla:	. . . I think so, you were turned off.
Doug:	Well I was . . . there isn't a discussion about this, it's, "I'm ready, I'm leaving now." . . . Carla left; I could have stayed around; she didn't consult me. So, we get to the parking lot, and I'm OK despite the fact that I could've stayed longer.
Therapist:	You're still OK?
Doug:	Yeah I'm still looking forward to our being together; I told myself that even if it wasn't exactly cordial, it was assertive, and this going to dinner and shopping was what we had planned on doing, alright, fine this was our night out.
Carla:	But before the party, you said we don't have to go.
Doug:	Yeah, so then as we're walking out of the car then, I hugged her on the way into the restaurant, and I remember saying something like, "Where's my little sweet wife; I wish I could find my sweet wife again."
Carla (angrily):	Mmm, nice!
Doug:	. . . It wasn't an aggressive gesture;—and then, that was the change.
Carla:	Well, what do you mean by my sweet wife?
Therapist:	OK, this is important. You're both agreeing that was the moment, that was the beginning of the bad vibes.
Doug:	I try to make an affectionate gesture, so we can go on and have a nice evening and suddenly she's angry.
Carla:	But Doug! What's my little sweet? . . .
Therapist:	[*The therapist could work with Doug here as he is denying his anger that she didn't negotiate with him about when to leave the party. It is also an option to work with Carla, who overreacts to Doug's negativity and contributes to the ruined evening.*] Carla, you have some power here, this is more in your hands than you think it is. [*Empower the client.*] Let's say Doug would have preferred to stay, and now he's feeling that you're not so sweet; you have a couple of options here; you have some power! You can choose the way you think about his negativity. [*Identify*

the emotion that is most troubling as focus of training.] You can think, "Oh god he wants me to be a passive wife again." And we've talked before about this being infuriating to imagine, and scary. But you have another option. [*Identify alternative, more adaptive strategies for managing emotions.*] You can focus on your end goal, which is to have a nice time and then think to yourself, "how can I get him over this hump?" So, how would you think about it differently if you were focused on having a good time instead of focusing on how unjust it was that he said that to you?

Carla: But it's very difficult for me to let that slide by because I did that for our whole marriage, let it slide by and it got me where? So today, I just want him to be aware that it hurts; I don't deserve this.

Therapist: OK—sometimes you really can let things that irritate you slide, but when it sounds like he's wanting you to be the submissive housewife, that really activates your fear scenario. And now that you're so much closer to being who you want to be, you worry that Doug is going to want you to go back and be submissive again.

Carla: . . . The point is it's never enough. He always wants more.

Therapist: What's your interpretation here, Carla? What does he want more of?

Carla: It wasn't enough that I went to the party with him. I didn't have to. But now, I have to stay and stay, even though the people are boring. If I don't do just what he wants me to, then I'm not sweet.

Therapist: OK, so you aren't just reacting to one small incident but to your fear that it's part of a larger effort on his part to turn you back into a submissive housewife. Is that right?

Carla: That's right.

Therapist: Does this sound like your fear scenario then?

Carla: No, I'm not afraid. I will never go back there.

Therapist: [*Empower the client.*] OK, no fear then, but you have to generate a lot of anger to resist what you interpret are his efforts to put you back there.

Carla: Well, he has no right.

Therapist: Right or not, what could he say or do to put you back there?

Carla: Nothing! I'll never go back there.

Therapist: Listen to yourself! What do you hear? [*Validate healthy goals associated with current functioning.*]

Carla: I hear my determination!

Therapist: There's no way you're ever going back to that place. It can't happen. Do you believe that?

Carla: I have to fight for it.

Therapist: OK, so the fighting part, could that be the part that doesn't quite believe that the passive housewife is gone forever?

Carla: I get tired, you know. When I get tired, I do wonder if it wouldn't be easier to just stop fighting.

Therapist: [*Identify alternative, more adaptive strategies for managing emotions.*] Until you are fully confident within yourself that you are no longer that person, then you may continue to worry about this, right? Once you know he has no power to turn you into that, why overreact to him?

Carla: He can't make me do it.

Therapist: [*Experiment with new strategies.*] Try just sitting for a minute with a feeling of calm confidence that you're never going back there no matter what.

Carla: I feel that. I know it's true.

Therapist: Stay with that feeling of confidence for a minute. . . . Now, (slowly) whenever your confidence is shaken, you can revisit this confident feeling, remind yourself of this certainty. . . .

Therapist: [*Then to Doug.*] Although you don't really want her to go back to being passive again, you can be aware that this is what Carla hears from you, even if you're not saying it. She's worried, right Carla? Sometimes you're going to walk into that without meaning to, and it's going to set her off you know. But the more secure she feels that it's not any more what you want, and the more she knows that you love her strength and want her just like that, the less reactive she's going to be when you say something that activates the old fear scenario.

Doug: I like you strong. I want you to be strong. We're better when you're strong.

[*Carla is quiet.*]

Therapist (to Doug): You can work on your own reactions to Carla. When she shuts down like that [on Friday], could you remind yourself, actively, that Carla's fear scenario, as far as what she fears you want from her, it's been activated

> and that's why she seems to overreact to what you say. It may help you to think sympathetically about her internal struggle—you'll take her reactions less personally and you might just fight less frequently.

This example shows the connection between Carla's fear of enmeshment and her emotional overreactivity. Carla's fear scenario is deeply embedded in a chain of automatic thoughts and not fully within her awareness until the therapist helps her connect the dots between the automatic thoughts to see how the fear scenario controls her emotions. The emotion regulation training should, in turn, help partners to comfort themselves and stay calm when their fear scenarios are activated.

Conclusion

Perhaps it is not surprising that so many couples lack deep intimate connections and find ways to compromise with less. The demands that intimate relationships place upon the self are formidable. Schnarch (1997) describes marriage as the best "growing up" process we know of and nothing illustrates that point with more force than the struggles associated with I versus we dilemmas. In order to sustain a satisfying and intimate connection, partners must often increase their psychological differentiation; that is, they must learn to assert themselves as individuals and simultaneously show respect and understanding toward their partner, all while maintaining a deep intimate connection between them.

10

DILEMMA #3: THE PAST LIVES IN THE PRESENT

Many things, which cannot be overcome when they are together, yield themselves up when taken little by little.

Plutarch, Lives

Psychologists have argued that with each stage of development, we add new sets of social skills and increasingly refined assumptions about relationships, as our social circle expands from family to include peers, teachers, neighbors, caregivers, and others. These complicated sets of assumptions and expectations about relationships are grounded in our experiences with others and our interpretations of the meanings of those experiences. These assumptions and expectations are the building blocks of our intimacy schemas, which in turn shape our emotions, our thinking processes, and our behavior in our adult intimate relationships. For all of us, then, intimacy schemas, and the habits that accompany them, connect us inexorably with our relational past and ensure that our past lives in our present.

For those who struggle unsuccessfully to form and sustain enriching intimate relationships, a haunting, disturbing past that lives in the present is often the hurdle that stands between them and the relationships they desire. Some may find it difficult to convey warmth and positive regard to others because they experienced rejection or neglect as children (Smetana, Campione-Barr, & Metzger, 2006). Others' struggle with fears that stem from traumatic losses or abuse during childhood. Still others are unable to enjoy romantic encounters, because they were teased or rejected by peers as teenagers. Individuals who lack skills or resources for finding, establishing and sustaining intimate relationships, due to difficulties in the past that prevented them from acquiring those skills, struggle with Intimacy Dilemma #3, the past lives in the present. Treatment for these individuals serves to make up for opportunities they missed in their families of origin, or in their childhood and adolescent peer relationships.

There are many points in the process of forming and sustaining intimate relationships where deficits stemming from early experiences can interfere.

Some people find that potentially romantic relationships never progress beyond a casual conversation. These individuals yearn for intimacy but do not attract potential partners. For others, painful social anxiety prevents them from letting others know them. Still others avoid potential rejection by hiding where they are unlikely to meet a potential partner. Still other individuals find that many are attracted but few stay. For them, beauty and charm draw people in, but something else pushes them away.

For those who attract and develop relationships, there are other problems. These individuals might meet and make a romantic connection with another only to have the relationship end as soon as it is established. Some are like Lori from Chapter 9, who fall in love but don't stay in love. Then there are those who seem to pick the wrong partner every time and are inexplicably attracted to the alcoholic, the philanderer, the mentally unstable, the abusive, or the narcissistic. Others, perhaps because of insecure attachments with parents or other early caregivers, may remain overly vigilant for signs of abandonment and exhaust their partners with bids for reassurance and angry recriminations when that reassurance is not adequate to their needs (Mikulincer & Shaver, 2007). Finally, there are those individuals who form relationships that are adequate for their own needs but leave their relationship partners unhappy and complaining about the lack of intimacy in the relationship. These are the people who get pulled into therapy by their intimacy-starved partners.

For all of these reasons and more, some individuals spend most of their lives without an intimate relationship, yet they long for one nevertheless. Individuals with these relationship problems likely ask themselves, "Is there something wrong with me? Why can't I find the right person? Why can't I fall in love? Why does no one seem interested? Why do my partners leave me?" Patterns repeat themselves because individuals confront relationship situations that overtax their resources and skills. It is always the same situations because it is the same set of skills and resources that they lack in each case. An important challenge for the mental health professional begins with the identification of the common deficits in each failed relationship effort.

This chapter organizes individual intimacy problems by the relationship stage during which the problems become manifest, and by the skills and resources required to deepen or sustain a relationship at each stage. I suggest linkages between patterns of relationship failure and the missed opportunities, faulty thinking patterns, and emotional vulnerabilities that people bring with them from their early years and apply to new encounters to their own detriment. Finally, I discuss ways to intervene with each pattern of difficulty.

There is likely some overlap between treatments for individual problems with intimacy and programs for treating personality disorders (e.g., Benjamin, 1996; Linehan, 1993; Young, Klosko, & Weishaar, 2003). This is as it should be, because personality disorders are defined in part by the pattern of disrupted intimate relationships that accompany them and are nearly always the result of long-standing interpersonal difficulties rooted in childhood experiences. For clinicians who are treating personality disorders, these recommendations serve best as an adjunct to individually oriented treatment for those disorders.

Stages of Relationship Development and Psychological Challenges

Individual intimacy resources can be organized according to the stage of intimate relationship development that first demands them—see Figure 10.1. Initiating, developing, and sustaining intimate relationships each require individual skills and resources, some of which may not be demanded during earlier relationship stages. For example, creating social opportunities demands some social assertiveness, basic conversation and listening skills, an ability to show a genuine interest in others, and a willingness to demonstrate warmth and friendliness. A person must also be able to tolerate disinterest or rejection from others to create social opportunities. Building a romantic relationship, however, requires additional skills including intimate self-disclosure, flirting and romance, emotional expressiveness, and comfort with sexuality.

When an individual's relationship consistently blows up at a particular point, he or she may well benefit from enhancing stage-specific skills and resources that relationships require at that point. Some steps in the relationship development process are difficult or impossible without certain relationship skills (e.g., sustaining relationships requires psychologically realistic interpretations of others' motives and behavior, emotion regulation and self-soothing skills, and so forth).

I have identified five *intimacy stuck points* that represent *milestones* for identifying the demands placed upon the individual's intimacy resources: (1) creating social opportunities and meeting new people, (2) developing and deepening relationships with potential romantic partners, (3) engaging in romantic, sexual interactions with partners, (4) sustaining romantic

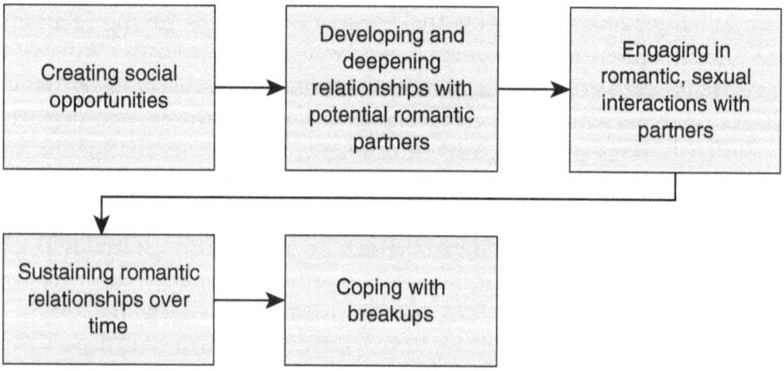

Figure 10.1 Stages of relationship development

relationships over time, and (5) coping with breakups. Each intimacy stuck point requires distinct skills and capacities. Each of these challenges can overwhelm the resources of a vulnerable individual and result in the person or the potential partner backing away from or sabotaging a developing relationship. A cognitive-behavioral approach demands that the skills, problematic thinking patterns, and emotion management deficits associated with problems with each stage be specified for purposes of assessment and treatment.

Creating Social Opportunities

The first step in the process, creating social opportunities and meeting new people, requires that the person be able to present an attractive appearance, take some initiative to attend or create social events, risk exposing him- or herself to situations in which romantic connection *and* rejection are possible,

Table 10.1 Challenges associated with creating social opportunities

Challenge	*Skills and Abilities Required*
Present an attractive appearance	Willing to pay attention to grooming, hairstyle, clothing, exercise
Plan or attend social events	Open to meeting new people Willing to extend invitations and risk rejection Willing to combat inertia and go out and meet other people
Make casual friendly conversation	Social conversation skill: Can introduce self, raise conversation topics, find commonalities with others, listen and activate one's curiosity about other people, avoid excessive self-focus
Self-disclose moderately to new acquaintances Increase self-disclosure as acquaintance increases in depth	Aware of social norms and able to apply them to enhance one's own social effectiveness Able to function as an "opener," someone who encourages others to self-disclose Good listener
Respond to others' initiatives in a friendly, open manner	Avoids excessive self-focus
Cultivate a permissive, forgiving attitude toward oneself as a social person	Able to avoid criticizing one's own social skills excessively

manage his or her social anxiety, and initiate and make conversation with new acquaintances in a way consistent with social norms—see Table 10.1. A good sense of humor and an easy laugh can also help. The therapist can use the items in Table 10.1 as a checklist for assessing the social skills of isolated individuals who do not function well in social situations (see also Appendix A–3).

The skills listed in Table 10.1 are "pre-intimacy" skills. These skills help a person to make a favorable impression on a potential intimate partner. These are skills that most individuals learn through peer relationships in childhood and adolescence (Prager, 1995). Children also learn these skills from socially adroit parents who model them and who instruct them in how to get along with others.

People who lack these skills can suffer because of that lack and yearn to feel more comfortable in social situations and to obtain more positive feedback from others. Some of these individuals go on to form a romantic relationship and perhaps a close friend or two, but others will find that their skill deficit is always a barrier between themselves and a deep intimate connection.

Building skills for creating new social opportunities. Social skills involve what we do and what we do not do when we are in a social situation. Although "don't do" lists can be overwhelming and do not teach a client what does work, if a client is practicing a "don't do" behavior, it is important to point it out and work on alternatives. Table 10.2 lists "don't do" behaviors that are worth focusing on if they are present.

Willing to present an attractive appearance. For some individuals, failing to make an effort to enhance their own attractiveness is an expression of ambivalence about their sexuality. It allows them to verbalize the desire, "I'm eager to meet someone" while still saying nonverbally, "I'd just as soon discourage any takers." This person may endorse the self-schema introduced in Chapter

Table 10.2 Social behaviors that interfere with relationship building

Eliminate potential partners because they are not conventionally attractive.
Fail to make eye contact or smile.
Talk too much about self (or about impersonal subject matter that may not interest the other person).
Fail to ask questions about the other person.
Disclose nothing about self or disclose too much information that is private and personal.
Talk too loudly or too softly.

6, "I'm unattractive" and find it easier to tolerate rejection over something he or she can control (e.g., "He didn't pursue me because I didn't wash my hair that day) than something less controllable ("Maybe I am a bore").

People who are paralyzed by a fear of rejection and who sabotage their efforts to attract others may fear that their "I'm unlovable as I am" self-schema will be validated. If events seem to validate this schema, the emotional impact can be devastating; it is therefore tempting to deliberately sabotage their own efforts to meet new people in order to protect themselves from evidence that seems to confirm it. Young et al. (2003) call these self-sabotaging behaviors "compensatory strategies," because they allow a person to avoid "confirming" a negative self-schema through unsuccessful interactions with others.

Intervention: Conduct a social experiment. Julie struggles with a common self-schema, "I am undesirable as a romantic partner." In her teens, Julie believed that she couldn't compete with the other girls when it came to attracting boys and decided to stop trying. She made friends with a group of teenagers who dressed "goth" and who rejected the "preppie" scene of school dances, clubs, cheerleading, and sports. Even after she graduated, Julie resisted making an effort. If Julie got rejected by men now, she wrote it off to the shallowness of men and their focus on beauty and did not get upset about it.

One way a therapist can help a client who deliberately invites rejection for one reason in order to avoid a more painful reason is by encouraging the client to set up an experiment. With this experiment, the client tests his or her mettle and determines whether he or she still needs the protection of the rejection-inviting behavior.

Here is how Julie's therapist presented this strategy to Julie:

Therapist: Julie, I'm having a hard time reconciling two things about you—your desire, your readiness, to meet a man, fall in love, and start a family, with your casual attention to your appearance.

Julie: I don't want to meet a man who only likes me for my outside. . . . They're the ones missing out. Don't you agree that this is the healthy attitude I should have?

Therapist: You are so right, they are really missing out. But yet, you're not getting what you want—as you said earlier, here you are 29 and you haven't met anyone for quite a while. . . .

Julie (tearing up): That's why I'm here.

Therapist: Would you be willing to do an experiment with your appearance?

Julie: What kind of experiment?

Therapist: Would you be willing to see what happens—how you feel—if you were to go to the next event [singles function] looking as smashing as you can? And then see how you feel being at the party that way. . . . What if you had taken a chance and really knocked yourself out to look smashing, and you still didn't meet anyone. What then?

Julie: I don't know—but the thought of that gives me this feeling in my chest—almost like I want to cry.

Therapist: So, what if you are setting yourself up for one kind of rejection, which hurts but not that much, in order to avoid another kind of rejection that really does hurt?

Julie: Maybe I do. I remember when I used to try really hard to get dates and attend parties and stuff with my friends and how awful it was to not be invited. I can't imagine going through that again.

Therapist: So, it would feel really bad to get rejected for some other reason? One you didn't even know about?

Julie: I don't know if I could stand that. *["I am fragile" schema.]*

Therapist: What if we worked together to prepare you to stand it? Would you be willing to do the experiment?

The therapist proposes that Julie check out how she feels about a rejection that she cannot attribute to her own behavior, a rejection that is out of her control. Through this experiment, Julie can test her tolerance for the pain of rejection and can experience herself surviving the episode without being crushed. She can also test out her cognitive therapy skills, such as monitoring her negative automatic thoughts and countering them with rational alternative interpretations of events. The therapist might want to follow up the suggestion of the experiment by working with Julie's automatic thoughts in connection with carrying it out. This would give the therapist an opportunity to hear the automatic thoughts that discourage Julie's following through with the experiment and to help her come up with alternative perspectives that would encourage her to try it. Finally, the experiment will give Julie the opportunity to acknowledge the aspects of social interaction that are in her control and other aspects that are not. The experiment may set Julie up with a new therapeutic goal: to increase her tolerance for the anxiety associated with the risks of creating social opportunities.

Intervention: Working with self-schemas. People who avoid social opportunities sometimes believe that in order to meet the "right one," one must avoid the appearance of looking for the "right one." Probably, many of these singles felt vulnerable as adolescents and young adults and strove to cover up their vulnerability by appearing not to care about love. Singles fear that they will appear "desperate" and can fail to put themselves into situations in which the potential for meeting new people exists. The automatic thought is that normal efforts to meet people are "desperate" and will fail. In order to avoid appearing desperate, these individuals may sabotage their efforts to meet new people.

The therapist working with this "bashful single" can make headway through a two-step process in which, first, the therapist helps the client identify the faulty negative automatic thought and, second, the therapist uses Socratic questioning to help the client behaviorally define the negative self-schema ("desperate") and evaluate the accuracy of the label. For example, a therapist might help a client to distinguish between "desperate" and "goal-oriented," the latter being a concept that most clients would value.

Intervention: Social skills training. Creating social opportunities requires certain basic social skills. Individuals who disclose too much or too little about themselves upon meeting a new person lack the skill of appropriate disclosure. There are powerful norms that regulate self-disclosure with a new acquaintance, and people who do not know these norms or accommodate their behavior to them are more likely to be rejected (Prager, 1995). The most useful social skills training programs for our purpose here are those targeting individuals with social anxiety (e.g., Antony & Swinson, 2000). The most effective combine education about social life and social norms, goal-setting, relaxation and anxiety management, cognitive restructuring, exposure, and skill-building in the areas of making conversation and appropriate self-disclosure. These interventions are especially helpful in groups where they are available.

The therapist can introduce skill-building work as follows, "Making conversation is a skill, like riding a bicycle. You learn it through exposure to the skills and practice. You may have missed out on learning some of this because you moved around so much when you were young and didn't get a chance to make friends. Just like you learn to ride a bike by trying over and over, falling off some of the time, so also you learn to make conversation the same way, through practice. You don't have to be super-wit in order to make conversation. Some people are that way and more power to them, but most of us settle for being nice and friendly, and you can learn to do that. We start with teaching you how to relax yourself on the spot and then practice effective conversation to increase your self-confidence." As part of social skills practice, the therapist can provide the client with a list of conversation openers.

Social skills training and behavior rehearsal are described in detail in Datillo (2010) and in Epstein and Baucom (2003). Table 10.3 summarizes the steps involved in rehearsing social skills for establishing social relationships.

Cultivate an accepting attitude toward oneself as a social person. Research on loneliness has shown that chronically lonely individuals focus more

Table 10.3 Steps in social skills training for creating social opportunities

Step in Training	*Sample Therapist Statement*
Describe the specific behaviors involved in increasing social skill.	"Making good conversation involves showing an interest in your new acquaintance by being a good listener and asking questions like those in your handout. Getting good at coming up with conversation topics takes practice, and we will practice here so that when you go out in the future, you will have some topics memorized."
	"Research shows that people are most attracted to others who disclose moderately: they're not sphinxes, saying nothing about themselves, and they're not waterfalls, spilling their guts about all their personal issues. Moderate self-disclosure involves telling a person where you're from, what you do for a living or what you study in school, what kinds of things you like to do, how you spend your free time, and so forth."
Describe the behavioral rehearsal process.	"Here's the most effective way for us to practice. First we agree on what skill you will practice. Then, I can show you a couple of different ways to do it through role-playing. I'll play you, and you play someone you've met at the dinner next week. Then we can talk about what I did and think together about how that works for you. Next, you'll practice being you, and I'll role-play the stranger at the dinner. You might start out by saying what I said, just trying it on to see how it fits. Then, we'll stop, you can say how you felt about it, and I'll give you feedback on how you sounded. Then we do it over again, with you incorporating any of the feedback you found valuable."

(*Continued*)

Table 10.3 (*Continued*)

Step in Training	*Sample Therapist Statement*
The therapist role-plays skillful conversation.	"Alright, I'm playing you here. So first, I scope out the dinner and find someone who's not talking to anyone and introduce myself. 'Hi, I don't believe we've met. I'm Phil Abelson.' . . . 'Nice to meet you. How do you know the Barristers?'"
The client and therapist talk about why the therapist did what he or she did.	"I picked that first topic because the couple who are giving the dinner are the one thing I know we have in common. But I could have started with anything on the list there. Notice that I didn't say anything terribly witty? I was just focusing on learning a few things about the person to see if there was something in common that we could talk about."
The client and therapist reverse roles, with the client practicing the conversation openers.	"Now you play yourself, and I'll play a new person at the dinner."
The client and therapist talk about what the client did and how the therapist felt, and the therapist gives the client feedback.	"I really liked the way you used open-ended questions to draw me out of myself, like you were really interested. How did you feel about doing that? . . . etc." "Practice is the way to make it more automatic so let's do it again. This time, I encourage you to make eye contact with me when you ask me about myself. Eye contact tends to convey more warmth."

on themselves and how they are coming across than do nonlonely people (Nurmi, Jyväskylä, Toivonen, Salmela-Aro, & Eronen, 1997). Further, they tend to be painfully self-critical as they imagine how socially awkward and unattractive they appear to be to others.

Cognitive interventions can help lonely people focus on others rather than on themselves and thereby increase their social appeal and decrease their social anxiety simultaneously. These interventions help people to modify self-critical thinking patterns learned in their early years and increase their curiosity about others. Table 10.4 lays out the steps involved in helping a lonely individual increase his or her social self-acceptance.

Table 10.4 Cognitive intervention to increase efficacy with creating social relationships

Step in Treatment
Describe the problem specifically as a problematic thinking pattern.
Teach and then demonstrate the connection between the thinking pattern and other aspects of the problem.
Teach how to catch, evaluate, and modify automatic negative thoughts to soothe negative emotions like anxiety.
Help the client generate his or her own realistic positive alternative thinking.
Explore the emotional consequences of the more positive versus the negative thoughts.
Create a homework assignment; teach the client how to use it outside of therapy.

In sum, there are individuals who do not have rewarding intimate romantic relationships because they have difficulty creating social opportunities. Some of these individuals may have good intimacy skills, and yet their self-defeating thinking patterns and associated awkward social behavior cause them to miss out on opportunities to attract potential partners and deepen those relationships. Behavioral interventions aimed at improving social skills, and cognitive interventions aimed at decreasing negative attitudes about the self in social situations, can help a person experience less social anxiety and improve his or her social effectiveness.

Deepening Social Relationships

The second stage of intimate relationship development is the stage of deepening relationships. At this stage, the goal is to develop a relationship to the point where the pair is no longer following the conventions of casual acquaintances (e.g., self-disclosure reciprocity; Prager, 1995), but the two are relaxing around one another, having fun together, and desiring more contact. Children and adolescents, who are introverted, shy, or withdrawn, who keep themselves occupied with solitary activities rather than other children risk missing out on learning how to deepen their peer relationships. Children who are neglected or mistreated in their families of origin also have difficulty with deepening relationships, because they have never felt secure (e.g., Hazan & Shaver, 1987) and never learned that people can be trustworthy or that they themselves can be loved generously. The skills and abilities involved with deepening social relationships are shown in Table 10.5 (although more research is needed in this area; see Dindia, Timmerman, & Greene, 2003).

Table 10.5 Challenges involved with deepening social relationships

Challenge	*Skills and Personal Qualities Required*
Initiate and plan social activities	Risk taking the initiative Overcome doubt and shame
Increase interactional intimacy	Active listening Express empathy, take the other's perspective Intimate self-disclosure
Increase opportunities for companionship	Comfort with sharing leisure activities and time
Establish equity in a relationship	A willingness to make compromises Feelings of generosity toward the other person that translate into cooperative behavior

Table 10.6 Progressive social initiatives

Week 1	Attend an event, get one phone number.
Week 2	Call the person on the phone to say hello; suggest they meet for coffee.
Week 3	Repeat Week 1.
Week 4	Call the person on the phone to say hello; suggest they meet for ice cream.
Week 5	Evaluate whether further meetings are desirable. Call the person and make a dinner date (or equivalent in time and involvement).

Individuals who have difficulty deepening their relationships can meet people and attract others but do not succeed in moving their relationships beyond the level of casual conversation. A behavioral approach can be effective with individuals who want to get out more but can't think through the maze of etiquette to determine the best way to follow up on a potential new friend. The therapist functions as a cheerleader with the client in this case and also helps the client break down the large task of "getting to know someone" into small tasks that he or she can accomplish each week as homework assignments. Table 10.6 shows a graded task assignment plan that a therapist would introduce, one assignment at a time, to a client who is not deepening his or her relationships.

The first step in helping individuals deepen their social relationships is to explain the skills that are involved. The therapist and client collaborate to identify necessary steps toward deepening a relationship; the therapist then teaches the client some ways of accomplishing the next step. Each step is assigned as homework; the client tries out the new behavior and returns to the therapist, reporting on the thoughts and feelings he or she had at the time. When the client reports on how the homework went (or, on why he or she did not follow through on the homework), the client is now ready to examine any thinking process that may have interfered with the performance of the homework. Therapists must take care not to make the steps too anxiety provoking or risk losing the client.

Intervention: Evaluating and modifying the automatic thoughts. For each task, the therapist works with the client to identify "task-orienting" versus "task-interfering" cognitions (Burns, 1999). This time-honored intervention involves having the person draw a line down the middle of a page and write down all the thoughts he or she had about taking the social initiative. For each task-interfering thought that the individual identifies, he or she is encouraged to create reasonable, alternative thoughts, or task-orienting cognitions, with which to counter the task interfering thoughts. The client then practices the realistic thoughts as he or she thinks about taking the initiative and following through.

For example, Victor's therapist listened carefully when he talked about why he didn't follow up with a woman he met over the weekend and helped him to identify and label his task-interfering cognitions ("I waited too late to call, so now I can't call"). The therapist walked Victor through a brief process of creating (and eventually practicing) alternative, task-orienting cognitions that would encourage him to take the risk ("e.g., "I can call—the worst things that can happen are that she won't remember me or will say no. I can handle either outcome").

Intervention: Social skill training. Some individuals have difficulty with the conversational demands of the deepening stage of relationship development. This individual fails to engage in active listening or self-disclosure for any number of reasons, with the result that the other person eventually breaks off contact. Typically, the individual with this problem was slow to mature and did not get the normal opportunities as an adolescent to practice these social skills and learn from peers.

For these individuals, I recommend the same process as described in Table 10.3 for social skill training, except that now the focus of the training is on active listening and appropriate self-disclosure. The therapist's role is to explain the social norms governing conversations that promote intimacy and to structure role-plays that will give the client a chance to see the therapist engage in these behaviors and then to try out these behaviors him- or herself. After having practiced in session, the client is encouraged to try the behaviors out with a new person who he or she is getting to know or with someone more comfortable like a family member, if the former is too anxiety-provoking.

In the example below, the therapist uses social skills training for two purposes with Elizabeth, who wanted a romantic relationship and had not been able to form one. In this session, Elizabeth reported having made plans for dinner that weekend with Michael, whom she had just met. Elizabeth's therapist hoped to use behavior rehearsal to provide her with practice deepening a new relationship through conversation and also to help her to feel less nervous through exposing her beforehand to a practice conversation.

Therapist: Why don't we role-play with me demonstrating some of the social behaviors that will help you and Michael get to know each other better when you go out this weekend? As we go through it, I'll tell you what I'm doing. And we can work with your reactions, OK?

Elizabeth: OK, although I'm a bit nervous.

Therapist: The practices help you to feel less nervous. Let's go for it. So I'm you, and you're Michael, but if you start having feelings about anything that's going on, we'll stop and you'll be you, OK?

Elizabeth: OK.

Therapist as Elizabeth: Hi Michael. Good to see you. *[See how you can be positive, even with a simple greeting.]*

Elizabeth as Michael (giggling): Hi Elizabeth. How are you doing?

Therapist as Elizabeth: Good! I had a nice day today. I slept in this morning and made myself a really nice brunch—eggs, the whole bit.

Elizabeth as Michael (giggling): That sounds good. And very relaxing. Something I would enjoy doing a lot.

Therapist as Elizabeth: What did you do with your Saturday? *[See how I'm sharing a little bit about myself and then asking him about himself? That's a good technique for breaking the ice.]*

Elizabeth as Michael: *[Hmmm. What would Michael do on a Saturday?]* I washed my car—it was nice being outside this morning, the weather was so great. . . . *[The two continue with casual, personal conversation.]* . . .

Therapist as Elizabeth: *[OK. I'm going to ask one of those opener questions to try to get into more depth.]* So what kinds of things do you like to do for fun, Michael? Besides your motorcycle?

Elizabeth as Michael: *[Boy I really don't know how to answer that. I guess we didn't talk much yet. I'll make something up.]* In the summer, I like to go to the lake, swim, and water ski.

Therapist as Elizabeth: I enjoy boating; I love to go fast on the water. *[Is this close enough to accurate?]* . . .

Therapist: OK, Elizabeth, let's pause. How are you feeling about this conversation?

Elizabeth: It's pretty easy.

Therapist: Great! It felt easy from my end, too. Now we can go one of two ways:

We can reverse roles, and you can practice some of what I was doing, or we can imagine the two of you at dinner when you're going to have a more intimate, self-disclosing conversation.

Elizabeth: Let's practice that. I'd like to see how you do that.

Therapist: OK. I'll be you some more. Why don't you try opening up a more intimate topic as Michael, for practice?

Elizabeth as Michael: Ummmm. *[Sits quietly for a moment.]* Tell me about your family, Elizabeth.

Therapist as Elizabeth: *[Good—you left it open for Elizabeth to say as much or as little personal stuff as she's inclined to. I'm going to share a moderate amount, show you what that sounds like. See how it feels to be on the receiving end.]* Well, I'm originally from the Midwest—Cincinnati to be exact. I grew up there, but never liked the cold, so I was happy to take a job here. . . . *[Conversation continues for a couple of rounds.]*

Therapist: How did you feel during that conversation?

Elizabeth: A little uncomfortable. Like I didn't know what to say. Some of that may come from trying to play Michael, and I don't know him that well.

Therapist: How did you feel about what I was saying as you when I was playing Elizabeth?

Elizabeth: It was OK. As Michael, I was interested. And I think I got the idea about saying some personal stuff but not too much.

Therapist: OK let's reverse roles back, and I'll be Michael. Let's pick a different topic; I'll open it. And you can practice opening up about yourself at that moderate level.

Coping with intimacy ambivalence that prevents the deepening of relationships. Some individuals can take the initiative and get involved only to "freeze out" the partner as the relationship progresses. As one articulate young woman put it, "I stand outside of my body and watch as I close off emotionally from the other person. I seem to become numb to the normal feelings I should be experiencing at this stage, and this leads to the end before it begins." This individual, like those described in Chapter 7, struggles with Dilemma #1 and thereby has difficulty accepting the vulnerability to hurt that comes with increasing intimacy in a relationship. However, unlike those discussed in Chapter 7 who establish relationships and commit to them, this individual does not permit relationships to mature. Rather, when most people would start having feelings and looking forward to being with the person they are getting to know, this person bails out psychologically, either turning off his or her own feelings or behaving in a way that drives the new person away. The therapist can help this individual using some of the same techniques described in Chapter 7:

1 Teach the intimacy-distance regulation model, particularly the concepts of intimacy ambivalence and intimacy-distance regulation, and normalize the need to both approach and self-protect.
2 Help the client make the connection between his or her behavior—withdrawing from relationships or freezing out the potential partners—and his or her emotions. If the client can't identify emotions, suggest that he or she is possibly being very successful at avoiding having feelings at all, either positive or anxious, about the people he or she is going out with. Use self-awareness training (Chapter 5) to help him or her become aware of his or her feelings.
3 Help the client identify the sources of his or her resistance to becoming involved. The therapist can introduce this identification process by saying, "In order to have a relationship, you have to learn to tolerate the uncertainty of getting closer to someone. One way to do that is to create a kind voice in your head that helps you get through the rough spots. In order to create the kind voice, we have to explore your concerns and fears so that the voice can be effective in soothing you as you face the uncertainties of building a relationship. Be assured, though, that everyone feels anxious and uncertain when they are building a new relationship."
4 With the client, do a verbal walk through of his or her last dating experience and why it fizzled. Through questioning, help the client identify his or her thoughts and feelings at each stage of the process and how he or she behaved in response. Help the client notice any self-protective benefits that came from the behavior and comment on them. It is sometimes a good idea to congratulate the client on being so effective at self-protection, as this is an important skill. Here is an example from Ellen's work with her therapist.

Therapist: OK, let's talk about the two of you in the car driving over. What went on? . . .

Therapist: Ellen, you're usually so much more expressive. What's going on as you tell the story of your date with Stan? Your voice is different.

Ellen: Yeah? Hmmmm, I don't know.

Therapist: Your voice is kind of flat—like this is boring maybe?

Ellen: I guess I'm feeling anxious, just remembering the date. Getting back and remembering the details.

Therapist: Can you make it OK that you're feeling anxious? Because one of the reasons we get into the details is so that we can recapture what you were feeling and thinking and see where this went wrong?

Ellen: OK. I remember wanting to seem calm and nonchalant, and maybe that's what I'm doing now.

Therapist: Hmmmm well, you're good at sounding nonchalant. Maybe too good. What do you think?

Ellen: Hmmm, I didn't think I was that good because I don't feel that nonchalant.

Therapist: So maybe you overdo it in order to hide your nervousness? . . . Did you know you were good at that?

Ellen: I suppose I must be. People don't comment on my being nervous or anything.

Therapist: Can you think of any disadvantages of being good at hiding your nervousness?

The walk-through should help the therapist and client identify the problematic thoughts and feelings that motivated the distancing behavior. Depending upon the thoughts that emerge, the therapist can now educate the client about any unrealistic assumptions or expectations, work on some alternative, more benign thoughts that are more realistic than the ones that motivated the distancing behavior, or help the client find alternative ways to regulate anxiety in the face of increasing intimacy.

When intimacy ambivalence leans too much toward the negative side and prevents an individual from allowing his or her relationships to deepen, it is possible that the past is making its way into the present. It is important to take a thorough history when individuals report that their relationships begin but do not develop. Fears or negative expectations that are strong enough to overwhelm an individual's yearning to make an intimate connection with another likely stem from earlier experiences of loss, betrayal, deprivation, or abuse.

Many adults are quite aware of the deprivations and traumas that they experienced as children and the fact that those experiences still affect their adult relationships. The therapist can encourage the client to tell his or her story and to notice the relationship between the events in the story and his or her presenting problem. Once the client has told his or her story, the therapist is then in a good position to implement one or more interventions that can assist the client in seeing the current problem as an extension of historical events whose influence in adult life can be minimized.

Guided fantasy can be effective in helping individuals explore and come to terms with difficult experiences in their families of origin. By encouraging the client to take a fantasy journey back to significant times in his or her history, the therapist helps the client increase the client's awareness of the emotional impact of those times and the extent to which those emotions are still very much alive in him or her.

In the following example, the therapist guides the client back to a fantasy visit to herself as a child. The client's presenting complaint was that her relationships never developed. The client had reported that she thought she might have been sexually abused as a young child, although she had no explicit memory of it. She had hypothesized that her problem with men had something to do with sexual abuse but was not sure.

Therapist: *[Link the guided fantasy to the client's goals for herself.]* Sometimes, feelings can get lost in childhood—I mean lost from awareness—and yet still be affecting us as adults just below the surface of our awareness. Would you be willing to revisit yourself as a child in a guided fantasy to see if you can bring up any of the feelings that you had then, whether related to sexual abuse or not?

Wanda: What would that involve? I feel a little nervous just thinking about it.

Therapist: It involves you getting really relaxed and then letting your mind go backward and recreating yourself as a child in your mind and living there for awhile, here with me in the session. The idea is for you to be really curious about what kinds of feelings and thoughts will come up as you experience the fantasy. You will be free to come out of the fantasy any time you want.

Wanda: OK, let's try it.

Therapist: [*Induction.*] OK, start by putting both of your feet on the floor and getting a relaxed posture. When you're ready, close your eyes, and I'll walk you through some relaxation instructions. . . . Let me know when you're feeling relaxed.

Wanda: I'm feeling pretty relaxed right now.

Therapist: *[Begin guided fantasy.]* Now I'd like you to imagine that you're standing next to a magical form of transportation, maybe a magic carpet. Can you see that?

Wanda: Yes, I have a rocket ship.
Therapist: OK, when you're ready, get into the rocket ship (short pause).
Wanda: OK, I'm inside.
Therapist: What do you see?
Wanda: It's kind of cramped in here; I see a big window in front, a lot of instruments in a kind of dashboard, and my seat is tall. The ceiling is low.
Therapist: Great. *[A vivid image is very helpful.]* OK, when you're ready, the rocket ship will begin taking you on a journey into your past. Let me know when you've started.
Wanda (short pause): OK, I'm going.
Therapist: The rocket is going to travel through the years until it gets to a year that is significant for you and can teach you something. Take your time, let me know when you've arrived.
Wanda: It's still going.
Therapist: OK (pause).
Wanda: It's slowing; it's stopping, and I'm four, maybe even three.
Therapist: OK. You're what, three and a half?
Wanda: Maybe four.
Therapist: OK, you're four. Can you get out of the rocket?
Wanda: The door opened for me.
Therapist: OK. When you're ready, get out and see what you see.
Wanda: OK. . . . I'm in my front yard, of the house we lived in when we lived in Harrisburg.
Therapist: [*Deepening the fantasy.*] What does it look like?
Wanda: There aren't any trees in the front yard. Just grass and some hedges along the house.
Therapist: No trees and some hedges.
Wanda: And the sky is dark—like it's going to rain.
Therapist: OK. Is this expected, in Harrisburg?
Wanda: Yes, it's rainy, and the winters are long.
Therapist: How do you feel being in the front yard of your home?
Wanda: I feel fine. I have a positive feeling about the yard.
Therapist: Walk around; see what you want to do next. Take your time.
Wanda: I want to go inside, but I hesitate.
Therapist: OK, stay with that feeling. See what the hesitation is about.
Wanda: I feel a little afraid.
Therapist: Stay with that feeling. Let it grow in you, so it can speak to you (pause).
Wanda: I want to get out of the rain, but I don't know if it's safe in there.

Therapist:	Where do you feel the fear?
Wanda:	In my stomach, it's like an empty place but also kind of cold.
Therapist:	Stay with that feeling. See what it has to tell you.
Wanda:	It's getting stronger, the more I think about going inside.
Therapist:	Stay with it.
Wanda:	I feel a bit nauseous.
Therapist:	Stay with it.
Wanda:	I'm getting wet. The rain is coming.
Therapist:	OK. Do what is best.
Wanda:	I think I want to get back in the rocket.
Therapist:	OK, get in the rocket.
Wanda:	I'm in the rocket now, and the door closed.
Therapist:	How do you feel in the rocket?
Wanda:	Safe. I feel so much safer.
Therapist:	The rocket will bring you back to the present when you're ready.
Wanda (quiet):	We're flying now, me and the rocket.
Therapist:	Take your time; let me know when you're back.
Wanda (quiet):	I'm back.
Therapist:	Take some deep breaths; let yourself just be for a minute or two. You can open your eyes when you're ready. . . .
Wanda:	I'm ready.
Therapist (debriefing):	How are you feeling now?
Wanda:	A little shaky but relieved to be back. That was really strange, that feeling, but it was also very familiar.
Therapist:	Sometimes our emotions know things that our heads don't know.
Wanda:	Yes, as a four-year-old, I knew something was wrong.
Therapist:	Yes, there is a wisdom that you had, you still have, that tells you when something is wrong.
Wanda:	I don't know what I was afraid of, just that it was scary enough to come back and not go in.
Therapist:	Do you want to know?
Wanda:	I'm not sure.
Therapist:	So when you felt afraid, was your first impulse to turn around? To leave?
Wanda:	Yes.
Therapist:	What would have happened if you went inside?
Wanda:	I don't know. Something bad. It seemed like I should leave if I could leave. It was a real relief to realize that I could leave. The rocket prevented me from being trapped there.

Therapist: So the rocket—your transportation away—is very important.

Wanda: It's my security, I'm realizing that.

Therapist: Perhaps you use that rocket even now, as an adult?

Wanda: I definitely use it. I think I keep it with me all the time. So I can always escape.

Therapist: And it works to prevent you from feeling that uncomfortable feeling?

Wanda: It must because I haven't felt that in a while, maybe in a long time.

Therapist: What's happening now, Wanda, is that your self-awareness is really increasing. Now you know what you feel, and you know about your rocket and how safe it makes you feel. You can expand your self-awareness to your everyday life, too. Monitor when you feel safe and when you feel the scary feeling. Notice the circumstances and what you do. Don't try to change anything yet. This homework is just for you to understand yourself better, to increase your self-awareness.

Guided fantasy is an excellent intervention for clients who believe that the past is living in the present and affecting their relationships but unable to say exactly how that influence is operating. In this example, the therapist helped the client recover a forgotten, but still vivid, emotion that she had experienced as a child and that was associated with her home. The client also became aware of how much she coped by escaping and how safe and secure she felt knowing she could escape, as symbolized by the rocket. The homework assignment gave Wanda the opportunity to explore her feelings and her coping method more fully as they affected her day to day. The therapist can follow up this session by encouraging Wanda to take another rocket trip and to give her the opportunity to experience more of the feelings that she still has about her past, and to also give her the opportunity to use the fantasy to explore other coping strategies.

The next dialogue between Wanda and her therapist illustrates the way that guided fantasy can be used to help a client increase his or her self-empowerment while revisiting a troubled childhood. In this session, Wanda is traveling back in time but retaining her adult self. She is traveling to go visit her younger self and to help her with whatever is scaring her.

Therapist (pauses): Let me know when you've disembarked and where you are.

Wanda: I'm back at the house in Harrisburg, front yard.

Therapist: OK. Look around, is anything different?

Wanda: This time, it's sunny.

Therapist: What else?

Wanda: The front door is open. That's odd, we wouldn't have left it open.
Therapist: Hmmm.
Wanda: I think four-year-old Wanda has just gone inside.
Therapist: What will you do?
Wanda: I'm going in after her.
Therapist: Take just a moment and pause; check your feelings.
Wanda: I feel the shaky, scary feeling, but I also feel very powerful.
Therapist: Where is that feeling of power located in your body?
Wanda: Ummm—my shoulders, my arms.
Therapist: Take a minute to focus that feeling; capture it; treasure it.
[Wanda pauses and reflects, stays in the fantasy.]
Therapist: What's going on?
Wanda: I'm noticing, the house is smaller than I remembered. The yard is too.
Therapist: Hmmm, interesting.
Wanda: I'm ready to go in. In fact, I'm worried about four-year-old Wanda.
Therapist: Can you locate the worried feeling?
Wanda: It's in my throat—I feel a choking feeling, but it's not as strong as the feeling I had the last time.
Therapist: OK when you're ready, go in.
Wanda: I'm going in. The hallway is dark. I see four-year-old Wanda playing in the den.
Therapist: Say more; what do you see?
Wanda: She keeps looking up; she looks afraid.
Therapist: What next for adult Wanda?
Wanda: I feel sad for her.
Therapist: Would you like to visit with her?
Wanda: Yes, I'd like to reassure her that she'll be alright.
Therapist: Go for it.
Wanda: OK, I'm with little Wanda in the den (long pause); I think I comforted her. I hugged her. She seemed a little less scared but not totally comfortable.
Therapist: Good that you were able to ease her fears even a little.
Wanda: Yes, I think it is good *(long pause)*. She looks so innocent, playing there.
Therapist: Who's in the house taking care of her? She can't be alone, right?
Wanda: I think my mother must be out. She'd be looking in on little Wanda.
Therapist: Who is there then?
Wanda: Must be my father *(long pause)*.
Therapist: Do you want to visit with him?
Wanda: Not especially. But I have to stay here to keep little Wanda safe.
Therapist: So the adult you can protect her?
Wanda: Yes. I think I could stand up to him now.

Therapist:	Think or know?
Wanda:	I know I would. I wouldn't let him hurt little Wanda (tearing up, crying softly, long pause). I'm feeling like I could leave now, and she'll be alright, eventually.
Therapist:	You've left her in a safe place?
Wanda:	Well, it's not exactly safe.
Therapist:	Could you leave something there for her that would symbolize the protection that your presence can offer?
Wanda:	Hmmmm . . . my grandmother's pendant. My grandmother made me feel safe and secure when I was with her, so this pendant should help little Wanda feel safe and secure.
Therapist (long pause):	Take your time and decide how you want to give it to her.
Wanda:	I've given it to her, and I'm really ready to head to my rocket.
Therapist:	Have you said goodbye?
Wanda:	I did. I hugged her.
Therapist:	Would you be willing to say one last thing? Say something reassuring about how whenever she feels afraid, she can think about adult you and how powerful you are and be comforted.
Wanda (pause):	Alright, I'm telling her (tearing up).
Therapist:	And your rocket is ready to take you forward to the present whenever you're ready (long pause). Let me know when you've arrived; take your time though coming back—whatever time you need.
Wanda (after another pause):	I'm back. That was nice. I feel lighter somehow.
Therapist:	Where is that light feeling in you?
Wanda:	In my chest. It feels open.
Therapist:	Maybe your heart opened a little too?
Wanda:	That's it. I think so.
Therapist:	What was it like, being powerful adult Wanda back there in Harrisburg?
Wanda:	It was different. I realized I could take whatever he dished out and dish it back. Or at least, not accept it. . . .
Wanda:	I'd like to hold onto this strong feeling. It's nice.
Therapist:	Each time you want to recover it, just close your eyes and imagine yourself taking care of little Wanda, helping her to be less sad.

This time, Wanda's therapist used guided fantasy to provide Wanda with an experience of strength and adult savvy in the context of her childhood trauma. Through the fantasy, Wanda had her first and most potent experience of caring for her vulnerable self. The fantasy also gave Wanda the opportunity to hear herself saying that she had sources of comfort within herself that she could give to herself and share.

Deepening Romantic Intimacy

Deepening romantic intimacy is a step that usually occurs in parallel with Step 2, above, deepening social relationships. However, some individuals function very well when they are deepening relationships as long as those relationships are not romantic relationships. As soon as a possible romance is on the horizon, they behave differently and less effectively, even though they very much want a romantic relationship for themselves.

Table 10.7 lists the most likely reasons for individuals to have problems with romantic relationships who do not otherwise have social problems. Some of these overlap with the problems people have with creating social opportunities.

Both paths in Figure 10.2 describe a person who has a negative self-schema that is specific to his or her appeal as a romantic partner. In the first case, the person's negative schema is "I'm physically unattractive," and the most devastating experience the person can imagine is one that would appear to confirm the truth of that schema. In the second case, the person also has a

Table 10.7 Common problems people have forming romantic relationships

Problem	*Behaviors with Attractive Others*
Not attracting others	Poor grooming, other physical problem
	Distant, unfriendly
	Doesn't flirt, show interest
	Doesn't initiate
Attracts others, but romance does not develop	Avoids sexual contact, encounters
	Inappropriate self-disclosure (too high, too low)
	Maintains multiple partners and never chooses
Loses interest, gets bored as soon as romance develops	Distancing, dismissive behavior pushes partners away
Gets clingy as soon as romance develops	Gets demanding, insatiable, pushes partners away

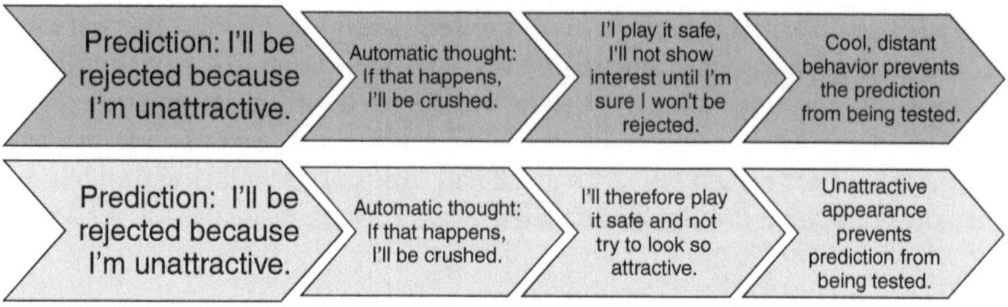

Figure 10.2 Two self-sabotaging paths that prevent deepening of romantic intimacy

negative schema regarding his or her romantic appeal which is more global. In this case, the person actually has fears of eliciting a positive response from a potential partner because it would put him or her in the position of being romantic and eventually sexual with that person. So projecting an unavailable, uninterested surface keeps people from being attracted in the first place. If no one has the desire to touch, then there is no pressure. However intense their anxiety about romance, such individuals are usually quite lonely and therefore ambivalent about their "successful" bid to keep others away.

Dealing with negative body image. For both paths in Figure 10.2, it can be helpful to work with people on improving their relationship with their bodies. The therapist makes no assumptions about what the client wants or needs in order to feel more confident in her skin, but rather suggests that therapist and client together set up a series of experiments, in which the client tries out options like a new exercise program or regular manicures, and then monitors her feelings about herself as a result of trying it. The therapist will focus on what makes the client feel prettier when she walks out the door, what buoys her up. Those will be the things that the therapist and client will then work on integrating into her routine.

For clients who are on Path 1, and who just need to perceive their own attractive features, incorporating one or more self-improvement activities may be sufficient to get them to take more risks with potential romantic partners. However, some clients who appear to be on Path 1 are in fact more afraid of being rejected for their "true selves" than of being rejected for their appearance.

When the therapist works with the client to identify and follow through with a self-improvement activity, the client on Path 2 will likely demonstrate resistance. The therapist should then consider the possibility that the second path is operating, with Figure 10.3 being one way of doing so. Individuals who have difficulty with the romantic, sexual aspect of new relationships may use their "undesirable" appearance as protection against confirming a schema that they

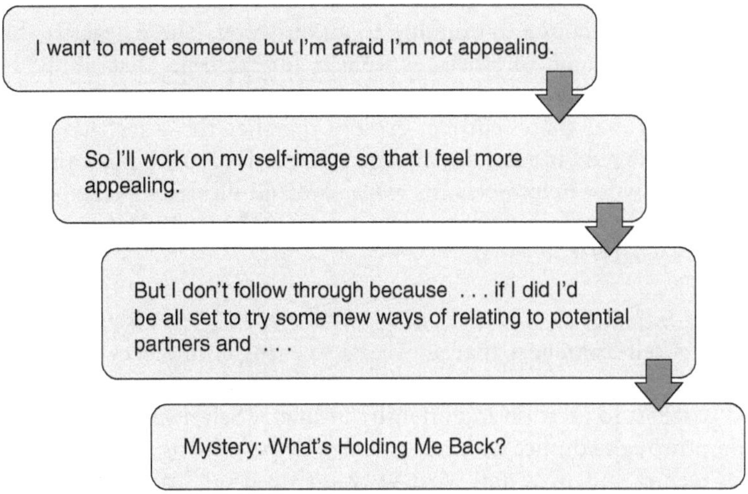

Figure 10.3 The mystery at the end of Path 2

are unlovable or undesirable at a deeper level. The "mystery" at the end is the "black box" that the therapist and client can work together to open and work on.

The therapist can use Figure 10.3 to introduce Path 2, which will begin a process in which the client and therapist identify, explore, and reinterpret experiences that led the client to conclude that the client was somehow unfit for romance. Some questions that will access critical experiences shaping intimacy schemas include: "What did you learn about yourself as a girl (boy) growing up? What messages did you get about what it meant to be a woman (man)? Did you hear offhand or deliberate comments about the way that women (men) looked, came across, that gave you messages about what was important, what counted? How did your family members, parents, grandparents, siblings, treat you when you started going through puberty? What was their reaction to your breasts growing larger (your voice deepening)? What about your friends at school? Did they tease you about anything in particular? What about the boys (girls)? Was there anything in particular that they did to make you feel rejected? What do you think about those messages today? Might there be some advantages to reconsidering them? . . . If you're like most of us humans, you absorbed those messages as a young person because they were your primary source of information about yourself. Now that you're an adult, you have the wherewithal to reevaluate them and to come up with your own thoughts about your womanhood (manhood)."

Exploring influences from the past helps to bring self-schemas about attractiveness, desirability, and lovability to the foreground, as these experiences were instrumental in the formation of these schemas. The therapist and client can talk together about the way that early experiences can "program" our thinking, and how we get into thinking habits that are not beneficial, especially when it comes to thinking about ourselves. These negative thought habits can also extend to others, as we fear, for example, that adults that we meet will behave the way that the other teens did when we were younger. The therapist and the client can explore together the ways that the social world has changed (and has not changed) since. Table 10.8 presents the step-by-step process for helping clients reevaluate and ultimately change negative self-schemas that was introduced in Chapter 6, here applied specifically to romantic-sexual self-schemas.

Increasing intimacy through increasing self-awareness. As discussed in Chapter 5, it is self-awareness that allows us to bring immediacy into our self-disclosures and into our sexual encounters. Immediacy in their interactions allows partners to increase and intensify intimacy. Self-awareness also helps us to think through conflict with our partners by permitting us to identify what we are feeling and why, and what we want from our partners. Sharing our

Table 10.8 Step-by-step process for changing negative romantic-sexual self-schemas

Step 1:	Educate: Introduce the cognitive model of emotions, emphasizing self schemas.
Step 2:	Assess and explore automatic negative thoughts.
Step 3:	Educate about previous experiences as sources of schemas and why schemas persist despite experiences to the contrary.
Step 4:	Conduct a "developmental analysis." Encourage the client to remember where he or she learned to accept the schema as truth. Explore and reinterpret emotionally charged memories with the goal of empowering the client.[1]
Step 5:	Assess the schema(s). Evaluate the messages from the various sources for truth value, using a double column technique like "Evidence For, Evidence Against," "Advantages versus Disadvantages" (Beck et al., 1979), or *empathic confrontation* (Young et al., 2003). When dealing with Intimacy Dilemma #3, the past lives in the present, it is especially important to identify and thoroughly analyze the events that convinced the client initially of the truth of the negative self-schema.
Step 6:	Assess and change schemas: Separate the messages into two groups, based on whether the evidence supports or does not support the schema. The therapist then encourages the client to conduct experiments that test the schema's validity (Beck, 1976; see Chapter 6).

1 Readers may also be interested in a process developed earlier by McCullough (2006) for eliciting and identifying the source of schemas. McCullough uses significant other history and asks, "How did your mother influence you? How did your father influence you? How about peers, close friends, girlfriends, grandparents, teachers, and so forth?"

self-awareness allows us to have emotionally significant moments of intimacy, characterized by immediacy. Although individuals vary widely in their taste for such intensely intimate moments, this skill is nevertheless germane to the deepening of romantic relationships.

Self-awareness training is useful for helping people to become more aware of their inner selves, making them more accessible for intimate communication. The feeling-finding mission from Chapter 5 encourages people to sit quietly and focus on the sensations of their five senses. As they focus on their sensations, the therapist asks them to describe what they are sensing with each sense, because a goal of this exercise is to help people to become accustomed to putting words to their experiences. For those who have difficulty with this exercise, the therapist can begin by asking the client to close his or her eyes, focus on breathing, and describe the sensation accompanying the breathing—is it tight and rapid or slow and relaxed. Once the client has tracked the sensations associated with breathing, he or she is ready to track other sensations in the body. The instruction is to (1) notice any sensations, (2) label them, and (3) let them be—see what they become or change into as you monitor them. Once clients have done self-awareness training with their therapists, they can practice at home.

Self-awareness training can also be a useful technique for someone who is unaware of sexual feelings. Heiman, Lopiccolo, and Palladini (1988) suggest that relationship partners rate themselves several times each day on a three-point scale: (1) absolutely no interest in sex, (2) you could go either way, and (3) watch out I'm ready! This self-rating exercise encourages them to think of sexual desire on a continuum and encourages even low-desire people to notice that there are times when they could be persuaded by an ardent partner.

Developing comfort with sexuality. For some individuals, the stalling of romantic relationships at the point at which sexual intimacy would reasonably follow is due to negative or ambivalent feelings about sexuality per se. In my experience, there are particular kinds of negative sexual self-schemas that are primarily experienced by women. These negative sexual self-schemas are related to body image and to an inability to feel sexual desire.

Discomfort with sexuality often stems from early experiences that led the individual to feel embarrassment or shame about her body. Culprits include teasing by peers, rejection by potential dates or boyfriends, overprotective parents who warned too fiercely about the dangers of premature sexuality, physical and sexual abuse at home, and sometimes, a parent who shares his or her negative view of the other sex with the child. Children may develop a negative attitude toward their bodies if their parents are overly uncomfortable with touch, hugging, bathing, diaper-changing, feeding, and other physical contact with the child. Traumas such as rape and other assaults can also create problems with sexuality later on.

Therapeutic work can begin by incorporating into therapy one of the books available for women on increasing comfort with sexuality. Heiman and colleagues' *Becoming Orgasmic: A Sexual and Personal Growth Program for Women* is in its second edition and continues to get positive reviews from therapists and from women who use it. Heiman et al. (1988) address multiple contributors to women's sexual unresponsiveness beginning with a personal sex history and continuing with a discussion of sexual myths such as, "Normal (feminine, sexual, or real) women have an orgasm every time they have sex" or "A sexually responsive woman can always be 'turned on' by her partner." They also include in their program relaxation exercises, kegeling (i.e., exercise for the pelvic floor muscles), and—for later in the program—self-touching and pleasuring exercises. The therapist can be an important support system for a woman making her way through the book, helping her to identify and evaluate the negative automatic thoughts and self-schemas elicited by a focus on her body and sexuality. For that majority of women that are concerned about their weight, a useful exercise is to encourage the woman to find great works of art, painting or sculpture, that celebrate the beauty and sensuality of normal-weight women and to find a conspicuous place to display them. Images of celebrity women who are considered beautiful yet who are not skinny can also serve as potential schema-altering stimuli. For a focus on body image, the book *Transforming Body Image: Love the Body You Have* (Hutchinson, 1985) is useful. The latter has exercises helping the woman to explore sources of displeasure with herself from her family of origin and encourages her to engage in movement exercises as a way of increasing the pleasure she takes in her own grace. I have also recommended that my clients watch TLC's "What Not to Wear," a show in which Stacy London and Clinton Kelly help women to appreciate and enhance their own unique beauty.

Lovers and good friends, too. One of the roadblocks individuals can experience as they deepen their relationships is a lack of flexibility in how they relate to their new love interest. Flexibility involves being able to relate romantically and also in a plain friendly way to the same person. Experience suggests that this problem may be more prevalent in men than in women. Young men grow up in a peer climate in which women are routinely dehumanized in casual conversations, and sexual encounters are still perceived as conquests rather than mutually agreed upon intimacies. Cool guys can take or leave the woman of the hour without experiencing grief, according to contemporary myths of masculinity (Levant & Pollack, 1995; Tolman, Spencer, Harmon, Rosen-Reynoso, & Striepe, 2004).

Coming out of this masculine socialization are young men who are mystified as to why they are not more successful at getting beyond the level of casual acquaintance with the young women they meet. Their problems stem from having little practice as youth with demonstrating interest in, curiosity, concern, and caring about the inner life of a woman. For some of these individuals, teaching and practice in the skills required to ask questions and listen and track an intimate conversation will be sufficient. Some may have failed to expand their interactional repertoire from that learned in the all-boy play groups of their youth. Research by Maccoby (1990) and others has shown that the level of intimacy acceptable for day-to-day interaction in all-boy peer groups is low. When adolescent boys begin to spend time with adolescent girls, they can be unprepared for the level of intimacy that girls expect in their conversations and may thereby fail to deepen their interactions because they are unaccustomed to intimate conversation with peers. Further, some young men may have inhibitions about sharing their vulnerable selves and stop themselves, even when they know that this is what is expected and makes sense in context.

Sustaining Romantic Relationships

Here I address the beginning stages of a romantic relationship as two people are in the process of becoming a couple. At this stage, each person is beginning to feel fond of the other, and the beginnings of a mutual attachment are present. This is the point at which the pair begins to change their schedules and routines to allow the other into their lives (or at least, it's the stage when one of the partners begins to expect the other to do so). People can experience anxiety in conjunction with the uncertainties of this stage in a relationship, asking themselves if this person can give them what they want, if they are ready to make the sacrifices that a relationship requires, if the other person really loves them, if the other person is trustworthy enough, sufficiently committed to making it work, and so forth. A person's ability to tolerate the uncertainty and associated anxiety at this stage will contribute to the person's ability to stay the course and let the relationship develop.

Two embedded challenges. Sustaining an intimate romantic relationship has two challenges embedded within it: (1) committing to the relationship and (2) sustaining a deep intimate connection with the partner. Some individuals who falter at this stage are aware of their distancing behavior and may even distance on purpose because they are not ready for a relationship, but others will distance without being aware of their own motivations. Inordinate anxiety or distancing behavior during uncertain times in a relationship is characteristic of someone with an insecure attachment history (e.g., Mikulincer & Shaver, 2007).

Problems with attachment security. Children are born with a need to feel secure and safe; to feel secure, infants seek to maintain proximity to an *attachment figure,* that is, a person who loves and takes care of the infant (Bowlby, 1969). When the environment seems dangerous or threatening, the infant stops what he or she was doing, searches insistently for the attachment figure, and begins to cry and crawl toward that person's likely location. When the attachment figure is able to comfort the infant, the infant achieves a positive emotional state, "felt security" (Bowlby, 1969).

The experiences young children accumulate with their attachment figures in childhood are significant for later personality development because these experiences are represented as "internal working models" or *attachment schemas.* These schemas classify expectations about others' availability to provide comfort in a stressful situation, and they classify expectations of the self and the self's ability to be loved, cared for, and comforted in times of stress. Attachment schemas carry expectations of comfort and security from past relationships into current ones.

For adults, the romantic partner is the most likely person to serve as an attachment figure, being that adults are most likely to turn to their romantic partners when they need comfort. Research on attachment relationships in adulthood supports Bowlby's contention that romantic partners serve adults as attachment figures (Collins & Feeney, 2004).

Intimacy in romantic relationships fosters the attachment between romantic partners just as extensive holding and touch foster an attachment between a parent and child (Brennan, Wu, & Love, 1998; Guerrero & Andersen, 1991). However, there is evidence that people who do not have a history of secure attachment with at least one caregiver will respond to a growing attachment in a romantic relationship with anxiety or avoidance (Mikulincer & Shaver, 2007).

People respond with anxiety as they form new attachments because attachments are difficult to break; breakups engender a predictable and often prolonged grief process (Bowlby, 1969). Ironically, then, people's desires to have an attachment relationship with a romantic partner are accompanied by the risk that the relationship will not work out and will cause them grief.

Individuals with histories of secure attachments experience less attachment-related anxiety in their relationships. A capacity to form a secure attachment facilitates the sustaining of intimate relationships but does not seem to be necessary to form them (Mikulincer & Shaver, 2007). People with secure attachment schemas maintain a higher level of intimacy in those relationships than insecure individuals do (Mayseless & Scharf, 2007).

Treating people with insecure attachment schemas. It is the newly developing, not yet committed relationship that may be most challenging to individuals with insecure attachment histories. These individuals have learned that others cannot wholly be counted on (if they can be counted on at all) to be loving, emotionally available, and faithful when the individual needs security and comfort. Individuals with insecure attachment schemas form intimate relationships that are less satisfying, less secure, less intimate, more prone to conflict, less committed, less supportive, and less communicative (Mikulincer & Shaver, 2007) than those who are secure.

Anxious individuals often face their new relationships with indiscriminate trepidation. In other words, regardless of the signals that they are picking up from their new partners, they are vigilant for signs of untrustworthiness and demanding of reassurance and even perfect consideration in the other person's behavior.

Helping someone with an anxious attachment schema to relax and enjoy a budding intimate romantic relationship often requires that the therapist determine whether the person should trust their insecure feelings with the new partner or whether their insecure feelings are part of a more global, individual response to a growing attachment in a romantic relationship. Before engaging in work on modifying attachment schemas, it is a good idea to rule out the following:

1 That the new partner is conveying implicit or even explicit messages that he or she is untrustworthy or is not especially enamored with the client.
2 That there are circumstances surrounding the new partner or the new relationship that suggest that it is likely to be short-lived (e.g., a married lover).
3 That the client is ignoring his or her own negative feelings about the new partner and possibly projecting those negative feelings onto the other person.
4 That there are irreconcilable problems that would make a successful relationship unlikely, such as differences in age, religion, values, or temperament.

It is important to rule out these potential relationship problems because the therapist should avoid helping the client rationalize away potential warning signs of difficulty.

The four concerns above will sometimes be difficult to separate from the client's own longstanding anxious attachment schema. In this case, it is a good idea to ask the client about previous relationships. If there is a pattern of aborted relationships in the client's past, then it is useful to take a closer look at issues that were common from the earlier relationships. Then the assessment issue is in identifying whether there is a pattern of choosing poor prospects for partners, or a pattern of the individual's own behavior, that compromises relationship quality and drives partners away.

Coping with Breakups

The breakup of a romantic relationship is difficult for almost anyone. Whether people bring Dilemma #3 issues with them or not, a breakup creates a complicated grief process (Rhoades, Dush, Atkins, Stanley, & Markman, 2011). The person misses and grieves for the company of the partner and the love both given and received before the breakup. There is also a dream to be mourned in the shared future the bereft individual imagined with the partner. People usually feel anger toward the romantic partner for not living up to their expectations, for being difficult to be with, or for betraying them. They may feel jealous of the former partner's new love interests. They may suffer a blow to self-esteem if they have been rejected as a lover by the other. They may also need to grieve a loss of identity that was tied up in being boyfriend, girlfriend, husband, or wife to the other. It means loss of status as a couple in a coupled world. Finally, distance and fading memory may encourage the client to idealize the former lover and yearn to be back with him or her. Idealization is commonly accompanied by high levels of anxiety, obsessive thinking about the former lover, and doubt about one's own judgment.

People who break up often cannot stop thinking about the former lover, their conversations, what led up to and necessitated the breakup, what they could or should have said, and what might have been. This continuous returning to the image of the formerly beloved represents the persistence of the attachment, even if the love is gone. The ex-spouse who keeps coming around knows the attachment (and comfort) is there, even as he or she knows that pain and sorrow are also there. Anxiously attached individuals are particularly distressed following a breakup (Davis, Shaver, & Vernon, 2003).

I often help individuals complaining about obsessive thoughts about a former lover to reinterpret the image of the formerly beloved as a symbol rather than as the actual person of the beloved. People are distressed about being unable to stop thinking about the ex-partner as this is very confusing to them, particularly if they saw the breakup as the best move for the two of them. They are further confounded because the more they try to stop thinking about the partner, the more they are unable to stop. Thought-stopping techniques do not seem to help. I suggest to clients that the image in their heads is what they had hoped the lover would be, rather than who the lover actually turned out to be. Once they became infatuated with the former partner, the image of that person's face and body filled in a blank space in their minds where the face of the perfect attachment figure should fit. While they were in the relationship, they hoped that the partner would turn into a perfect lover, but that did not happen. Unfortunately for their distress, this knowledge does not dislodge the former partner's face from the yearned for perfect attachment figure that we dream about and talk to in our minds. When working with individuals who are disturbed by obsessive thinking about their former lover, it is useful to explain the difference between love and attachment (Weiss, 1976). Other alternative frameworks that can be helpful include:

"Breakups are so stressful and leave us all so desperately needing comfort that, I believe, our minds take over and take us back to the last attachment relationship as though it could still be a source of comfort. Jim, for you, has become a mental stand-in for the partner that you want in your life."

"When you think about him, notice how differently he behaves in your imagination than how he behaves in real life. Remind yourself that it's not the same person. Eventually you will replace Jim's image with someone else. But for now, your broken heart needs that image stand-in because you're grieving."

The confidence to say yes to intimacy. In order to say yes, people must believe that they could tolerate a breakup if they had to. This doesn't mean that we don't have to make judicious choices about the people with whom we become involved, because the warning signs are often there from the beginning. Avoiding relationships that are likely to break up is smart. Nevertheless, we have to take the risk that we might fail in order to succeed in finding a lasting, sustainable intimate relationship. In order to take the risk, we must have some confidence that we will be able to weather the emotional storm of the breakup in the event the relationship fails.

Past experience usually makes people wary. If a person has been through a breakup, he or she may compromise intimacy (or differentiation) in order to keep the relationship stable. Knowing from previous experience that he or she does not cope well with a breakup, the person may cling to an unrewarding relationship in order to avoid going through the experience again. Alternatively, some may find ways to avoid being engaged at all in romantic relationships, however much they yearn to have one. Fearing that one cannot weather a breakup is the other side of the fear of intimacy and has the same effect. The therapist can discover a fear of breakups by asking the individual about previous romances and their outcomes, and finding out what they went through in the past and whether they are afraid of repeating the experience. Fear of breakups can be addressed using the same cognitive and affective interventions that are used for other sources of intimacy-related anxiety.

Conclusion

Intimacy Dilemma #3, the past lives in the present, occurs when lessons about relationships learned (or not learned) in the past are generalized to the current interpersonal situation. If those lessons were negative or difficult, problems may occur. Because these problems stem from behavior learned in previous emotionally charged, negative circumstances, the behavior, and the assumptions and expectations that guide the behavior, resist change even when circumstances are different.

Sometimes we encounter interpersonal situations as adults that couldn't have occurred during childhood, and we must learn new social skills and interpersonal sensitivities in order to cope successfully with their challenges.

In particular, the risks of relating to potential romantic partners may seem too great to the inexperienced and awkward teen who puts off the inevitable only to find him- or herself in young adulthood, more than ready for romance and feeling incompetent about the emotional risks and demands involved. Alternatively, a young person who marries early may find him- or herself, after a divorce, similarly unprepared after years of an unhappy marriage, to mingle with potential partners, get to know them, develop an intimate connection, and commit to a long-term relationship.

Earlier relationships may also have been traumatizing for some intimacy-seekers, leaving them with self and other schemas that appropriately and accurately represent those traumatizing relationships, but serve them poorly in their efforts to find and retain a fulfilling intimate relationship as adults. Further, schemas that develop in the context of trauma are anxiety-charged and create a hyper-vigilance in young adults that often leaves them unable to respond appropriately to the normal intimacy dilemmas they encounter as they attempt to establish and build relationships.

The strategies offered in this chapter are designed to aid in the conceptualization, assessment, and intervention with people who did not acquire the psychological resources that they need for intimate romantic relating. These individuals can examine their past relationships for lessons inadvertently or deliberately learned that motivate self-defeating behavior and can develop new ways of thinking and interacting, so that they are open to new opportunities for gratifying love relationships.

11

EPILOGUE

Intimacy problems are some of the toughest to treat. Individuals whose defenses have been carefully (if not deliberately) developed to protect them from hurt will resist dropping them. One the one hand, they want to take a chance on enriching their relationships with new levels of intimacy. On the other hand, most adults seeking treatment have already experienced a world of hurt and are reluctant to risk more. Therapists who attempt to help these couples may find themselves in the position of trying to force intimacy down the throats of reluctant clients who seem to want nothing more than to stay in their safe and lonely corners.

I have written this book because, in the course of simultaneously conducting research on intimacy and treating couples with intimacy problems, I have been able to help many couples attain more satisfying intimate relationships. I close with a list of 11 ideas about intimate relating, drawn from this book, that are useful to keep in mind when treating people with intimacy-related problems.

1. *Intimacy problems stem primarily from one of three intimacy dilemmas:* #1, joy versus protection from pain, #2, I versus we, and #3, the past lives in the present.
2. *Intimacy ambivalence is normal.* People have a need for intimacy and feel lonely when the need is not met. Yet intimacy is also emotionally risky. Intimacy ambivalence is a normal response to intimacy's dual potential.
3. *Couples are always in an intimacy-distance regulating process.* Relational intimacy is not a constant but rather fluctuates between moments of intimacy and times of separateness. Smooth intimacy-distance regulation requires effective initiations, reciprocations, postponements, and regrets, all of which should avoid communicating rejection as much as possible.
4. *Intimacy needs exist in creative tension with "opposing" needs.* Needs for separateness and autonomy can, in their fulfillment, add zest and excitement to relationships. They can also compete with intimacy in their fulfillment by interfering with the couple's togetherness. Intimacy-distance regulation is the process by which couples find a creative and workable tension between opposing needs.

5 *Individual intimacy needs are only modestly changeable.* Aspects of personality are inherited, and change potential is finite. Our partners are "package deals" with good qualities having predictable downsides. Mutual acceptance maintains intimacy in the face of any disappointment.
6 *Intimate relating creates experiences of oneness and togetherness; paradoxically, it also fosters awareness of differences.* Intimate communication, to the extent that it is honest and self-revealing, shows partners their differences as well as their similarities.
7 *Psychological differentiation can be conceptualized behaviorally and is a useful concept for understanding intimacy dilemmas.* The ability to express the self emphatically while maintaining a respectful and loving stance toward the partner and upholding the intimate connection is critical for maintaining a rewarding relationship.
8 *Couples who struggle with psychological differentiation may find themselves at one of two extreme poles.* Unrelated partners distance themselves from one another in order that they avoid feeling too much emotion about what the other says or does. Enmeshed partners strive to be more alike: submerging their own wants and needs or pushing the other to change.
9 *Couples' "power struggles" are less about power than about the unrealistic hope or belief that two can become one.* More realistic beliefs about the frequency with which two people can think alike can ease the struggle.
10 *Fear scenarios interfere with an individual's ability to enjoy intimate relating or lead a person to sabotage that which he or she longs for most fervently.* Fear scenarios may cause partners to overreact to each other's behavior. Unrealistic fear scenarios interfere with realistic thinking about the relationship.
11 *Individual problems with intimacy may stem from dysfunctional attitudes or habits developed in one's formative years.* Adults can learn new relationship skills that they missed obtaining in their younger years.

It is possible for couples to fight less and cooperate more while still missing a critical ingredient in their relationship. Along with love, intimacy captures the lifeblood of a couple relationship, the process that keeps the relationship thriving rather than just surviving. Intimacy fulfills psychological needs and enhances our health, well-being, quality of life, and relationship satisfaction. The interventions provided in this book can, for some couples, offer a way to recover, sustain, and more thoroughly enjoy the deep intimate connection that brought them together.

REFERENCES

Ainsworth, M. D. S. (1989). Attachments beyond infancy. *American Psychologist, 44,* 709–716.

Antony, M. & Swinson, R. (2008, 2nd edition). *Shyness and Social Anxiety Workbook: Proven, Step-by-Step Techniques for Overcoming your Fear.* Oakland, CA: New Harbinger.

Aron, A., & Aron, E. N. (1996). Self and self-expansion in relationships. In G. J. O. Fletcher & J. Fitness (Eds.), *Knowledge structures in close relationships: A social psychological approach* (pp. 325–344). Hillsdale, NJ: Erlbaum.

Aron, A. P., Mashek, D. J., & Aron, E. N. (2004). Closeness as including other in the self. In D. J. Mashek & A. P. Aron (Eds.), *Handbook of closeness and intimacy* (pp. 27–41). Mahwah, NJ: Erlbaum.

Aron, A. P., Norman, C. C., Aron, E. N., & Lewandowski, G. (2002). Shared participation in self-expanding activities: Positive effects on experienced marital quality. In P. Noller & J. Feeney (Eds.), *Understanding marriage: Developments in the study of couple interaction* (pp. 177–194). New York, NY: Cambridge University Press.

Bakan, D. (1966). *The duality of human existence.* Chicago, IL: Rand McNally.

Bartholomew, K., & Horowitz, I.M. (1991). Attachment styles among young adults: A test of a four-category model. *Journal of Personality & Social Psychology, 61,* 226-244.

Basco, M. R., Birchler, G., Kalal, B., Talbott, R., & Slater, M. A. (1991). The clinician rating of adult communication (CRAC): A clinician's guide to the assessment of interpersonal communication skill. *Journal of Clinical Psychology, 47,* 368–380.

Baucom, D., & Epstein, N. (1990). *Cognitive-behavioral couple therapy.* New York, NY: Brunner/Mazel.

Baucom, D. H., Epstein, N., Daiuto, A. D., Carels, R. A., Rankin, L. A., & Burnett, C. K. (1996). Cognitions in marriage: The relationship between standards and attributions. *Journal of Family Psychology, 10,* 209–222.

Baucom, D. H., Epstein, N., Rankin, L. A., & Burnett, C. K. (1996). Assessing relationship standards: The inventory of specific relationship standards. *Journal of Family Psychology, 10,* 72–88.

Baucom, D. H., Gordon, K. C., Snyder, D. K., Atkins, D. C., & Christensen, A. (2006). Treating affair couples: Clinical considerations and initial findings. *Journal of Cognitive Psychotherapy: An International Quarterly, 20,* 375–392.

Baxter, L. A., & Simon, E. P. (1993). Relationship maintenance strategies and dialectical contradictions in personal relationships. *Journal of Social and Personal Relationships, 10,* 225–242.

Beach, S. R. H. (2001). Expanding the study of dyadic conflict: The potential role of self-evaluation maintenance processes. In A. Booth, A. C. Crouter, & M. Clements (Eds.), *Couples in conflict* (pp. 83–94). Mahwah, NJ: Erlbaum.

Beach, S. R. H., Tesser, A., Fincham, F., Mendolia, M., Anderson, P., Crelia, R., & Whitaker, D. (1996). Self-evaluation maintenance in marriage: Toward a performance ecology of the marital relationship. *Journal of Family Psychology, 10,* 379–396.

Beck, A. T. (1976). *Cognitive therapy and the emotional disorders.* Oxford, England: International Universities Press.

Beck, A. T., Rush, A. J., Shaw, B. F., & Emery, G. (1979). *Cognitive therapy of depression.* New York, NY: Guilford Press.

Benjamin, L. S. (1996). *Interpersonal Diagnosis and Treatment of Personality Disorders.* New York: Guilford

Berscheid, E. (1983). Emotion. In H. H. Kelley, E. Berscheid, A. Christensen, J. H. Harvey, T. L. Huston, G. Levinger, ... D. R. Peterson (Eds.), *Close relationships: Development and change.* New York, NY: W. W. Freeman.

Blatt, S. J., & Bass, R. B. (1996). Relatedness and self-definition: A dialectic model of personality development. In G. G. Noam & K. W. Fischer (Eds.), *Development and vulnerability in close relationships* (pp. 309–338). Hillsdale, NJ: Erlbaum.

Boszormenyi-Nagy, I., & Spark, G. M. (1973). *Invisible loyalties: Reciprocity in intergenerational family therapy.* Oxford, England: Harper & Row.

Bowen, M. (1960). Family concept of schizophrenia. In D. Jackson (Ed.), *Etiology of schizophrenia.* New York, NY: Basic Books.

Bowen, M. (1978). *Family therapy in clinical practice.* Northvale, NJ: Aronson.

Bowlby, J. (1969). *Attachment.* New York, NY: Basic Books.

Brennan, K. A., Wu, S., & Love, J. (1998). Adult romantic attachment and individual differences in attitudes toward physical contact in the context of adult romantic relationships. In J.A. Simpson & W. S. Rholes (Eds.), *Attachment theory and close relationships* (pp. 394-428). New York: Guilford.

Burns, D. (1999). *Feeling good: The new mood therapy.* New York, NY: Harper.

Campbell, L., Simpson, J. A., Boldry, J., & Kashy, D. A. (2005). Perceptions of conflict and support in romantic relationships: The role of attachment anxiety. *Journal of Personality and Social Psychology, 88,* 510–531.

Christensen, A., & Jacobson, N. S. (1996). *Acceptance and change in couple therapy: A therapist's guide to transforming relationships.* New York, NY: Norton.

Clark, D.A., & Steer, R. A. (1996). Empirical status of the cognitive model of anxiety and depression. In P. M. Salkovskis (Ed.), *Frontiers of cognitive therapy* (pp. 75–96). New York, NY: Guilford Press.

Collins, N. L., & Feeney, B. C. (2004). An attachment theory perspective on closeness and intimacy. In D. J. Mashek & A. P. Aron (Eds.), *Handbook of closeness and intimacy* (pp. 163–187). Mahwah, NJ: Erlbaum.

Cordova, J. A., Gee, C. B., & Warren, L. (2005). Emotional skillfulness in marriage: Intimacy as a mediator of the relationship between emotional skillfulness and marital satisfaction. *Journal of Social and Clinical Psychology, 24,* 218–235.

Cuber, J. F., & Haroff, P. B. (1965). *Sex and the significant Americans.* New York, NY: Penguin.

Datillo, F. M. (2005). The critical component of cognitive restructuring in couples therapy: A case study. *Australia & New Zealand Journal of Family Therapy, 26,* 73–78.

Datillo, F. M. (2010). *Cognitive-behavioral therapy with couples and families.* New York, NY: Guilford Press.

Davis, D., Shaver, P. R., & Vernon, M. L. (2003). Physical, emotional, and behavioral reactions to breaking up: The roles of gender, age, emotional involvement, and attachment style. *Personality and Social Psychology Bulletin, 29,* 871–884.

Derlega, V. J., & Grzelak, J. (1979). Appropriateness of self disclosure. In G. J. Chelune (Ed.), *Self disclosure: Origins, patterns, and implications of openness in interpersonal relationships* (p. 151–176). San Francisco, CA: Jossey Bass.

Dindia, K., Timmerman, L., & Greene, J. O. (2003). Accomplishing romantic relationships. In B. R. Burleson (Ed.), *Handbook of communication and social interaction skills* (pp. 685–721). Mahwah, NJ: Erlbaum.

Dobson, K. S., & Breiter, H. J. (1983). Cognitive assessment of depression: Reliability and validity of three measures. *Journal of Abnormal Psychology, 92,* 107–109.

Eidelson, R., & Epstein, N. (1982). Cognition and relationship maladjustment: Development of a measure of dysfunctional relationship beliefs. *Journal of Consulting and Clinical Psychology, 50,* 715–720.

Ellis, A. (1962). *Reason and emotion in psychotherapy.* Oxford, England: Lyle Stuart.

Epstein, N. (2006). Introduction to the special issue on cognitive-behavioral couple therapy. *Journal of Cognitive Psychotherapy: An International Quarterly, 20,* 339–340.

Epstein, N., & Baucom, D. (2003). *Enhanced cognitive behavioral couple therapy.* Washington, DC: American Psychological Association.

Epstein, S. (2003). Cognitive-experiential self theory of personality. In *Handbook of Psychology: Personality and Social Psychology V, T. Millon and M.J. Lerner (Eds.).* (pp. 159-184). Hoboken, NJ: Wiley.

Erikson, E. H. (1950). *Childhood and society.* New York, NY: Norton.

Evans, P. (1996). *The verbally abusive relationship: How to recognize it and how to respond.* Avon, MA: Adams Media.

Ferreira, A. J. (1963). Family myth and homeostasis. *Archives General Psychiatry, 9,* 457–463.

Fruzzetti, A. (2006). *The high conflict couple.* Oakland, CA: New Harbinger.

Gable, S. L., Gonzaga, G. C., & Strachman, A. (2006). Will you be there for me when things go right? Supportive responses to positive event disclosures. *Journal of Personality and Social Psychology, 91,* 904–917.

Gore, J. S., Cross, S. E., & Morris, M. L. (2006). Let's be friends: Relational self-construal and the development of intimacy. *Personal Relationships, 13,* 83–102.

Gottman, J. M. (1999). *The marriage clinic: A scientifically based marital therapy.* New York, NY: Norton.

Greenberger, D., & Padesky, C. (1995). *Mind over mood.* New York, NY: Guilford Press.

Grossmann, K. E., Grossmann, K., & Waters, E. (Eds.). (2005). *Attachment from infancy to adulthood: The major longitudinal studies.* New York, NY: Guilford Press.

Guerrero, L. K., & Andersen, P. A. (1991). The waxing and waning of relational intimacy: Touch as a function of relational stage, gender and touch avoidance. *Journal of Social and Personal Relationships, 8,* 147–165.

Guisinger, S., & Blatt, S. J. (1994). Individuality and relatedness: Evolution of a fundamental dialectic. *American Psychologist, 49,* 104–111.

Haaga, D. A., Dyck, M. J., & Ernst, D. (1991). Empirical status of cognitive theory of depression. *Psychological Bulletin, 110,* 215–236.

Haley, J. (1987). *Problem-solving therapy* (2nd ed.). San Francisco, CA: Jossey-Bass.

Hatfield, E., & Rapson, R. (1992). Similarity and attraction in close relationships. *Communication Monographs, 59,* 268–287.

Hazan, C., & Shaver, P. (1987). Romantic love conceptualized as an attachment process. *Journal of Personality and Social Psychology, 52,* 511–524.

Heiman, J. R., Lopiccolo, J., & Palladini, D. (1988). *Becoming orgasmic: A sexual and personal growth program for women.* New York, NY: Prentice-Hall.

Horberg, E. J., & Chen, S. (2010). Significant others and contingencies of self-worth: Activation and consequences of relationship-specific contingencies of self-worth. *Journal of Personality and Social Psychology, 98*(1), 77–91.

Hutchison, M. G. (1985). *Transforming body image: Learning to love the body you have.* Berkeley, CA: The Crossing Press.

Jackson, D. D. (1957). The question of family homeostasis. *Psychiatric Quarterly, 1,* 79–90.

Jacobson, E. (1938). *Progressive relaxation.* Chicago, IL: University of Chicago Press.

Jacobson, N. S., & Christensen, A. (1996). *Acceptance and change in couple therapy.* New York, NY: Norton.

Jacobson, N. S., & Margolin, G. (1979). *Marital therapy: Strategies based on social learning and behavior exchange principles.* New York, NY: Brunner/Mazel.

Johnson, S. M. (2004). *The practice of emotionally focused therapy* (2nd ed.). New York, NY: Brunner-Routledge.

Johnson, S. M. (2005). *Emotionally focused couple therapy with trauma survivors: Strengthening attachment bonds.* New York, NY: Guilford Press.

Johnson, S., & Greenberg, L. (1994). Emotion in intimate relationships: Theory and implications for therapy. In S. Johnson & L. Greenberg (Eds.), *The heart of the matter: Perspectives on emotion in marital therapy* (pp. 3–22). Philadelphia, PA: Brunner/Mazel.

Johnson, S. M., & Williams-Keeler, L. (1998). Creating healing relationships for couples dealing with trauma: The use of emotionally focused marital therapy. *Journal of Marital and Family Therapy, 24,* 25–40.

Jourard, S. J. (1971). *Self-disclosure: An experimental analysis of the transparent self.* Oxford, England: Wiley-Interscience.

Joyce, P., & Sills, C. (2001). *Skills in Gestalt counseling and psychotherapy.* London, England: Sage.

Karpel, M. (1976). Individuation: From fusion to dialogue. *Family Process, 15,* 65–82.

Karpel, M. (1994). *Evaluating couples: A handbook for practitioners.* New York, NY: Norton.

Kelley, H. H. (1984). Interdependence theory and its future. *Representative Research in Social Psychology, 14,* 2–15.

Kirby, J. S., Baucom, D. H., & Peterman, M. A. (2005). An investigation of unmet intimacy needs in marital relationships. *Journal of Marital and Family Therapy, 31,* 313–325.

Knee, R., Lonsbury, C., Canevello, A., & Patrick, H. (2005). Self-determination and conflict in romantic relationships. *Journal of Personality and Social Psychology, 29,* 997–1009.

Knee, C., Patrick, H., & Lonsbary, C. (2003). Implicit theories of relationships: Orientations toward evaluation and cultivation. *Personality And Social Psychology Review*, 7(1), 41–55.

Larson, R.W. (1990). The solitary side of life: An examination of the time people spend alone from childhood to old age. *Developmental Review, 10,* 155–183.

Laurenceau, J. P., Barrett, L. F., Pietromonaco, P. R. (1998). Intimacy as an interpersonal process: The importance of self-disclosure, partner disclosure, and perceived partner responsiveness in interpersonal exchanges. *Journal of Personality and Social Psychology, 74,* 1238–1251.

Laurenceau, J-P., Barrett, L. F., & Rovine, M. J. (2005). The interpersonal process model of intimacy in marriage: A daily-diary and multilevel modeling approach. *Journal of Family Psychology, 9,* 314–323.

Levant, R., & Pollack, W. S. (1995). *A new psychology of men.* New York, NY: Basic Books.

Linehan, M. M. (1993). *Cognitive-behavioral treatment of borderline personality disorder.* New York, NY: Guilford Press.

Lippert, T., & Prager, K. J. (2001). Daily experiences of intimacy: A study of couples. *Personal Relationships, 8,* 283–298.

Maccoby, E. E. (1990). Gender and relationships. *American Psychologist, 45,* 513–520.

Maris, R.W., Berman, A. L., Maltsberger, J.T., & Yufit, R.I. (1992). *Assessment and prediction of suicide.* New York: Guilford.

Markus, H. (1977). Self-schemata and processing information about the self. *Journal of Personality and Social Psychology, 35,* 63–78.

Maslow, A. H. (1968). *Toward a psychology of being.* New York, NY: Van Nostrand Reinhold.

May, R. (1969). *Existential psychology.* New York, NY: Crown/Random House.

Mayseless, O., & Scharf, M. (2007). Adolescents' attachment representations and their capacity for intimacy in close relationships. *Journal of Research on Adolescence, 17,* 23–50.

McCarthy, B., & McCarthy, E. (2003). *Rekindling desire: A step-by-step program to help low-sex and no-sex marriages.* New York, NY: Taylor & Francis.

McCullough, J. P. (2006). *Treating chronic depression with disciplined personal involvement: Cognitive behavioral analysis system of psychotherapy (CBASP).* New York, NY: Springer.

Mikulincer, M., & Shaver, P. R. (2007). *Attachment in adulthood: Structure, dynamics, and change.* New York, NY: Guilford Press.

Minuchin, S. (1978). *Psychosomatic families: Anorexia nervosa in context.* Cambridge, MA: Harvard University Press.

Monsour, M. (1992). Meanings of intimacy in cross- and same-sex friendships. *Journal of Social and Personal Relationships, 9,* 277–295.

Montgomery, B. M. (1986). Interpersonal attraction as a function of open communication and gender. *Communication Research Reports, 3,* 140–145.

Murray, H.A. (1938). *Explorations in personality.* New York, NY: Oxford University Press.

Murray, S. L. (2005). Regulating the risks of closeness: A relationship-specific sense of felt security. *Psychological Science, 14,* 74–78.

Nurmi, J. E., Jyväskylä, U., Toivonen, S., Salmela-Aro, K., & Eronen, S. (1997). Social strategies and loneliness. *Journal of Social Psychology, 137,* 764–777.

O'Farrell, T. J., & Fals-Stewart, W. (2000). Behavioral couples therapy for alcoholism and drug abuse. *Journal of Substance Abuse Treatment, 18,* 51–54.

O'Rourke, N., Neufeld, E., Claxton, A., & Smith, J. Z. (2010). Knowing me-knowing you: Reported personality and trait discrepancies as predictors of marital idealization between long-wed spouses. *Psychology and Aging, 25,* 412–421.

Perls, F. S. (1969). *Gestalt therapy verbatim.* Lafayette, CA: Real People Press.

Prager, K. J. (1995). *The psychology of intimacy.* New York, NY: Guilford Press.

Prager, K.J. (1999). The intimacy dilemma: A guide for couple therapists. In J. Carlson & L. Sperry, (Eds.), *The Intimate Couple.* (pp. 109-157). New York: Brunner/Mazel.

Prager, K. J., & Buhrmester, D. (1998). Intimacy and need fulfillment in couple relationships. *Journal of Social and Personal Relationships, 15,* 435–469.

Prager, K. J., Fuller, D. O., & Gonzalez, A. S. (1989). The function of self disclosure in social interaction. *Journal of Social Behavior and Personality, 4,* 563–580.

Prager, K. J., & Roberts, L. J. (2004). Deep intimate connection: Self and intimacy in couple relationships. In D. J. Mashek & A. P. Aron (Eds.), *Handbook of closeness and intimacy* (pp. 43–60). Mahwah, NJ: Erlbaum.

Reis, H.T. (2006). Implications of attachment theory for research on intimacy. In M. Mikulincer & G. S. Goodman (Eds.), *Dynamics of romantic love: Attachment, caregiving, and sex* (pp. 383–403). New York, NY: Guilford Press.

Reis, H. T., & Patrick, B. C. (1996). Attachment and intimacy: Component processes. In E. T. Higgins & A. W. Kruglanski (Eds.), *Social psychology: Handbook of basic principles* (pp. 523–563). New York, NY: Guilford Press.

Reis, H. T., & Shaver, P. (1988). Intimacy as an interpersonal process. In S. Duck, D. F. Hay, S. E. Hobfoll, W. Ickes, & B. M. Montgomery (Eds.), *Handbook of personal relationships: Theory, research and interventions* (pp. 367–389). Oxford, England: Wiley.

Rhoades, G. K., Dush, C. M. K., Atkins, D. C., Stanley, S. M., & Markman, H. J. (2011). Breaking up is hard to do: The impact of unmarried relationship dissolution on mental health and life satisfaction. *Journal of Family Psychology, 25,* 366–374.

Rogers, C. (1958). A process conception of psychotherapy. *American Psychologist, 13,* 142–149.

Rogers, C. R. (1959). A theory of therapy, personality and interpersonal relationships, as developed in the client-centered framework. In S. Koch (Ed.), *Psychology: A study of a science* (Vol. 3, pp. 184–526). New York, NY: McGraw Hill.

Rotenberg, K.J. (1997). Loneliness and the perception of the exchange of disclosures. *Journal of Social and Clinical Psychology, 16,* 259–276.

Rubin, L. B. (1984). *Intimate strangers.* New York, NY: Harper Perennial.

Ryan, R. M., & Deci, E. (2010). Self-determination theory and the role of basic psychological needs in personality and the organization of behavior. In O. P. John, R.W. Robins, & L.A. Pervin (Eds.), *Handbook of personality: Theory and research* (3rd ed.). New York, NY: Guilford Press.

Sartre, J. P. (1956). *Being and nothingness: An essay in phenomenological ontology.* New York, NY: Citadel.

Satir, V. (1967). Family systems and approaches to family therapy. *Journal of the Fort Logan Mental Health Center, 4,* 81–93.
Schaefer, M. T., & Olson, D. H. (1981). Assessing intimacy: The PAIR Inventory. *Journal of Marital and Family Therapy, 7,* 47–60.
Schnarch, D.M. (1991). *Constructing the sexual crucible: An integration of sexual and marital therapy.* New York, NY: Norton.
Schnarch, D. (1997). *Passionate couples: Keeping love and intimacy alive in committed relationships.* New York, NY: Norton.
Silverman, L.H., Lachman, F.M., & Milich, R.H. (1982). *The search for oneness.* New York, NY: International Universities Press.
Smetana, J. G., Campione-Barr, N., & Metzger, A. (2006). Adolescent development in interpersonal and societal contexts. *Annual Review of Psychology, 57,* 255–284.
Snyder, D. K. (November, 2009). *Integrative couple therapy: An informed pluralistic approach.* Paper presented at the annual meeting of the Association for Behavioral and Cognitive Therapy, New York, NY.
Snyder, D. K., Baucom, D. H., & Gordon, K. C. (2007). *Getting past the affair: A program to help you cope, heal, and move on—Together or apart.* New York, NY: Guilford Press.
Snyder, D. K., Castellani, A., & Whisman, M. (2006). Current status and future directions in couple therapy. *Annual Review Psychology, 57,* 317–344.
Sookman, D., Pinard, G., & Beauchemin, N. (1994). Multidimensional schematic restructuring treatment for obsessions: Theory and practice. *Journal of Cognitive Psychotherapy, 8,* 175–194.
Sprecher, S. (1987). The effects of self-disclosure given and received on affection for an intimate partner and stability of the relationship. *Journal of Social and Personal Relationships, 4,* 115–127.
Sprecher, S., & Hendrick, S. S. (2004). Self-disclosure in intimate relationships: Associations with individual and relationship characteristics over time. *Journal of Social and Clinical Psychology, 23,* 857–858.
Sprecher, S., Metts, S., Burleson, B., Hatfield, E., & Thompson, A. (1995). Domains of expressive interaction in intimate relationships: Associations with satisfaction and commitment. *Family Relations, 44,* 203–210.
Spring, J. (1996). *After the affair: Healing the pain and rebuilding trust when a partner has been unfaithful.* New York, NY: Harper Collins.
Stith, S. M., McCollum, E., & Rosen, E. E. (2011). The changing face of intimate partner violence treatment. In S. M. Stith, E. E. McCollum, & K. H. Rosen (Eds.), *Couples therapy for domestic violence* (pp. 7 19). Washington, DC: Ameri can Psychological Association.
Stuart, R. B. (1980). *Helping couples change: A social learning approach to marital therapy.* New York, NY: Guilford Press.
Sullivan, H. S. (1953). *Conceptions of modern psychiatry.* New York, NY: Norton.
Tillich, P. (1952). *The courage to be.* New Haven, CT: Yale University Press.
Tolman, D. L., Spencer, R., Harmon, T., Rosen-Reynoso, M., & Striepe, M. (2004). Getting close, staying cool: Early adolescent boys' experiences with romantic relationships. In N. Way & J. Y. Chu (Eds.), *Adolescent boys: Exploring diverse cultures of boyhood* (pp. 235–255). New York: New York University Press.
Tornstam, L. (1992). Loneliness in marriage. *Journal of Social and Personal Relationships, 9,* 197–217.

Vittengl, J. R., & Holt, C. S. (2000). Getting acquainted: The relationship of self-disclosure and social attraction to positive affect. *Journal of Social and Personal Relationships, 17,* 53–66.
Wakefield, P. J., Williams, R. E., Yost, E. B., & Patterson, K. M. (1996). *Couple therapy for alcoholism: A cognitive-behavioral treatment manual.* New York, NY: Guilford Press.
Weiss, R. S. (1976). The emotional impact of marital separation. *Journal of Social Issues, 32*(1), 135–145.
Weitzman, M. L., McHugh, R., & Otto, M. W. (2011). The association between affect amplification and urgency. *Depression and Anxiety, 28,* 1105–1110.
Whitbourne, S. K., & Weinstock, C. S. (1986). *Adult development.* Westport, CT: Praeger Publishers.
Wright, J., & Basco, M. (2001). *Getting your life back: The complete guide to recovery from depression.* New York, NY: Free Press.
Young, J. E., Klosko, J. S., & Weishaar, M. E. (2003). *Schema therapy: A practitioner's guide.* New York, NY: Guilford Press.

INDEX

Note: page numbers in *italics* indicate figures or tables.